THE CULTURAL TURN

Radical Thinkers ▼

Theodor Adorno
*In Search of Wagner,
Minima Moralia*

Theodor Adorno et al.
Aesthetics and Politics

Giorgio Agamben
Infancy and History

Aijaz Ahmad
In Theory

Louis Althusser
*For Marx,
On Ideology,
Politics and History*

Louis Althusser,
Étienne Balibar
Reading Capital

Étienne Balibar
Spinoza and Politics

Jean Baudrillard
*Fragments,
The Perfect Crime,
The System of Objects,
The Transparency of Evil*

Walter Benjamin
*The Origin of German
Tragic Drama*

Roy Bhaskar
*A Realist Theory
of Science*

Norberto Bobbio
*Liberalism and
Democracy*

Simon Critchley
*Ethics-Politics-
Subjectivity*

Guy Debord
Panegyric

Jacques Derrida
The Politics of Friendship

Derrida et al.
Ghostly Demarcations

Peter Dews
Logics of Disintegration

Terry Eagleton
*The Function of
Criticism,
Walter Benjamin*

Fredric Jameson
*The Cultural Turn,
Late Marxism*

Ernesto Laclau
Emancipation(s)

Georg Lukács
Lenin

Herbert Marcuse
A Study on Authority

Franco Moretti
Signs Taken for Wonders

Chantal Mouffe
*The Democratic Paradox,
The Return of the
Political*

Antonio Negri
The Political Descartes

Jacques Rancière
*On the Shores of
Politics*

Gillian Rose
Hegel Contra Sociology

Jacqueline Rose
*Sexuality in the Field
of Vision*

Kristin Ross
*The Emergence
of Social Space*

Jean-Paul Sartre
*Between Existentialism
and Marxism*

Göran Therborn
*What Does the Ruling
Class Do When It Rules?*

Paul Virilio
*The Information
Bomb,
Open Sky,
Strategy of Deception,
War and Cinema*

Raymond Williams
*Culture and Materialism,
Politics of Modernism*

Slavoj Žižek
*For They Know Not
What They Do,
The Indivisible
Remainder,
The Metastases of
Enjoyment*

THE CULTURAL TURN

Selected Writings on the Postmodern 1983–1998

Fredric Jameson

VERSO

London • New York

This collection first published by Verso 1998
© Frederic Jameson 1998
Reprinted 2009
All rights reserved

The moral rights of the author have been asserted

1 3 5 7 9 10 8 6 4 2

Verso
UK: 6 Meard Street, London W1F 0EG
US: 20 Jay Street, Suite 1010, Brooklyn, NY 11201
www.versobooks.com

Verso is the imprint of New Left Books

ISBN-13: 978-1-84467-349-0

British Library Cataloguing in Publication Data
A catalogue record for this book is available from the British Library

Library of Congress Cataloging-in-Publication Data
A catalog record for this book is available from the Library of Congress

Typeset by SetSystems Ltd, Saffron Walden
Printed in the US by Maple Vail

For Masao Miyoshi

Contents

Acknowledgements   ix

Foreword *by Perry Anderson*   xi

82(84) 1 Postmodernism and Consumer Society   1

82(83) 2 Theories of the Postmodern   21

89 3 Marxism and Postmodernism   33

91(94) 4 The Antinomies of Postmodernity   50

94 5 'End of Art' or 'End of History'?   73

95 6 Transformations of the Image in Postmodernity   93

96 7 Culture and Finance Capital   136

97 8 The Brick and the Balloon: Architecture, Idealism
       and Land Speculation   162

Notes   191

Index   201

Acknowledgements

'Postmodernism and the Consumer Society' was first published in *Postmodernism and Its Discontents: Theories, Practices*, ed. E. Ann Kaplan (London: Verso, 1988), and combines elements from 'Postmodernism and the Consumer Society', in *The Anti-Aesthetic*, ed. Hal Foster (Port Townsend, WA: Bay Press, 1983) and 'Postmodernism: the Cultural Logic of Late Capitalism', *New Left Review* 146 (July–August 1984).

'Theories of the Postmodern' was first published as 'The Politics of Theory: Ideological Positions in the Debate', *New German Critique* no. 53, Fall 1984.

'Marxism and Postmodernism' was first published in *Postmodernism/Jameson/Critique*, ed. Douglas Kellner (Washington DC: Maisonneuve Press, 1989) and in *New Left Review* 176 (July–August 1989).

'The Antinomies of Postmodernity' is an extract from *The Seeds of Time* (New York, NY: Columbia University Press, 1989).

'The Brick and the Balloon: Architecture, Idealism and Land Speculation' is the text of a talk delivered at the seventh annual ANY conference in Rotterdam, June 1997, and is reprinted with permission of the organizers; it was also published in *ANYHOW*, ed. Cynthia Davidson (Cambridge, Mass.: MIT Press, 1998) and in *New Left Review* 228 (March–April 1998).

Foreword

Exploding like so many magnesium flares in a night sky, Fredric Jameson's writings have lit up the shrouded landscape of the postmodern, suddenly transforming its shadows and obscurities into an eerie, refulgent tableau. The contours of the scenery revealed are on display below. *The Cultural Turn* offers the most compact and complete résumé of the development of his thinking on the subject, across two decades of intensely productive reflections, from his earliest sorties to his latest assessments. At once introduction and overview, it offers the best scroll of Jameson's work on the postmodern to date.

The relation of this work to the prior history of ideas of the postmodern – a complicated story of anticipations, displacements and inversions, that can at times look arbitrary or enigmatic, yet possesses its own underlying logic – forms a striking topic in its own right.[1] What any such genealogy makes clear, however, is the unique position occupied by Jameson in the field. No other writer has produced as searching or comprehensive a theory of the cultural, socio-economic and geo-political dimensions of the postmodern. The log-book of its development lies open below.

The volume opens with three foundational texts from the eighties. 'Postmodernism and Consumer Society', originally

---

1 I have attempted to explore this in *The Origins of Postmodernity*, London 1998, which offers a more extensive reading of Jameson.

delivered as an address to the Whitney Museum of Contemporary Arts in the fall of 1982, and subsequently expanded into a famous essay for *New Left Review* in 1984, sets out the core theses of Jameson's theory of the passing of modernism and arrival of a new postmodern configuration, as transcriptions of the cultural logic of late capitalism. This original intervention has remained the cornerstone of all the work by Jameson that has followed. Virtually concurrent with it (actually written a few months earlier, in the spring of 1982, and published in *New German Critique* in 1983), 'Theories of the Postmodern' supplies a crisp map of the various stances – intellectual and political – adopted towards postmodernism up to the time of Jameson's own entry into the field, in the form of a combinatory of possible positions. Here Jameson makes clear the distinctive standpoint from which he has consistently written: a Marxism eschewing any facile moralism for a sober materialist analysis of the historical ground of major cultural transformations. This was an outlook that has disconcerted many readers on the Left. The third essay below, 'Marxism and Postmodernism', composed in early 1989, is Jameson's calm reply to such critics, setting his own project within the classic enterprises of the Marxist tradition.

All these texts were written in the era of Reagan, whose Presidency they effectively span. This was a time of prolonged speculative boom, on the back of massive rearmament for the struggle against Communism, and a vast redistribution of income towards the rich in the United States and more generally the West. The domestic euphoria of these years forms the immediate backdrop for Jameson's diagnosis of the logic of postmodernism. As the world crossed into the nineties, this context abruptly altered. With the collapse of the Soviet bloc, the global triumph of capitalism was widely proclaimed, as henceforward the necessary pattern of all economic and political life. In its most ambitious interpretation, the elimination of any alternatives was read as a definitive terminus: in a categorical, if not chronological sense, nothing less than the end of history itself. It was to the paradoxes of this new meaning of postmodernity, as the cancellation of time and *Gleichschaltung* of space, that Jameson addressed himself in the fourth text included here.

FOREWORD

'The Antinomies of Postmodernity', originally delivered as a
Wellek Library Lecture in 1991, was published in expanded
form as the first chapter of *The Seeds of Time* in 1994. It is a
tour de force of formidable power.

The final texts below are a quartet of hitherto unpublished
essays, that mark a critical new phase in Jameson's writing.
'"End of Art" or "End of History"?', which dates from 1994,
is a complex reflection on two Hegelian themes that have gained
renewed currency today. It offers both a trenchant analysis of
the conservative tropes at work in this revival, and an ingeniously radical reinterpretation of them – in which Francis Fukuyama's famous claim emerges in an unexpected light. The
uncompromising note struck here is carried through in the next
essay, 'Transformations of the Image in Postmodernity', first
presented to a conference in Venezuela in 1995, which starts
by registering a sort of regression within the evolution of postmodernism itself, to intellectual or aesthetic positions once cast
aside. Jameson then proceeds to one particular such parabola,
in the metamorphoses of the 'look' as it was successively
understood by Sartre and Fanon, Foucault and Robbe-Grillet,
and finally Guy Debord – whose theory of the spectacle ushers
us into a contemporary world where modernist attachment to
the sublime has receded before a renewed cult of the beautiful
that, in Jameson's view, can now only be meretricious.

The last two essays form a natural pair. Jameson's writing on
postmodern culture has always been closely informed by a sense
of the economic transformations accompanying and shaping it.
His original theorization of postmodernism was stimulated by
Ernest Mandel's classic study of *Late Capitalism* in the seventies. He now turns Giovanni Arrighi's landmark *Long Twentieth Century* of the nineties to remarkable account in 'Culture
and Finance Capital' (1996), to yield a quite new way of seeing
typical mechanisms of the contemporary cinema – even such
pregnant by-products of the industry as the preview. Likewise
in 'The Brick and the Balloon' (1997), Robert Fitch's recent
investigation of land speculation in Manhattan – *The Assassination of New York* – is set to work in a wide-ranging
meditation on the relations between ground-rent and architectural forms, under the sway of Marx's 'fictitious capital', that

ends with a characteristically sudden, deft swerve to the spectral in Hong Kong.

In a brief compass, *The Cultural Turn* traces the movement of one of the leading cultural intelligences of our time, in pursuit of the mutable forms of the postmodern world. The results will leave few indifferent.

Perry Anderson
April 1998

Postmodernism and Consumer Society

The concept of postmodernism is not widely accepted or even understood today. Some of the resistance to it may come from the unfamiliarity of the works it covers, which can be found in all the arts: the poetry of John Ashbery, for instance, as well as the much simpler talk poetry that came out of the reaction against complex, ironic, academic modernist poetry in the 1960s; the reaction against modern architecture and in particular against the monumental buildings of the International Style; the pop buildings and decorated sheds celebrated by Robert Venturi in his manifesto *Learning from Las Vegas*; Andy Warhol, pop art and the more recent Photorealism; in music, the moment of John Cage but also the later synthesis of classical and 'popular' styles found in composers like Philip Glass and Terry Riley, and also punk and new wave rock with such groups as the Clash, Talking Heads and the Gang of Four; in film, everything that comes out of Godard – contemporary vanguard film and video – as well as a whole new style of commercial or fiction films, which has its equivalent in contemporary novels, where the works of William Burroughs, Thomas Pynchon and Ishmael Reed on the one hand, and the French new novel on the other, are also to be numbered among the varieties of what can be called postmodernism.

This list would seem to make two things clear at once. First, most of the postmodernisms mentioned above emerge as specific reactions against the established forms of high modernism, against this or that dominant high modernism which conquered the university, the museum, the art gallery network and the foundations. Those formerly subversive and embattled styles – Abstract Expressionism; the great modernist poetry of Pound, Eliot or Wallace Stevens; the International Style (Le Corbusier, Gropius, Mies van der Rohe); Stravinsky; Joyce, Proust and Mann – felt to be scandalous or shocking by our grandparents are, for the generation which arrives at the gate in the 1960s, felt to be the establishment and the enemy – dead, stifling, canonical, the reified monuments one has to destroy to do anything new. This means that there will be as many different forms of postmodernism as there were high modernisms in place, since the former are at least initially specific and local reactions against those models. That obviously does not make the job of describing postmodernism as a coherent thing any easier, since the unity of this new impulse – if it has one – is given not in itself but in the very modernism it seeks to displace.

The second feature of this list of postmodernisms is the effacement of some key boundaries or separations, most notably the erosion of the older distinction between high culture and so-called mass or popular culture. This is perhaps the most distressing development of all from an academic standpoint, which has traditionally had a vested interest in preserving a realm of high or elite culture against the surrounding environment of philistinism, of schlock and kitsch, of TV series and *Reader's Digest* culture, and in transmitting difficult and complex skills of reading, listening and seeing to its initiates. But many of the newer postmodernisms have been fascinated precisely by that whole landscape of advertising and motels, of the Las Vegas strip, of the Late Show and B-grade Hollywood film, of so-called paraliterature with its airport paperback categories of the gothic and the romance, the popular biography, the murder mystery and the science fiction or fantasy novel. They no longer 'quote' such 'texts' as a Joyce might have done, or a Mahler; they incorporate them, to the point where the line between high art and commercial forms seems increasingly difficult to draw.

A rather different indication of this effacement of the older categories of genre and discourse can be found in what is sometimes called contemporary theory. A generation ago there was still a technical discourse of professional philosophy – the great systems of Sartre or the phenomenologists, the work of Wittgenstein or analytical or common language philosophy – alongside which one could still distinguish that quite different discourse of the other academic disciplines – of political science, for example, or sociology or literary criticism. Today, increasingly, we have a kind of writing simply called 'theory' which is all or none of those things at once. This new kind of discourse, generally associated with France and so-called French theory, is becoming widespread and marks the end of philosophy as such. Is the work of Michel Foucault, for example, to be called philosophy, history, social theory or political science? It's undecidable, as they say nowadays, and I will suggest that such 'theoretical discourse' is also to be numbered among the manifestations of postmodernism.

Now I must say a word about the proper use of this concept: it is not just another word for the description of a particular style. It is also, at least in my use, a periodizing concept whose function is to correlate the emergence of new formal features in culture with the emergence of a new type of social life and a new economic order – what is often euphemistically called modernization, post-industrial or consumer society, the society of the media or the spectacle, or multinational capitalism. This new moment of capitalism can be dated from the post-war boom in the United States in the late 1940s and early 1950s or, in France, from the establishment of the Fifth Republic in 1958. The 1960s are in many ways the key transitional period, a period in which the new international order (neo-colonialism, the Green Revolution, computerization and electronic information) is at one and the same time set in place and is swept and shaken by its own internal contradictions and by external resistance. I want here to sketch a few of the ways in which the new postmodernism expresses the inner truth of that newly emergent social order of late capitalism, but will have to limit the description to only two of its significant features, which I will call pastiche and schizophrenia; they will give us a chance to sense the specificity of the postmodernist experience of space and time respectively.

3

Pastiche Eclipses Parody

One of the most significant features or practices in postmodern-ism today is pastiche. I must first explain this term (from the language of the visual arts), which people generally tend to confuse with or assimilate to that related verbal phenomenon called parody. Both pastiche and parody involve the imitation or, better still, the mimicry of other styles and particularly of the mannerisms and stylistic twitches of other styles. It is obvious that modern literature in general offers a very rich field for parody, since the great modern writers have all been defined by the invention or production of rather unique styles: think of the Faulknerian long sentence or of D. H. Lawrence's character-istic nature imagery; think of Wallace Steven's peculiar way of using abstractions; think also of mannerisms of the philos-ophers, of Heidegger for example, or Sartre; think of the musical styles of Mahler or Prokofiev. All of these styles, however different from one another, are comparable in this: each is quite unmistakable; once one of them is learned, it is not likely to be confused with something else.

Now parody capitalizes on the uniqueness of these styles and seizes on their idiosyncrasies and eccentricities to produce an imitation which mocks the original. I won't say that the satiric impulse is conscious in all forms of parody: in any case, a good or great parodist has to have some secret sympathy for the original, just as a great mimic has to have the capacity to put himself/herself in the place of the person imitated. Still, the general effect of parody is – whether in sympathy or with malice – to cast ridicule on the private nature of these stylistic manner-isms and their excessiveness and eccentricity with respect to the way people normally speak or write. So there remains some-where behind all parody the feeling that there is a linguistic norm in contrast to which the styles of the great modernists can be mocked.

But what would happen if one no longer believed in the existence of normal language, of ordinary speech, of the linguis-tic norm (the kind of clarity and communicative power cel-ebrated by Orwell in his famous essay 'Politics and the English

Language', say)? One could think of it in this way: perhaps the immense fragmentation and privatization of modern literature – its explosion into a host of distinct private styles and mannerisms – foreshadows deeper and more general tendencies in social life as a whole. Supposing that modern art and modernism – far from being a kind of specialized aesthetic curiosity – actually anticipated social developments along these lines; supposing that in the decades since the emergence of the great modern styles society had itself begun to fragment in this way, each group coming to speak a curious private language of its own, each profession developing its private code or idiolect, and finally each individual coming to be a kind of linguistic island, separated from everyone else? But then in that case, the very possibility of any linguistic norm in terms of which one could ridicule private languages and idiosyncratic styles would vanish, and we would have nothing but stylistic diversity and heterogeneity.

That is the moment at which pastiche appears and parody has become impossible. Pastiche is, like parody, the imitation of a peculiar or unique style, the wearing of a stylistic mask, speech in a dead language: but it is a neutral practice of such mimicry, without parody's ulterior motive, without the satirical impulse, without laughter, without that still latent feeling that there exists something *normal* compared with which what is being imitated is rather comic. Pastiche is blank parody, parody that has lost its sense of humour: pastiche is to parody what that curious thing, the modern practice of a kind of blank irony, is to what Wayne Booth calls the stable and comic ironies of the eighteenth century.[1]

The Death of the Subject

But now we need to introduce a new piece into this puzzle, which may help to explain why classical modernism is a thing of the past and why postmodernism should have taken its place. This new component is what is generally called the 'death of the subject' or, to say it in more conventional language, the end of individualism as such. The great modernisms were, as we have said, predicated on the invention of a personal, private style, as unmistakable as your fingerprint, as incomparable as your own body. But this means that the modernist aesthetic is in some way organically linked to the conception of a unique self and private identity, a unique personality and individuality, which can be expected to generate its own unique vision of the world and to forge its own unique, unmistakable style.

Yet today, from any number of distinct perspectives, the social theorists, the psychoanalysts, even the linguists, not to speak of those of us who work in the area of culture and cultural and formal change, are all exploring the notion that this kind of individualism and personal identity is a thing of the past; that the old individual or individualist subject is 'dead'; and that one might even describe the concept of the unique individual and the theoretical basis of individualism as ideological. There are in fact two positions on all this, one of which is more radical than the other. The first one is content to say: yes, once upon a time, in the classic age of competitive capitalism, in the heyday of the nuclear family and the emergence of the bourgeoisie as the hegemonic social class, there was such a thing as individualism, as individual subjects. But today, in the age of corporate capitalism, of the so-called organization man, of bureaucracies in business as well as in the state, of demographic explosion – today, that older bourgeois individual subject no longer exists.

Then there is a second position, the more radical of the two – what one might call the poststructuralist position. It adds: not only is the bourgeois individual subject a thing of the past, it is also a myth; it never really existed in the first place; there have never been autonomous subjects of that type. Rather, this construct is merely a philosophical and cultural mystification which sought to persuade people that they 'had' individual subjects and possessed some unique personal identity.

For our purposes, it is not particularly important to decide which of these positions is correct (or rather, which is more interesting and productive). What we have to retain from all this is rather an aesthetic dilemma: because if the experience and the ideology of the unique self, an experience and ideology which informed the stylistic practice of classical modernism, is over and done with, then it is no longer clear what the artists and writers of the present period are supposed to be doing. What is clear is merely that the older models – Picasso, Proust, T. S. Eliot – do not work any more (or are positively harmful), since nobody has that kind of unique private world and style to express any longer. And this is perhaps not merely a 'psychological' matter: we also have to take into account the immense weight of seventy or eighty years of classical modernism itself. This is yet another sense in which the writers and artists of the present day will no longer be able to invent new styles and worlds – they've already been invented; only a limited number of combinations are possible; the unique ones have been thought of already. So the weight of the whole modernist aesthetic tradition – now dead – also 'weighs like a nightmare on the brain of the living', as Marx said in another context.

Hence, once again, pastiche: in a world in which stylistic innovation is no longer possible, all that is left is to imitate dead styles, to speak through the masks and with the voices of the styles in the imaginary museum. But this means that contemporary or postmodernist art is going to be about art itself in a new kind of way; even more, it means that one of its essential messages will involve the necessary failure of art and the aesthetic, the failure of the new, the imprisonment in the past.

The Nostalgia Mode

As this may seem very abstract, I want to give a few examples, one of which is so omnipresent that we rarely link it with the kinds of developments in high art discussed here. This particular practice of pastiche is not high-cultural but very much within mass culture, and it is generally known as the 'nostalgia film' (what the French neatly call *la mode rétro* – retrospective styling). We must conceive of this category in the broadest way. Narrowly, no doubt, it consists merely of films about the past and about specific generational moments of that past. Thus, one of the inaugural films in this new 'genre' (if that's what it is) was Lucas's *American Graffiti*, which in 1973 set out to recapture all the atmosphere and stylistic peculiarities of the

1950s United States: the United States of the Eisenhower era. Polanski's great film *Chinatown* (1974) does something similar for the 1930s, as does Bertolucci's *The Conformist* (1969) for the Italian and European context of the same period, the fascist era in Italy; and so forth. We could go on listing these films for some time. But why call them pastiche? Are they not, rather, work in the more traditional genre known as the historical film – work which can more simply be theorized by extrapolating that other well-known form, the historical novel?

I have my reasons for thinking that we need new categories for such films. But let me first add some anomalies: supposing I suggested that *Star Wars* (George Lucas, 1977) is also a nostalgia film. What could that mean? I presume that we can agree that this is not a historical film about our own intergalactic past. Let me put it somewhat differently: one of the most important cultural experiences of the generations that grew up from the 1930s to the 1950s was the Saturday afternoon serial of the Buck Rogers type – alien villains, true American heroes, heroines in distress, the death ray or the doomsday box, and the cliff-hanger at the end whose miraculous solution was to be witnessed next Saturday afternoon. *Star Wars* reinvents this experience in the form of a pastiche; there is no point to a parody of such serials, since they are long extinct. Far from being a pointless satire of such dead forms, *Star Wars* satisfies a deep (might I even say repressed?) longing to experience them again: it is a complex object in which on some first level children and adolescents can take the adventures straight, while the adult public is able to gratify a deeper and more properly nostalgic desire to return to that older period and to live its strange old aesthetic artefacts through once again. This film is thus *metonymically* a historical or nostalgia film. Unlike *American Graffiti*, it does not reinvent a picture of the past in its lived totality; rather, by reinventing the feel and shape of characteristic art objects of an older period (the serials), it seeks to reawaken a sense of the past associated with those objects. *Raiders of the Lost Ark* (1981), meanwhile, occupies an intermediary position here: on some level it is about the 1930s and 1940s, but in reality it too conveys that period metonymically through its own characteristic adventure stories (which are no longer ours).

Now let me discuss another anomaly which may take us further towards understanding nostalgia film in particular and pastiche generally. This one involves a recent film called *Body Heat* (Lawrence Kasdan, 1981), which, as has abundantly been pointed out by the critics, is a kind of distant remake of *Double Indemnity* (1944). (The allusive and elusive plagiarism of older plots is, of course, also a feature of pastiche.) Now *Body Heat* is technically not a nostalgia film, since it takes place in a contemporary setting, in a little Florida village near Miami. On the other hand, this technical contemporaneity is most ambiguous indeed: the credits – always our first cue – are all lettered in a 1930s Art-Deco style which cannot but trigger nostalgic reactions (first to *Chinatown*, no doubt, and then beyond it to some more historical referent). Then the very style of the hero himself is ambiguous: William Hurt is a new star but has nothing of the distinctive style of the preceding generation of male superstars like Steve McQueen or Jack Nicholson, or rather, his persona here is a kind of mix of their characteristics with an older role of the type generally associated with Clark Gable. So here too there is a faintly archaic feel to all this. This spectator begins to wonder why this story, which could have been situated anywhere, is set in a small Florida town, in spite of its contemporary reference. One begins to realize after a while that the small town setting has a crucial strategic function: it allows the film to do without most of the signals and references which we might associate with the contemporary world, with consumer society – the appliances and artefacts, the high rises, the object world of late capitalism. Technically, then, its objects (its cars, for instance) are 1980s products, but everything in the film conspires to blur that immediate contemporary reference and to make it possible to receive this too as nostalgia work – as a narrative set in some indefinable nostalgic past, an eternal 1930s, say, beyond history. It seems to me exceedingly symptomatic to find the very style of nostalgia films invading and colonizing even those movies today which have contemporary settings, as though, for some reason, we were unable today to focus our own present, as though we had become incapable of achieving aesthetic representations of our own current experience. But if that is so, then it is a terrible indictment of consumer capitalism itself – or, at the very least, an alarming and pathological symptom of a society that has become incapable of dealing with time and history.

So now we come back to the question of why nostalgia film or pastiche is to be considered different from the older historical novel or film. I should also include in this discussion the major literary example of all this, to my mind: the novels of E. L. Doctorow – *Ragtime*, with its turn-of-the-century atmosphere, and *Loon Lake*, for the most part about our 1930s. But these are, in my opinion, historical novels in appearance only. Doctorow is a serious artist and one of the few genuinely left or radical novelists at work today. It is no disservice to him, however, to suggest that his narratives do not represent our historical past so much as they represent our ideas or cultural stereotypes about that past. Cultural production has been driven back inside the mind, within the monadic subject: it can no longer look directly out of its eyes at the real world for the referent but must, as in Plato's cave, trace its mental images of the world on its confining walls. If there is any realism left here, it is a 'realism' which springs from the shock of grasping that confinement and of realizing that, for whatever peculiar reasons, we seem condemned to seek the historical past through our own pop images and stereotypes about the past, which itself remains forever out of reach.

Postmodernism and the City

Now, before I try to offer a somewhat more positive conclusion, I want to sketch the analysis of a full-blown postmodern building – a work which is in many ways uncharacteristic of that postmodern architecture whose principal names are Robert Venturi, Charles Moore, Michael Graves and more recently Frank Gehry, but which to my mind offers some very striking lessons about the originality of postmodernist space. Let me amplify the figure which has run through the preceding remarks, and make it even more explicit: I am proposing the notion that we are here in the presence of something like a mutation in built space itself. My implication is that we ourselves, the human subjects who happen into this new space, have not kept pace with that evolution; there has been a mutation in the object, unaccompanied as yet by any equivalent mutation in the subject; we do not yet possess the perceptual equipment to match this new hyperspace, as I will call it, in part because our perceptual habits were formed in that older kind of space I have called the space of high modernism. The newer architecture – like many of the other cultural products I have evoked in the preceding remarks – therefore stands as something like an imperative to grow new organs to expand our sensoria and our bodies to some new, as yet unimaginable, perhaps ultimately impossible, dimensions.

The Bonaventure Hotel

The building whose features I will enumerate here is the Westin Bonaventure Hotel, built in the new Los Angeles downtown by the architect and developer John Portman, whose other works include the various Hyatt Regencies, the Peachtree Center in Atlanta, and the Renaissance Center in Detroit. I must mention the populist aspect of the rhetorical defence of postmodernism against the elite (and utopian) austerities of the great architectural modernisms: it is generally affirmed that these newer buildings are popular works on the one hand; and that they respect the vernacular of the American city fabric on the other. That is to say that they no longer attempt, as did the masterworks and monuments of high modernism, to insert a different, distinct, an elevated, a new utopian language into the tawdry and commercial sign-system of the surrounding city, but on the contrary, seek to speak that very language, using its lexicon and syntax, that has been emblematically 'learned from Las Vegas'.

On the first of these counts, Portman's Bonaventure fully confirms the claim: it is a popular building, visited with enthusiasm by locals and tourists alike (although Portman's other buildings are even more successful in this respect). The populist insertion into the city fabric is, however, another matter, and it is with this that we will begin. There are three entrances to the Bonaventure: one from Figueroa, and the other two by way of elevated gardens on the other side of the hotel, which is built into the remaining slope of the former Beacon Hill. None of these is anything like the old hotel marquee, or the monumental *porte-cochère* with which the sumptuous buildings of yesteryear were wont to stage your passage from city street to the older interior. The entryways of the Bonaventure are, as it were, lateral and rather backdoor affairs: the gardens in the back admit you to the sixth floor of the towers, and even there you must walk down one flight to find the elevator by which you gain access to the lobby. Meanwhile, what one is still tempted to think of as the front entry, on Figueroa, admits you, baggage and all, onto the second-storey balcony, from which you must take an escalator down to the main registration desk. More about these elevators and escalators in a moment. What I first want to suggest about these curiously unmarked ways-in is that they seem to have been imposed by some new category of closure governing the inner space of the hotel itself (and this over and above the material constraints under which Portman had to work). I believe that, with a certain number of other characteristic postmodern buildings, such as the Beaubourg in Paris, or the Eaton Center in Toronto, the Bonaventure aspires to being a total space, a complete world, a kind of miniature city (and I would want to add that to this new total space corresponds a new collective practice, a new mode in which individuals move and congregate, something like the practice of a new and historically original kind of hyper-crowd). In this sense, then, the mini-city of Portman's Bonaventure ideally ought not to have entrances at all (since the entryway is always the seam that links the building to the rest of the city that surrounds it), for it does not wish to be a part of the city, but rather its equivalent and its replacement or substitute. That is, however, obviously not possible or practical, hence the deliberate downplaying and reduction of the entrance function to its bare minimum. But this disjunction from the surrounding city is very different from that of the great monuments of the International Style: there, the act of disjunction was violent, visible and had a very real symbolic significance – as in Le Corbusier's great *pilotis*, whose gesture radically separates the new utopian space of the modern from the degraded and fallen city fabric, which it thereby explicitly repudiates (although the gamble of the modern was that this new utopian space, in the virulence of its Novum, would fan out and transform that eventually by the power of its new spatial language). The Bonaventure, however, is content to 'let the fallen city fabric continue to be in its being' (to parody Heidegger); no further effects – no larger protopolitical utopian transformation – are either expected or desired.

This diagnosis is, to my mind, confirmed by the great reflective glass skin of the Bonaventure, whose function might first be interpreted as developing a thematics of reproductive technology. Now, on a second reading, one would want to stress the way in which the glass skin repels the city outside; a repulsion for which we have analogies in those reflective sunglasses which make it impossible for your interlocutor to see your own eyes and thereby achieve a certain aggressivity towards and power over the Other. In a similar way, the glass skin achieves a peculiar and placeless dissociation of the Bonaventure from its neighbourhood: it is not even an exterior, inasmuch as when you seek to look at the hotel's outer walls you cannot see the hotel itself, but only the distorted images of everything that surrounds it.

Now I want to say a few words about escalators and elevators. Given their very real pleasures in Portman's architecture – particularly these last, which the artist has termed 'gigantic kinetic sculptures' and which certainly account for much of the spectacle and the excitement of the hotel interior, especially in the Hyatts, where like great Japanese lanterns or gondolas they ceaselessly rise and fall – and given such a deliberate marking and foregrounding in their own right, I believe one has to see such 'people movers' (Portman's own term, adapted from Disney) as something a little more meaningful than mere functions and engineering components. We know in any case that recent architectural theory has begun to borrow from narrative analysis in other fields, and to attempt to see our physical trajectories through such buildings as virtual narratives or stories, as dynamic paths and narrative paradigms which we as visitors are asked to fulfil and to complete with our own bodies and movements. In the Bonaventure, however, we find a dialectical heightening of this process. It seems to me that not only do the escalators and elevators here henceforth replace movement, but also and above all designate themselves as new reflexive signs and emblems of movement proper (something which will become evident when we come to the whole question of what remains of older forms of movement in this building, most notably walking itself). Here the narrative stroll has been underscored, symbolized, reified and replaced by a transportation machine which becomes the allegorical signifier of that older promenade we are no longer allowed to conduct on our own. This is a dialectical intensification of the autoreferentiality of all modern culture, which tends to turn upon itself and designate its own cultural production as its content.

I am more at a loss when it comes to conveying the thing itself, the experience of space you undergo when you step off such allegorical devices into the lobby or atrium, with its great central column, surrounded by a miniature lake, the whole positioned between the four symmetrical residential towers with their elevators, and surrounded by rising balconies capped by a kind of greenhouse roof at the sixth level. I am tempted to say that such space makes it impossible for us to use the language of volume or volumes any longer, since these last are impossible to seize. Hanging streamers indeed suffuse this empty space in such a way as to distract systematically and deliberately from whatever form it might be supposed to have; while a constant busyness gives the feeling that emptiness is here absolutely packed, that it is an element within which you yourself are immersed, without any of that distance that formerly enabled the perception of perspective or volume. You are in this hyperspace up to your eyes and your body; and if it seemed to you before that the suppression of depth observable in postmodern painting or literature would necessarily be difficult to achieve in architecture itself, perhaps you may now be willing to see this bewildering immersion as its formal equivalent in the new medium.

Yet escalator and elevator are also, in this context, dialectical opposites; and we may suggest that the glorious movement of the elevator gondolas is also a dialectical compensation for this filled space of the atrium – it gives us the chance of a radically different, but complementary, spatial experience: that of rapidly shooting up through the ceiling and outside, along one of the four symmetrical towers, with the referent, Los Angeles itself, spread out breathtakingly and even alarmingly before us. But even this vertical movement is contained: the elevator lifts you to one of those revolving cocktail lounges, in which you, seated, are again passively rotated about and offered a contemplative spectacle of the city itself, now transformed into its own images by the glass windows through which you view it.

Let me quickly conclude all this by returning to the central space of the lobby itself (with the passing observation that the hotel rooms are visibly marginalized: the corridors in the residential sections are low-ceilinged and dark, most depressingly functional indeed, while one understands that the rooms – frequently redecorated – are in the worst taste). The descent is dramatic enough, plummeting back down through the roof to splash down in the lake; what happens when you get there is something else, which I can only try to characterize as milling confusion, something like the vengeance this space takes on those who still seek to walk through it. Given the absolute symmetry of the four towers, it is quite impossible to get your bearings in this lobby; recently, colour coding and directional signals have been added in a pitiful, rather desperate and revealing attempt to restore the co-ordinates of an older space. I will take as the most dramatic practical result of this spatial mutation the notorious dilemma of the shopkeepers on the various balconies: it has been obvious, since the very opening of the hotel in 1977, that nobody could ever find any of these stores, and even if you located the appropriate boutique, you would be most unlikely to be as fortunate a second time; as a consequence, the commercial tenants are in despair and all the merchandise is marked down to bargain prices. When you recall that Portman is a businessman as well as an architect, and a millionaire developer, an artist who is at one and the same time a capitalist in his own right, you cannot but feel that here too something of a 'return of the repressed' is involved.

So I come finally to my principal point here, that this latest mutation in space – postmodern hyperspace – has finally succeeded in transcending the capacities of the individual human body to locate itself, to organize its immediate surroundings perceptually, and to map cognitively its position in a mappable external world. And I have already suggested that this alarming disjunction between the body and its built environment – which is to the initial bewilderment of the older modernism as the velocities of spacecraft are to those of the automobile – can itself stand as the symbol and analogue of that even sharper dilemma, which is the incapacity of our minds, at least at present, to map the great global, multinational and decentred communicational network in which we find ourselves caught as individual subjects.

The New Machine

But as I am anxious that Portman's space not be perceived as something either exceptional or seemingly marginalized and leisure-specialized on the order of Disneyland, I would like in passing to juxtapose this complacent and entertaining (although bewildering) leisure-time space with its analogue in a very different area, namely the space of postmodern warfare, in particular as Michael Herr evokes it in his great book on the experience of Vietnam, *Dispatches*. The extraordinary linguistic innovations of this work may be considered postmodern in the eclectic way in which its language impersonally fuses a whole range of contemporary collective idiolects, most notably rock language and black language, but the fusion is dictated by problems of content. This first terrible postmodernist war cannot be recounted in any of the traditional paradigms of the war novel or movie – indeed, that breakdown of all previous narrative paradigms is, along with the breakdown of any shared language through which a veteran might convey such experience, among the principal subjects of the book and may be said to open up the place of a whole new reflexivity. Benjamin's account of Baudelaire, and of the emergence of modernism from a new experience of city technology which transcends all the older habits of bodily perception, is both singularly relevant here and singularly antiquated, in the light of this new and virtually unimaginable quantum leap in technological alienation:

He was a moving-target-survivor subscriber, a true child of the war, because except for the rare times when you were pinned or stranded the system was geared to keep you mobile, if that was what you thought you wanted. As a technique for staying alive it seemed to make as much sense as anything, given naturally that you were there to begin with and wanted to see it close; it started out sound and straight but it formed a cone as it progressed, because the more you moved the more you saw, the more you saw the more besides death and mutilation you risked, and the more you risked of that the more you would have to let go of one day as a 'survivor'. Some of us moved around the war like crazy people until we couldn't see which way the run was taking us anymore, only the war all over its surface with occasional, unexpected penetration. As long as we could have choppers like taxis it took real exhaustion or depression near shock or a dozen pipes of opium to keep us even apparently quiet, we'd still be running around inside our skins like something was after us, ha, ha, La Vida Loca. In the months after I got back the hundreds of helicopters I'd flown in began to draw together until they'd formed a collective meta-chopper, and in my mind it was the sexiest thing going; saver-destroyer, provider-waster, right hand-left hand, nimble, fluent, canny and human; hot steel, grease, jungle-saturated canvas webbing, sweat cooling and warming up again, cassette rock and roll in one ear and door-gun fire in the other, fuel, heat, vitality and death, death itself, hardly an intruder.[2]

In this new machine, which does not, like the older modernist machinery of the locomotive or the airplane, represent motion, but which can only be represented *in motion*, something of the mystery of the new postmodernist space is concentrated.

The Aesthetic of Consumer Society

Now I must try, in conclusion, to characterize the relationship of cultural production of this kind to social life in this country today. This will also be the moment to address the principal objection to concepts of postmodernism of the type I have sketched here: namely that all the features we have enumerated are not new at all but abundantly characterized modernism proper or what I call high modernism. Was not Thomas Mann, after all, interested in the idea of pastiche, and is not 'The Oxen of the Sun' chapter of *Ulysses* its most obvious realization? Can Flaubert, Mallarmé and Gertrude Stein not be included in an account of postmodernist temporality? What is so new about all of this? Do we really need the concept of postmodernism?

One kind of answer to this question would raise the whole issue of periodization and of how a historian (literary or other) posits a radical break between two henceforth distinct periods. I must limit myself to the suggestion that radical breaks between periods do not generally involve complete changes of content but rather the restructuring of a certain number of elements already given: features that in an earlier period or system were subordinate now become dominant, and features that had been dominant again become secondary. In this sense, everything we have described here can be found in earlier periods and most notably within modernism proper. My point is that until the present day those things have been secondary or minor features of modernist art, marginal rather than central, and that we have something new when they become the central features of cultural production.

But I can argue this more concretely by turning to the relationship between cultural production and social life generally. The older or classical modernism was an oppositional art; it emerged within the business society of the gilded age as scandalous and offensive to the middle-class public – ugly, dissonant, bohemian, sexually shocking. It was something to make fun of (when the police were not called in to seize the books or close the exhibitions): an offence to good taste and to common sense, or, as Freud and Marcuse would have put it, a provocative challenge to the reigning reality- and performance-principles of early twentieth-century middle-class society. Modernism in general did not go well with overstuffed Victorian furniture, with Victorian moral taboos, or with the conventions of polite society. This is to say that whatever the explicit political content of the great high modernisms, the latter were always in some mostly implicit ways dangerous and explosive, subversive within the established order.

If then we suddenly return to the present day, we can measure the immensity of the cultural changes that have taken place. Not only are Joyce and Picasso no longer weird and repulsive, they have become classics and now look rather realistic to us. Meanwhile, there is very little in either the form or the content of contemporary art that contemporary society finds intolerable and scandalous. The most offensive forms of this art – punk rock, say, or what is called sexually explicit material – are all taken in its stride by society, and they are commercially success- ful, unlike the productions of the older high modernism. But this means that even if contemporary art has all the same formal features as the older modernism, it has still shifted its position fundamentally within our culture. For one thing, commodity production and in particular our clothing, furniture, buildings and other artefacts are now intimately tied in with styling changes which derive from artistic experimentation; our adver- tising, for example, is fed by modernism in all the arts and inconceivable without. For another, the classics of high modern- ism are now part of the so-called canon and are taught in schools and universities – which at once empties them of any of their older subversive power. Indeed, one way of marking the break between the periods and of dating the emergence of postmodernism is precisely to be found there: at the moment (the early 1960s, one would think) in which the position of high modernism and its dominant aesthetics become established in the academy and are henceforth felt to be academic by a whole new generation of poets, painters and musicians.

But one can also come at the break from the other side, and describe it in terms of periods of recent social life. As I have suggested, Marxists and non-Marxists alike have come around to the general feeling that at some point following World War Two a new kind of society began to emerge (variously described as post-industrial society, multinational capitalism, consumer society, media society and so forth). New types of consumption; planned obsolescence; an ever more rapid rhythm of fashion and styling changes; the penetration of advertising, television and the media generally to a hitherto unparalleled degree throughout society; the replacement of the old tension between city and country, centre and province, by the suburb and by universal standardization; the growth of the great networks of superhighways and the arrival of automobile culture – these are some of the features which would seem to mark a radical break with that older pre-war society in which high modernism was still an underground force.

I believe that the emergence of postmodernism is closely related to the emergence of this new moment of late consumer or multinational capitalism. I believe also that its formal features in many ways express the deeper logic of this particular social system. I will only be able, however, to show this for one major theme: namely the disappearance of a sense of history, the way in which our entire contemporary social system has little by little begun to lose its capacity to retain its own past, has begun to live in a perpetual present and in a perpetual change that obliterates traditions of the kind which all earlier social information have had, in one way or another, to preserve. Think only of the media exhaustion of news: of how Nixon and, even more so, Kennedy, are figures from a now distant past. One is tempted to say that the very function of the news media is to relegate such recent historical experiences as rapidly as possible into the past. The informational function of the media would thus be to help us forget, to serve as the very agents and mechanisms for our historical amnesia.

But in that case the two features of postmodernism on which I have dwelt here – the transformation of reality into images, the fragmentation of time into a series of perpetual presents – are both extraordinarily consonant with this process. My own conclusion here must take the form of a question about the critical value of the newer art. There is some agreement that the older modernism functioned against its society in ways which are variously described as critical, negative, contestatory, subversive, oppositional and the like. Can anything of the sort be affirmed about postmodernism and its social moment? We have seen that there is a way in which postmodernism replicates or reproduces – reinforces – the logic of consumer capitalism; the more significant question is whether there is also a way in which it resists that logic. But that is a question we must leave open.

Theories of the Postmodern

The problem of postmodernism – how its fundamental characteristics are to be described, whether it even exists in the first place, whether the very *concept* is of any use, or is, on the contrary, a mystification – this problem is at one and the same time an aesthetic and a political one. The various positions that can logically be taken on it, whatever terms they are couched in, can always be shown to articulate visions of history in which the evaluation of the social moment in which we live today is the object of an essentially political affirmation or repudiation. Indeed, the very enabling premise of the debate turns on an initial, strategic presupposition about our social system: to grant some historic originality to a postmodernist culture is also implicitly to affirm some radical structural difference between what is sometimes called consumer society and earlier moments of the capitalism from which it emerged.

The various logical possibilities, however, are necessarily linked with the taking of a position on that other issue inscribed in the very designation postmodernism itself, namely, the evaluation of what must now be called high or classical modernism. Indeed, when we make some initial inventory of the varied cultural artefacts that might plausibly be characterized as postmodern, the temptation is strong to seek the 'family resemblance' of such heterogeneous styles and products not in themselves but in some common high modernist impulse and aesthetic against which they all, in one way or another, stand in reaction.

The architectural debates, however, the inaugural discussions of postmodernism as a style, have the merit of making the political resonance of these seemingly aesthetic issues inescapable and allowing it to be detectable in the sometimes more coded or veiled discussions in the other arts. On the whole, four general positions on postmodernism may be disengaged from the variety of recent pronouncements on the subject; yet even this relatively neat scheme, or *combinatoire*, is further complicated by one's impression that each of these possibilities is susceptible of either a politically progressive or a politically reactionary expression (speaking now from a Marxist or more generally left perspective).

One can, for example, salute the arrival of postmodernism from an essentially antimodernist standpoint.[1] A somewhat earlier generation of theorists (most notably Ihab Hassan) seem already to have done something like this when they dealt with the postmodernist aesthetic in terms of a more properly poststructuralist thematics (the *Tel quel* attack on the ideology of representation, the Heideggerian or Derridean 'end of Western metaphysics'), where what is often not yet called postmodernism (see the utopian prophecy at the end of Foucault's *The Order of Things*) is saluted as the coming of a whole new way of thinking and being in the world. But since Hassan's celebration also includes a number of the more extreme monuments of high modernism (Joyce, Mallarmé), this would be a relatively more ambiguous stance were it not for the accompanying celebration of a new informational high technology which marks the affinity between such evocations and the political thesis of a properly 'post-industrial society'.

All of which is largely disambiguated in Tom Wolfe's *From Bauhaus to Our House*, an otherwise undistinguished book on the recent architectural debates by a writer whose own New Journalism itself constitutes one of the varieties of postmodernism. What is interesting and symptomatic about this book, however, is the absence of any utopian celebration of the postmodern and, far more striking, the passionate hatred of the modern that breathes through the otherwise obligatory camp sarcasm of the rhetoric; and this is not a new, but a dated and archaic passion. It is as though the original horror of the first middle-class spectators of the very emergence of the modern itself – the first Corbusiers, as white as the first freshly built cathedrals of the twelfth century, the first scandalous Picasso heads with two eyes on one profile like a flounder, the stunning 'obscurity' of the first editions of *Ulysses* or *The Waste Land* – this disgust of the original philistines, *Spießbürger*, bourgeois or Main Street Babbitry, had suddenly come back to life, infusing the newer critiques of modernism with an ideologically very different spirit whose effect is, on the whole, to reawaken in the reader an equally archaic sympathy with the protopolitical, utopian, anti-middle-class impulses of a now extinct high modernism itself. Wolfe's diatribe thus offers a textbook example of the way in which a reasoned and contemporary theoretical repudiation of the modern – much of whose progressive force springs from a new sense of the urban and a now considerable experience of the destruction of older forms of communal and urban life in the name of a high-modernist orthodoxy – can be handily reappropriated and pressed into the service of an explicitly reactionary cultural politics.

These positions – antimodern, propostmodern – then find their opposite number and structural inversion in a group of counterstatements whose aim is to discredit the shoddiness and irresponsibility of the postmodern in general by way of a reaffirmation of the authentic impulse of a high-modernist tradition still considered to be alive and vital. Hilton Kramer's twin manifestos in the inaugural issue of his journal, *The New Criterion*, articulate these views with force, contrasting the moral responsibility of the 'masterpieces' and monuments of classical modernism with the fundamental irresponsibility and superficiality of a postmodernism associated with camp and the 'facetiousness' of which Wolfe's style is a ripe and obvious example.

What is more paradoxical is that politically Wolfe and Kramer have much in common; and there would seem to be a certain inconsistency in the way in which Kramer must seek to eradicate from the 'high seriousness' of the classics of the modern their fundamentally anti-middle-class stance and the protopolitical passion which informs the repudiation, by the great modernists, of Victorian taboos and family life, of commodification, and of the increasing asphyxiation of a desacralizing capitalism, from

Ibsen to Lawrence, from Van Gogh to Jackson Pollock. Kramer's ingenious attempt to assimilate this ostensibly anti-bourgeois stance of the great modernists to a 'loyal opposition' secretly nourished, by way of foundations and grants, by the bourgeoisie itself, while signally unconvincing, is surely itself enabled by the contradictions of the cultural politics of modernism proper, whose negations depend on the persistence of what they repudiate, and entertain – when they do not (very rarely indeed, as in Brecht) attain some genuine political self-consciousness – a symbiotic relationship with capital.

It is, however, easier to understand Kramer's move here when the political project of *The New Criterion* is clarified; for the mission of the journal is clearly to eradicate the sixties itself and what remains of its legacy, to consign that whole period to the kind of oblivion which the fifties was able to devise for the thirties, or the twenties for the rich political culture of the pre-World War One era. *The New Criterion* therefore inscribes itself in the effort, ongoing and at work everywhere today, to construct some new conservative cultural counterrevolution, whose terms range from the aesthetic to the ultimate defence of the family and religion. It is therefore paradoxical that this essentially political project should explicitly deplore the omnipresence of politics in contemporary culture – an infection largely spread during the sixties but which Kramer holds responsible for the moral imbecility of the postmodernism of our own period.

The problem with the operation – an obviously indispensable one from the conservative viewpoint – is that for whatever reason, its papermoney rhetoric does not seem to have been backed by the solid gold of state power, as was the case with McCarthyism or during the period of the Palmer raids. The failure of the Vietnam War seems, at least for the moment, to have made the naked exercise of repressive power impossible[2] and to have endowed the sixties with a persistence in collective memory and experience that it was not given to the traditions of the thirties or the pre-World War One period to know. Kramer's 'cultural revolution' therefore tends most often to lapse into a feeble and sentimental nostalgia for the fifties and the Eisenhower era.

In the light of what has been shown for an earlier set of positions on modernism and postmodernism, it will not be surprising that in spite of the openly conservative ideology of this second evaluation of the contemporary cultural scene, the latter can also be appropriated for what is surely a far more progressive line on the subject. We are indebted to Jürgen Habermas[3] for this dramatic reversal and rearticulation of what remains the affirmation of the supreme value of the modern and the repudiation of the theory and practice of postmodernism. For Habermas, however, the vice of postmodernism consists very centrally in its politically reactionary function, as the attempt everywhere to discredit a modernist impulse Habermas himself associates with the bourgeois Enlightenment and its still universalizing and utopian spirit. With Adorno himself, Habermas seeks to rescue and recommemorate what both see as the essentially negative, critical and utopian power of the great high modernisms. On the other hand, his attempt to associate these last with the spirit of the eighteenth-century Enlightenment marks a decisive break indeed with Adorno and Horkheimer's sombre *Dialectic of Enlightenment*, in which the scientific ethos of the *philosophes* is dramatized as a misguided will to power and domination over nature, and their desacralizing program as the first stage in the development of a sheerly instrumentalizing world-view which will lead straight to Auschwitz. This very striking divergence can be accounted for by Habermas's own vision of history, which seeks to maintain the promise of 'liberalism' and the essentially utopian content of the first, universalizing bourgeois ideology (equality, civil rights, humanitarianism, free speech and open media) despite the failure of those ideals to be realized in the development of capitalism itself.

As for the aesthetic terms of the debate, however, it will not be adequate to respond to Habermas's resuscitation of the modern by some mere empirical certification of the latter's extinction. We need to take into account the possibility that the national situation in which Habermas thinks and writes is rather different from our own: McCarthyism and repression are, for one thing, realities in the Federal Republic of Germany today, and the intellectual intimidation of the Left and the silencing of a left culture (largely associated, by the West German Right, with 'terrorism') has been on the whole a far more successful operation than elsewhere in the West.[4] The triumph of a new McCarthyism and of the culture of the *Spießbürger* and the philistine suggests the possibility that in this particular national situation Habermas may well be right, and the older forms of high modernism may still retain something of the subversive power they have lost elsewhere. In that case, a postmodernism which seeks to enfeeble and undermine that power may well also merit his ideological diagnosis in a local way, even though the assessment remains ungeneralizable.

Both of the previous positions – antimodern/propostmodern and promodern/antipostmodern – are characterized by an acceptance of the new term, which is tantamount to an agreement on the fundamental nature of some decisive break between the modern and the postmodern moments, however these are evaluated. There remain, however, two final logical possibilities, both of which depend on the repudiation of any conception of such a historical break and which therefore, implicitly or explicitly, call into question the usefulness of the very category of postmodernism. As for the works associated with the latter, they will then be assimilated back into classical modernism proper, so that the 'postmodern' becomes little more than the form taken by the authentically modern in our own period, and a mere dialectical intensification of the old modernist impulse toward innovation. (I must here omit yet another series of debates, largely academic, in which the very continuity of modernism as it is here reaffirmed is itself called into question by some vaster sense of the profound continuity of romanticism, from the late eighteenth century on, of which both the modern and the postmodern will be seen as mere organic stages.)

The two final positions on the subject thus logically prove to be a positive and negative assessment, respectively, of a postmodernism now assimilated back into the high-modernist tradition. Jean-François Lyotard[5] thus proposes that his own vital commitment to the new and the emergent, to a contemporary or postcontemporary cultural production now widely characterized as 'postmodern', be grasped as part and parcel of a reaffirmation of the authentic older high modernisms very much in Adorno's spirit. The ingenious twist, or swerve, in his own proposal involves the proposition that something called post-modernism does not *follow* high modernism proper, as the latter's waste product, but rather very precisely *precedes* and prepares it, so that the contemporary postmodernisms all around us may be seen as the promise of the return and the reinvention, the triumphant reappearance, of some new high modernism endowed with all its older power and with fresh life. This is a prophetic stance whose analyses turn on the antirepresentational thrust of modernism and postmodernism. Lyotard's aesthetic positions, however, cannot be adequately evaluated in aesthetic terms, since what informs them is an essentially social and political conception of a new social system beyond classical capitalism (our old friend 'post-industrial society'): the vision of a regenerated modernism is, in that sense, inseparable from a certain prophetic faith in the possibilities and promise of the new society itself in full emergence.

The negative inversion of this position will then clearly involve an ideological repudiation of modernism of a type which might conceivably range from Lukács's older analysis of modernist forms as the replication of the reification of capitalist social life all the way to some of the more articulated critiques of high modernism of the present day. What distinguishes this final position from the antimodernisms already outlined above is, however, that it does not speak from the security of an affirmation of some new postmodernist culture but rather sees even the latter itself as a mere degeneration of the already stigmatized impulses of high modernism proper. This particular position, perhaps the bleakest of all and the most implacably negative, can be vividly confronted in the works of the Venetian architecture historian Manfredo Tafuri, whose extensive analyses[6] constitute a powerful indictment of what we have termed the 'protopolitical' impulses in high modernism (the 'utopian' substitution of cultural politics for politics proper, the vocation to transform the world by transforming its forms, space or language). Tafuri is, however, no less harsh in his anatomy of the negative, demystifying, 'critical' vocation of the various modernisms, whose function he reads as a kind of Hegelian 'ruse of History' whereby the instrumentalizing and desacralizing tendencies of capital itself are ultimately realized through just such demolition work by the thinkers and artists of the modern movement. Their 'anticapitalism' therefore ends up laying the basis for the 'total' bureaucratic organization and control of late capitalism, and it is only logical that Tafuri should conclude by positing the impossibility of any radical transformation of culture before a radical transformation of social relationships themselves.

The political ambivalence demonstrated in the earlier two positions seems to me to be maintained here, but *within* the positions of both of these very complex thinkers. Unlike many of the previously mentioned theorists, Tafuri and Lyotard are both explicitly political figures with an overt commitment to the values of an older revolutionary tradition. It is clear, for example, that Lyotard's embattled endorsement of the supreme value of aesthetic innovation is to be understood as the figure for a certain kind of revolutionary stance, while Tafuri's whole conceptual framework is largely consistent with the classical Marxist tradition. Yet both are also, implicitly, and more openly at certain strategic moments, rewritable in terms of a post-Marxism which at length becomes indistinguishable from anti-Marxism proper. Lyotard has, for example, very frequently sought to distinguish his 'revolutionary' aesthetic from the older ideals of political revolution, which he sees as either Stalinist or archaic and incompatible with the conditions of the new post-industrial social order; while Tafuri's apocalyptic notion of the total social revolution implies a conception of the 'total system' of capitalism which, in a period of depoliticization and reaction, is only too fatally destined for the kind of discouragement which has so often led Marxists to a renunciation of the political altogether (Horkheimer and Merleau-Ponty come to mind, along with many of the ex-Trotskyists of the thirties and forties and the ex-Maoists of the sixties and seventies).

The combination scheme outlined above can now be schematically represented as follows, the plus and minus signs designating the politically progressive or reactionary functions of the positions in question:

THEORIES OF THE POSTMODERN

	ANTIMODERNIST	PROMODERNIST
PROPOSTMODERNIST	Wolfe − Jencks +	Lyotard $\left\{\begin{array}{l}+\\-\end{array}\right.$
ANTIPOSTMODERNIST	Tafuri $\left\{\begin{array}{l}-\\+\end{array}\right.$	Kramer − Habermas +

With these remarks we come full circle and can now return to the more positive potential political content of the first position in question, and in particular to the question of a certain *populist* impulse in postmodernism which it has been the merit of Charles Jencks (but also of Venturi and others) to have underscored – a question that will also allow us to deal a little more adequately with the absolute pessimism of Tafuri's Marxism itself. What must first be observed, however, is that most of the political positions which we have found to inform what is most often conducted as an aesthetic debate are in reality moralizing ones that seek to develop final judgments on the phenomenon of postmodernism, whether the latter is stigmatized as corrupt or, on the other hand, saluted as a culturally and aesthetically healthy and positive form of innovation. But a genuinely historical and dialectical analysis of such phenomena – particularly when it is a matter of a present of time and of history in which we ourselves exist and struggle – cannot afford the impoverished luxury of such absolute moralizing judgments: the dialectic is 'beyond good and evil' in the sense of some easy taking of sides, whence the glacial and inhuman spirit of its historical vision (something that already disturbed contemporaries about Hegel's original system). The point is that we are *within* the culture of postmodernism to the point where its facile repudiation is as impossible as any equally facile celebration of it is complacent and corrupt. Ideological judgment on postmodernism today necessarily implies, one would think, a judgment on ourselves as well as of the artefacts in question; nor can an entire historical period, such as our own, be grasped in any adequate way by means of global moral judgments or

29

their somewhat degraded equivalent, pop psychological diagnoses. On the classical Marxian view, the seeds of the future already exist within the present and must be conceptually disengaged from it, both through analysis and through political praxis (the workers of the Paris Commune, Marx once remarked in a striking phrase, '*have no ideals to realize*'; they merely sought to disengage emergent forms of new social relations from the older capitalist social relations in which the former had already begun to stir). In place of the temptation either to denounce the complacencies of postmodernism as some final symptom of decadence or to salute the new forms as the harbingers of a new technological and technocratic utopia, it seems more appropriate to assess the new cultural production within the working hypothesis of a general modification of culture itself with the social restructuring of late capitalism as a system.[7]

As for emergence, however, Jencks's assertion that postmodern architecture distinguishes itself from that of high modernism through its populist priorities[8] may serve as the starting point for some more general discussion. What is meant, in the specifically architectural context, is that where the now more classical high-modernist space of a Corbusier or a Wright sought to differentiate itself radically from the fallen city fabric in which it appeared – its forms thus dependent on an act of radical disjunction from its spatial context (the great *pilotis* dramatizing separation from the ground and safeguarding the Novum of the new space) – postmodernist buildings, on the contrary, celebrate their insertion into the heterogeneous fabric of the commercial strip and the motel and fast-food landscape of the postsuperhighway American city. Meanwhile, a play of allusion and formal echoes ('historicism') secures the kinship of these new art buildings with the surrounding commercial icons and spaces, thereby renouncing the high-modernist claim to radical difference and innovation.

Whether this undoubtedly significant feature of the newer architecture is to be characterized as *populist* must remain an open question. It would seem essential to distinguish the emergent forms of a new commercial culture – beginning with advertisements and spreading to formal *packaging* of all kinds, from products to buildings, and not excluding artistic commodities such as television shows (the 'logo') and best-sellers and films – from the older kinds of folk and genuinely 'popular' culture which flourished when the older social classes of a peasantry and an urban *artisanat* still existed and which, from the mid nineteenth century on, has gradually been colonized and extinguished by commodification and the market system.

What can at least be admitted is the more universal presence of this particular feature, which appears more unambiguously in the other arts as an effacement of the older distinction between high and so-called mass culture, a distinction on which modernism depended for its specificity, its utopian function consisting at least in part in the securing of a realm of authentic experience over against the surrounding environment of middle- and low-brow commercial culture. Indeed, it can be argued that the emergence of high modernism is itself contemporaneous with the first great expansion of a recognizably mass culture (Zola may be taken as the marker for the last coexistence of the art novel and the best-seller within a single text).

It is this constitutive differentiation which now seems on the point of disappearing: we have already mentioned the way in which, in music, after Schönberg and even after Cage, the two antithetical traditions of the 'classical' and the 'popular' once again begin to merge. In the visual arts the renewal of photography as a significant medium in its own right and also as the 'plane of substance' in pop art or photorealism is a crucial symptom of the same process. At any rate, it becomes minimally obvious that the newer artists no longer 'quote' the materials, the fragments and motifs, of a mass or popular culture, as Flaubert began to do; they somehow incorporate them to the point where many of our older critical and evaluative categories (founded precisely on the radical differentiation of modernist and mass culture) no longer seem functional.

But if this is the case, then it seems at least possible that what wears the mask and makes the gestures of 'populism' in the various postmodernist apologias and manifestos is in reality a mere reflex and symptom of a (to be sure momentous) cultural mutation, in which what used to be stigmatized as mass or commercial culture is now received into the precincts of a new and enlarged cultural realm. In any case, one would expect a term drawn from the typology of political ideologies to undergo basic semantic readjustments when its initial referent (that Popular Front class coalition of workers, peasants and petit bourgeois generally called 'the people') has disappeared.

Perhaps, however, this is not so new a story after all: one remembers, indeed, Freud's delight at discovering an obscure tribal culture, which alone among the multitudinous traditions of dream analysis had managed to hit on the notion that all dreams have hidden sexual meanings – except for sexual dreams, which meant something else! So also it would seem in the postmodernist debate, and the depoliticized bureaucratic society to which it corresponds, where all seemingly cultural positions turn out to be symbolic forms of political moralizing, except for the occasional overtly political note itself, which is now stigmatized as non- or anti-cultural.

Marxism and Postmodernism

Marxism and postmodernism: people often seem to find this combination peculiar or paradoxical, and somehow intensely unstable, so that some of them are led to conclude that, in my own case, having 'become' a postmodernist, I must have ceased to be a Marxist in any meaningful (or in other words stereotypical) sense.[1] For the two terms (in full postmodernism) carry with them a whole freight of pop nostalgia images, 'Marxism' perhaps distilling itself into yellowing period photographs of Lenin and the Soviet revolution, and 'postmodernism' quickly yielding a vista of the gaudiest new hotels. The over-hasty unconscious then rapidly assembles the image of a small, painstakingly reproduced nostalgia restaurant – decorated with the old photographs, with Soviet waiters sluggishly serving bad Russian food – hidden away within some gleaming new pink and blue architectural extravaganza. If I may indulge a personal note, it has happened to me before to have been oddly and comically identified with an object of study: a book I published years ago on structuralism elicited letters, some of which addressed me as a 'foremost' spokesperson for structuralism, while the others appealed to me as an 'eminent' critic and opponent of that movement. I was really neither of those things, but I have to conclude that I must have been 'neither' in some relatively complicated and unusual way that it seemed hard for people to grasp. As far as postmodernism is concerned, and despite the trouble I took in my principal essay on the subject to explain how it was not possible intellectually or politically simply to celebrate postmodernism or to 'disavow' it (to use a word to which I will return), avant-garde art critics quickly identified me as a vulgar Marxist hatchet-man, while some of the more simplehearted comrades concluded that, following the example of so many illustrious predecessors, I had finally gone off the deep end and become a 'post-Marxist' (which is to say, a renegade and a turncoat).

I am therefore particularly grateful to Doug Kellner for his thoughtful introductory demonstration of the ways in which this new topic is not alien to my earlier work but rather a logical consequence of it, something I want to rehearse again myself in terms of the notion of a 'mode of production', to which my analysis of postmodernism claims to make a contribution. It is first worth observing, however, that my version of all this – which obviously (but perhaps I haven't said so often enough) owes a great debt to Baudrillard, as well as to the theorists to whom he is himself indebted (Marcuse, McLuhan, Henri Lefebvre, the situationists, Sahlins, etc., etc.) – took form in a relatively complicated conjuncture. It was not only the experience of new kinds of artistic production (particularly in the architectural area) that roused me from the canonical 'dogmatic slumbers': I will want to make the point later on that as I use it, 'postmodernism' is not an exclusively aesthetic or stylistic term. The conjuncture also offered the occasion for resolving a long-standing *malaise* with traditional economic schemas in the Marxist tradition, a discomfort felt by a certain number of us not in the area of social class, whose 'disappearance' only true 'free-floating intellectuals' could be capable of entertaining, but in the area of the media, whose shock-wave impact on Western Europe enabled the observer to take a little critical and perceptual distance from the gradual and seemingly natural mediatization of North American society in the 1960s.

A Third Stage of Capitalism

Lenin on imperialism did not quite seem to equal Lenin and the media, and it gradually seemed possible to take his lesson in a different way. For he set the example of identifying a new stage of capitalism that was not explicitly foreseen in Marx: the so-called monopoly stage, or the moment of classical imperialism. That could lead you to believe either that the new mutation had been named and formulated once and for all; or that one might be authorized to invent yet another one under certain circumstances. But Marxists were all the more unwilling to draw this second, antithetical conclusion, because in the meantime the new mediatic and informational social phenomena had been colonized (in our absence) by the Right, in a series of influential studies in which the first tentative Cold War notion of an 'end of ideology' finally gave birth to the full-blown concept of a 'post-industrial society' itself. Ernest Mandel's book *Late Capitalism* changed all that, and for the first time theorized a third stage of capitalism from a usably Marxian perspective.[2] This is what made my own thoughts on 'postmodernism' possible, which are therefore to be understood as an attempt to theorize the specific logic of the cultural production of that third stage, and not as yet another disembodied culture critique or diagnosis of the spirit of the age.

It has not escaped anyone's attention that my approach to postmodernism is a totalizing one. The interesting question today is then not why I adopt this perspective, but why so many people are scandalized (or have learned to be scandalized) by it. In the old days, abstraction was surely one of the strategic ways in which phenomena, particularly historical phenomena, could be estranged and defamiliarized; when one is immersed in the immediate – the year-by-year experience of cultural and informational messages, of successive events, of urgent priorities – the abrupt distance afforded by an abstract concept, a more global characterization of the secret affinities between those apparently autonomous and unrelated domains, and of the rhythms and hidden sequences of things we normally remember only in isolation and one by one, is a unique resource, particularly since the history of the preceding few years is always what is least accessible to us. Historical reconstruction, then, the positing of global characterizations and hypotheses, the abstraction from the 'blooming, buzzing confusion' of immediacy, was always a radical intervention in the here-and-now and the promise of resistance to its blind fatalities.

But one must acknowledge the representational problem if

only to separate it out from the other motives at work in the 'war on totality'. If historical abstraction – the notion of a mode of production, or of capitalism, fully as much as of postmodernism – is something not given in immediate experience, then it is pertinent to worry about the potential confusion of this concept with the thing itself, and about the possibility of taking its abstract 'representation' for reality, of 'believing' in the substantive existence of abstract entities such as Society or Class. Never mind that worrying about other people's errors generally turns out to mean worrying about the errors of other intellectuals. In the long run there is probably no way of marking a representation so securely *as* representation that such optical illusions are permanently forestalled, any more than there is a way to ensure the resistance of a materialistic thought to idealistic recuperations, or to ward off the reading of a deconstructive formulation in metaphysical terms. Permanent revolution in intellectual life and culture means that impossibility, and the necessity for a constant reinvention of precautions against what my tradition calls conceptual reification. The extraordinary fortunes of the concept of postmodernism are surely a case in point here, calculated to inspire those of us responsible for it with some misgivings: but what is needed is not the drawing of the line and the confession of excess ('dizzy with success', as Stalin once famously put it), but rather the renewal of historical analysis itself, and the tireless reexamination and diagnosis of the political and ideological functionality of the concept, the part it has suddenly come to play today in our imaginary resolutions of our real contradictions.

There is, however, a deeper paradox rehearsed by the periodizing or totalizing abstraction which for the moment bears the name of postmodernism. This lies in the seeming contradiction between the attempt to unify a field and to posit the hidden identities that course through it and the logic of the very impulses of this field, which postmodernist theory itself openly characterizes as a logic of difference or differentiation. If what is historically unique about the postmodern is thus acknowledged as sheer heteronomy and the emergence of random and unrelated subsystems of all kinds, then, or so the argument runs, there has to be something perverse about the effort to grasp it as a unified system in the first place: the effort is, to say the least, strikingly inconsistent with the spirit of postmodernism itself; perhaps, indeed, it can be unmasked as an attempt to 'master' or to 'dominate' the postmodern, to reduce and exclude its play of differences, and even to enforce some new conceptual conformity over its pluralistic subjects? Yet, leaving the gender of the verb out of it, we all do want to 'master' history in whatever ways turn out to be possible: the escape from the nightmare of history, the conquest by human beings of control over the otherwise seemingly blind and natural 'laws' of socio-economic fatality, remains the irreplaceable will of the Marxist heritage, whatever language it may be expressed in. It can therefore not be expected to hold much attraction for people uninterested in seizing control over their own destinies.

System and Differentiation

But the notion that there is something misguided and contradictory about a unified theory of differentiation also rests on a confusion between levels of abstraction: a system that constitutively produces differences remains a system, nor is the idea of such a system supposed to be in kind 'like' the object it tries to theorize, any more than the concept of dog is supposed to bark or the concept of sugar to taste sweet. It is felt that something precious and existential, something fragile and unique about our own singularity, will be lost irretrievably when we find out that we are just like everybody else: in that case, so be it, and let's know the worst; the objection is the primal form of existentialism (and phenomenology), and it is the emergence of such things and such anxieties that needs to be explained. In any case, objections to the global concept of postmodernism in this sense seem to me to recapitulate, in other terms, the classical objections to the concept of capitalism: something scarcely surprising from the present perspective, which consistently affirms the identity of postmodernism with capitalism itself in its latest systemic mutation. Those objections turned essentially around one form or another of the following paradox: namely that although the various precapitalist modes of production achieved their capacity to reproduce themselves through various forms of solidarity or collective cohesion, the logic of capital is on the contrary a dispersive and atomistic, 'individualistic' one, an anti-society rather than a society, whose systemic structure, let alone its reproduction of itself, remains a mystery and a contradiction in terms. Leaving aside the answer to the conundrum ('the market'), what may be said is that this paradox is the originality of capitalism and that the verbally contradictory formulas we necessarily encounter in defining it point beyond the words to the thing itself (and also give rise to that peculiar new invention, the dialectic). We will have occasion to return to problems of this kind in what follows: suffice it to say all this more crudely by pointing out that the very concept of differentiation (whose most elaborate development we owe to Niklas Luhmann) is itself a systemic one, or, if you prefer, turns the play of differences into a new kind of identity on a more abstract level (it being understood that one must also distinguish between dialectical oppositions and differentiations of this random, dispersive type).

The 'war against totality' has finally its political motivation, which it is the merit of Horne's essay to reveal.[3] Following Lyotard, he makes it clear that the fear of utopia is in this case our old friend *1984*, and that a utopian and revolutionary politics, correctly associated with totalization and a certain 'concept' of totality, is to be eschewed because it leads fatally to Terror: a notion at least as old as Edmund Burke, but helpfully revived, after innumerable restatements during the Stalin period, by the Cambodian atrocities. Ideologically, this particular revival of Cold War rhetoric and stereotypes, launched in the demarxification of France in the 1970s, turns on a bizarre identification of Stalin's Gulag with Hitler's extermination camps (but see Arno Mayer's remarkable *Why Did the Heavens not Darken?* for a definitive demonstration of the constitutive relationship between the 'final solution' and Hitler's anti-communism[4]); what can be 'postmodern' about these hoary nightmare images, except for the depoliticization to which they invite us, is less clear. The history of the revolutionary convulsions in question can also be appealed to for a very different lesson, namely that violence springs from counterrevolution first and foremost, indeed, that the most effective form of counter-revolution lies precisely in this transmission of violence to the revolutionary process itself. I doubt if the current state of alliance or micro-politics in the advanced countries supports such anxieties and fantasies; they would not, for me at least, constitute grounds for withdrawing support and solidarity from a potential revolution in South Africa, say; finally, this general feeling that the revolutionary, utopian or totalizing impulse is somehow tainted from the outset and doomed to bloodshed by the very structure of its thoughts does strike one as idealistic, if not finally a replay of doctrines of original sin in their worst religious sense. At the end of this essay I will return to more concrete political issues and considerations.

The Social Determinants of Thought

Now, however, I want to return to the question of totalizing thought in a different way, interrogating it not for its truth content or validity but rather for its historical conditions of possibility. This is then no longer to philosophize exactly, or if you prefer to philosophize on a *symptomal* level, in which we step back and estrange our immediate judgments on a given concept ('the most advanced contemporary thinking no longer permits us to deploy concepts of totality or periodization') by way of asking the question about the social determinants that enable or shut down thought. Does the current taboo on totality simply result from philosophical progress and increased self-consciousness? Is it because we have today attained a state of theoretical enlightenment and conceptual sophistication, which permit us to avoid the grosser errors and blunders of the old-fashioned thinkers of the past (most notably Hegel)? That may be so, but it would also require some kind of historical explanation (in which the invention of 'materialism' would surely have to intervene). This hubris of the present and of the living can be avoided by posing the issue in a somewhat different way: namely, why it is that 'concepts of totality' have seemed necessary and unavoidable at certain historical moments, and on the contrary noxious and unthinkable at others. This is an inquiry which, working its way back on the outside of our own thought and on the basis of what we can no longer (or not yet) think, cannot be philosophical in any positive sense (although Adorno attempted, in *Negative Dialectic*, to turn it into a genuine philosophy of a new kind); it would certainly lead us to the intensified sense that ours is a time of nominalism in a variety of senses (from culture to philosophical thought). Such nominalism would probably turn out to have several pre-histories or overdeterminations: the moment of existentialism, for instance, in which some new social sense of the isolated individual (and of the horror of demography, or of sheer number or multiplicity, particularly in Sartre) causes the older traditional 'universals' to pale and lose their conceptual force and persuasiveness; the age-old tradition of Anglo-American empiricism as well, which emerges from this death of the concept with renewed force in a paradoxically 'theoretical' and hyper-intellectual age. There is of course a sense in which the slogan 'postmodernism' means all this too; but then in that case it is not the explanation, but what remains to be explained.

Speculation and hypothetical analysis of this kind that bears on the weakening of general or universalizing concepts in the present is the correlative of an operation that can often look more reliable, namely the analysis of moments in the past when such conceptuality seemed possible; indeed, those moments in which the emergence of general concepts can be observed have often seemed to be historically privileged ones. As far as the concept of totality is concerned, I am tempted to say about it what I once said about Althusser's notion of structure, namely that the crucial point to be made is this: we can acknowledge the presence of such a concept, provided we understand that there is only one of them: something otherwise often known as a 'mode of production'. Althusserian 'structure' is that, and so is 'totality', at least as I use it. As for 'totalizing' processes, that often means little more than the making of connections between various phenomena: thus, to take an influential contemporary example, although Gayatri Spivak offers her conception of a 'continuous sign-chain' as an alternative to dialectical thought,[5] on my usage that conception would also stand as a specific (and non-dialectical) form of 'totalizing'.

We must be grateful to the work of Ronald L. Meek for the prehistory of the concept of a 'mode of production' (as that will later be worked out in the writings of Morgan and Marx), which in the eighteenth century takes the form of what he calls the 'four stages theory'.[6] This theory comes together in the mid eighteenth century, in France and in the Scottish Enlightenment, as the proposition that human cultures historically vary with their material or productive basis, which knows four essential transformations: hunting and gathering, pastoralism, agriculture and commerce. What will then happen to this historical narrative, above all in the thought and work of Adam Smith, is that, having now produced that object of study which is the specifically contemporary mode of production, or capitalism, the historical scaffolding of the precapitalist stages tends to fall away and lend both Smith's and Marx's model of capitalism a synchronic appearance. But Meek wants to argue that the historical narrative was essential to the very possibility of thinking capitalism as a system, synchronic or not;[7] and something like that will remain my own position with respect to that 'stage' or moment of capitalism which projects the cultural logic of what some of us now seem to be calling 'postmodernism'.

I am here, however, essentially concerned with the conditions of possibility of the concept of a 'mode of production', that is to say, the characteristics of the historical and social situation which make it possible to articulate and formulate such a concept in the first place. I will suggest, in a general way, that thinking this particular new thought (or combining older thoughts in this new way) presupposes a particular kind of 'uneven' development, such that distinct and co-existing modes of production are registered together in the lifeworld of the thinker in question. This is how Meek describes the preconditions for the production of this particular concept (in its original forms as a 'four stages theory'):

> My own feeling is that thinking of the type we are considering which lays primary emphasis on the development of economic techniques and socio-economic relationships, is likely to be a function, first, of the rapidity of contemporary economic advance, and second, of the facility with which a contrast can be observed

between areas which are economically advancing and areas which are still in 'lower' stages of development. In the 1750s and 60s, in cities like Glasgow and areas such as the more advanced provinces in the north of France, the whole social life of the communities concerned was being rapidly and visibly transformed, and it was fairly obvious that this was happening as a result of profound changes taking place in economic techniques and basic socio-economic relationships. And the new forms of economic organiz-ation which were emerging could be fairly easily compared and contrasted with the older forms of organization which still existed, say, in the Scottish Highlands, or in the remainder of France – or among the Indian tribes in America. If changes in the mode of subsistence were playing such an important and 'progressive' role in the development of contemporary society, it seemed a fair bet that they must also have done so in that of past society.[8]

Historical Paradigms

This possibility of thinking the new concept of a mode of production for the first time is sometimes loosely described as one of the newly emergent forms of historical consciousness, or historicity. It is not necessary, however, to have recourse to the philosophical discourse of consciousness as such, since what are being described might equally well be termed new discursive paradigms, and this more contemporary way of talking about conceptual emergence is reinforced, for literary people, by the presence alongside this one of yet another new historical paradigm in the novels of Sir Walter Scott (as Lukács interprets it in *The Historical Novel*[9]). The unevenness that allowed French thinkers (Turgot, but also Rousseau himself!) to concep-tualize a 'mode of production' probably had as much as anything else to do with the pre-revolutionary situation in the France of that period, in which feudal forms stood out ever more starkly in their distinctive difference against a whole newly emergent bourgeois culture and class consciousness.

Scotland is in many ways a more complex and interesting case, for, as last of the emergent First World countries, or first of the Third World ones (to use Tom Nairn's provocative idea, in *The Break-up of Britain*[10]), Enlightenment Scotland is above all the space of a coexistence of radically distinct zones of production and culture: the archaic economy of the Highlanders and their clan system, the new agricultural exploitation of the Lowlands, the commercial vigour of the English 'partner' over the border, on the eve of its industrial 'take-off'. The brilliance of Edinburgh is therefore not a matter of Gaelic genetic material, but rather owing to the strategic yet eccentric position of the Scottish metropolis and intellectuals with respect to this virtually synchronic coexistence of distinct modes of production, which it is now uniquely the task of the Scottish Enlightenment to 'think' or to conceptualize. Nor is this merely an economic matter: Scott, like Faulkner later on, inherits a social and historical raw material, a popular memory, in which the fiercest revolutions and civil and religious wars now inscribe the coexistence of modes of production in vivid narrative form. The condition of thinking a new reality and articulating a new paradigm for it therefore seems to demand a peculiar conjuncture and a certain strategic distance from that new reality, which tends to overwhelm those immersed in it (this would be something like an epistemological variant of the well-known 'outsider' principle in scientific discovery).

All of which, however, has another secondary consequence of greater significance to us here and which bears on the gradual repression of such conceptuality. If the postmodern moment, as the cultural logic of an enlarged third stage of classical capitalism, is in many ways a purer and more homogeneous expression of this last, from which many of the hitherto surviving enclaves of socio-economic difference have been effaced (by way of their colonization and absorption by the commodity form), then it makes sense to suggest that the waning of our sense of history, and more particularly our resistance to globalizing or totalizing concepts like that of the mode of production itself, are a function of precisely that universalization of capitalism. Where everything is henceforth systemic the very notion of a system seems to lose its reason for being, returning only by way of a 'return of the repressed' in the more nightmarish forms of the 'total system' fantasized by Weber or Foucault or the *1984* people.

But mode of production is not a 'total system' in that

forbidding sense, and includes a variety of counterforces and new tendencies within itself, of 'residual' as well as 'emergent' forces, which it must attempt to manage or control (Gramsci's conception of hegemony): were those heterogeneous forces not endowed with an effectivity of their own, the hegemonic project would be unnecessary. Thus, differences are presupposed by the model: something which should be sharply distinguished from another feature which complicates this one, namely that capitalism also produces differences or differentiation as a function of its own internal logic. Finally, to recall our initial discussion of representation, it is also clear that there is a *difference* between the concept and the thing, between this global and abstract model and our own individual social experience, from which it is meant to afford some explanatory difference but which it is scarcely designed to 'replace'.

A number of other reminders about the 'proper use' of the mode of production model are probably also advisable: that what is called a 'mode of production' is not a productionist model, as it always seems worth saying. What also seems worth saying, in the present context, is that it involves a variety of levels (or orders of abstraction) which must be respected, if these discussions are not to degenerate into random shouting matches. I proposed a very general picture of such levels in *The Political Unconscious*, and in particular the distinctions that have to be respected between an examination of historical events, an evocation of larger class and ideological conflicts and traditions, and an attention to impersonal socio-economic patterning systems (of which the well-known thematics of reification and commodification are examples). The question of agency, which arises often in these pages, has to be mapped across these levels.

The Place of Cultural Production

Featherstone, for example, thinks that 'postmodernism' on my use is a specifically cultural category:[11] it is not, and was rather for better and for worse designed to name a 'mode of production' in which cultural production finds a specific functional place, and whose symptomatology is in my work mainly drawn from culture (this is no doubt the source of the confusion). He therefore advises me to pay closer attention to the artists themselves and to their publics, as well as to the institutions which mediate and govern this newer kind of production: nor can I see why any of those topics should be excluded, they are very interesting matters indeed. But it is hard to see how sociological inquiry at that level would become *explanatory*: rather, the phenomena he is concerned with tend at once to reform into their own semi-autonomous sociological level, one which then at once requires a diachronic narrative. To say what the art market is now, and the status of the artist or the consumer, means saying what it was before this transformation, and even at some outside limit leaving a space open for some alternative configuration of such activities (as is the case, for example, in Cuba, where the art market, galleries, investments in painting, etc., do not exist). Once you have written up that narrative, that series of local changes, then the whole thing gets added into the dossier as yet another space in which something like the postmodern 'great transformation' can be read.

Indeed, although with Featherstone's proposals concrete social agents seem to make their appearance (postmodernists are then these artists or musicians, these gallery or museum officials or record company executives, these specific bourgeois or youth or working-class consumers), here too the requirement of differentiating levels of abstraction must be maintained. For one can only plausibly assert that 'postmodernism' as an ethos and a 'life style' (truly a contemptible expression that one) is the expression of the 'consciousness' of a whole new class fraction that largely transcends the limits of the groups enumerated above: this larger and more abstract category has variously been labelled as a new petty bourgeoisie, a professional-managerial class, or more succinctly as 'the yuppies' (each of these expressions smuggling in a little surplus of concrete social representation along with itself).[12]

This identification of the class content of postmodern culture does not at all imply that 'yuppies' have become something like a new ruling class or 'a subject of history' – merely that their cultural practices and values, their local ideologies, have articulated a useful dominant ideological and cultural paradigm for this stage of capital. It is indeed often the case that cultural forms prevalent in a particular period are not furnished by the principal agents of the social formation in question (businessmen who no doubt have something better to do with their time, or are driven by psychological and ideological motive forces of a different type). What is essential is that the culture-ideology in question articulates the world in the most useful way functionally, or in ways that can be functionally reappropriated. Why a certain class fraction should provide these ideological articulations is a historical question as intriguing as the question of the sudden dominance of a particular writer or a particular style. There can surely be no model or formula given in advance for these historical transactions; just as surely, however, we have not yet worked this out for what is being called postmodernism. Meanwhile, another limitation of my own work on the subject (not mentioned by any of the contributors) now becomes clear, namely that the tactical decision to stage the account in cultural terms has made for a relative absence of any identification of properly postmodern 'ideologies'. Indeed, since I have been particularly interested in the formal matter of what I call some new 'theoretical discourse', and also because the paradoxical combination of global decentralization and small group institutionalization has seemed to me an important feature of the postmodern tendential structure, I have appeared mainly to single out intellectual and social phenomena like 'poststructuralism' and the 'new social movements'; thus, against my own deepest political convictions, all the 'enemies' have still seemed to be on the Left, an impression I will try to rectify in what follows.

But what has been said about the class origins of postmodernism has as its consequence the requirement that we now specify another higher (or more abstract and global) kind of agency than any so far enumerated. This is of course multinational capital itself: it may as a process be described as some 'non-human' logic of capital, and I would continue to defend the appropriateness of that language and that kind of description, in its own terms and on its own level. That that seemingly disembodied force is also an ensemble of human agents, trained

46

in specific ways and inventing original local tactics and practices according to the creativities of the human freedom – this is also obvious, from a different perspective, to which one would only wish to add that for the agents of capital also the old dictum holds that 'people make their history, but not in circumstances of their own choosing'. It is within the possibilities of late capitalism that people glimpse 'the main chance', 'go for it', make money, and reorganize firms in new ways (just like artists or generals, ideologists or gallery owners).

What I have tried to show here is that although my account of the postmodern may seem in the eyes of some of its readers and critics to 'lack agency', it can be translated or transcoded into a narrative account in which agents of all sizes and dimensions are at work. The choice between these alternate descriptions – focalizations on distinct levels of abstraction – is a practical rather than a theoretical one. It would however be desirable to link up this account of agency with that other very rich (psychoanalytic) tradition of psychic and ideological 'subject positions'. If it is now objected that the descriptions of agency described above are merely an alternative version of the base–superstructure model – an economic base for postmodernism on the one account, a social or class base on this other – then so be it, provided we understand that 'base and superstructure' is not really a model, but a starting point and a problem, something as undogmatic as an imperative simultaneously to grasp culture in and for itself, but also in relationship to its outside, its content, its context, and its space of intervention and of effectivity. How one does that, however, is never given in advance. Gross's beautiful adaptation of Benjamin – postmodernism as the 'afterimage' of late capitalism[13] – reminds us not only how wonderfully supple Benjamin was in his formulations of this relationship (elsewhere he says that the 'superstructure' is the *expression* of the 'base', something that also radically modifies our stereotypes), but also how many new paths of exploration the new figures open up and entail. Afterimages are objective phenomena which are also mirages and pathologies; they dictate attention to optical processes, to the psychology of perception, and also to the dazzling qualities of the object, and so on and so forth. I have proposed a 'model' of postmodernism, which is worth what it's worth and must now take its chances independently; but it is the construction of such a model that is ultimately the fascinating matter, and I hope it will not be taken as a knee-jerk affirmation of 'pluralism' if I say that alternative constructions are desirable and welcome, since the grasping of the present from within is the most problematical task the mind can face.

Remapping Class

Something is lost when an emphasis on power and domination tends to obliterate the displacement, which made up the originality of Marxism, towards the economic system, the structure of the mode of production, and exploitation as such. Once again, matters of power and domination are articulated on a different level from those systemic ones, and no advances are gained by staging the complementary analyses as an irreconcilable opposition, unless the motive is to produce a new ideology (in the tradition, it bears the time-honoured name of *anarchism*), in which case other kinds of lines are drawn and one argues the matter differently.

Saul Landau has observed, about our current situation, that there has never been a moment in the history of capitalism when this last enjoyed greater elbow-room and space for manoeuvre: all the threatening forces it generated against itself in the past – labour movements and insurgencies, mass socialist parties, even socialist states themselves – seem today in full disarray when not in one way or another effectively neutralized; for the moment global capital seems able to follow its own nature and inclinations, without the traditional precautions. Here then we have yet another, 'definition' of postmodernism, and a useful one indeed, which only an ostrich will wish to accuse of 'pessimism'. This is a transitional period between two stages of capitalism, in which the earlier forms of the economic are in the process of being restructured on a global scale, including the older forms of labour and its traditional organizational institutions and concepts. That a new international proletariat (taking forms we cannot yet imagine) will reemerge from this convulsive upheaval it needs no prophet to predict: we ourselves are still in the trough, however, and no one can say how long we will stay there. This is the sense in which two seemingly rather different conclusions to my historical essays on the current situation (one on the sixties and one on postmodernism)[14] are in reality identical: in the first, I anticipate the process of proletarianization on a global scale which I have just evoked here; in the second I call for something mysteriously termed 'cognitive mapping' of a new and global type.

But 'cognitive mapping' was in reality nothing but a code word for 'class consciousness': only it proposed the need for class consciousness of a new and hitherto undreamed of kind, while it also inflected the account of the direction of that new spatiality implicit in the postmodern (which Ed Soja's *Postmodern Geographies* now places on the agenda in so eloquent and timely a fashion[15]). I occasionally get just as tired of the slogan of 'postmodernism' as anyone else, but when I am tempted to regret my complicity with it, to deplore its misuses and its notoriety, and to conclude with some reluctance that it raises more problems than it solves, I find myself pausing to wonder whether any other concept can dramatize the issue in quite so effective and economical a fashion. 'We have to name the system': this high point of the sixties finds an unexpected revival in the postmodernism debate.

4

The Antinomies of Postmodernity

Even after the 'end of history', there has seemed to persist some historical curiosity of a generally systemic – rather than merely anecdotal – kind: not merely to know what will happen next, but as a more general anxiety about the larger fate or destiny of our system or mode of production. On this, individual experience (of a postmodern kind) tells us that it must be eternal, while our intelligence suggests this feeling to be most improbable indeed, without coming up with plausible scenarios as to its disintegration or replacement. It seems to be easier for us today to imagine the thoroughgoing deterioration of the earth and of nature than the breakdown of late capitalism; perhaps that is due to some weakness in our imaginations.

I have come to think that the word *postmodern* ought to be reserved for thoughts of this kind. The term and its various substantives seem instead to have evolved into various partisan expressions of value, mostly turning on affirmation or repudiation of this or that vision of pluralism. But these are arguments better conducted in concrete social terms (those of the various feminisms, or the new social movements, for example). Postmodernism as an ideology, however, is better grasped as a symptom of the deeper structural changes in our society and its culture as a whole, or in other words, in the mode of production.

Inasmuch as those changes still remain tendencies, however, and our analyses of actuality are governed by the selection of what we think will persist or develop, any attempt to say what postmodernism is can scarcely be separated from the even more problematic attempt to say where it is going – in short, to disengage its contradictions, to imagine its consequences (and the consequences of those consequences), and to conjecture the shape of its agents and institutions in some more fully developed maturity of what can now at best only be trends and currents. All postmodernism theory is thus a telling of the future, with an imperfect deck.

It is conventional to distinguish an antinomy from a contradiction, not least because folk wisdom implies that the latter is susceptible of a solution or a resolution, whereas the former is not. In that sense, the antinomy is a cleaner form of language than the contradiction. With it, you know where you stand; it states two propositions that are radically, indeed absolutely, incompatible, take it or leave it. Whereas the contradiction is a matter of partialities and aspects – only some of it is incompatible with the accompanying proposition – indeed, it may have more to do with forces, or the state of things, than with words or logical implications. Contradictions are supposed, in the long run, to be productive; whereas antinomies – take Kant's classic one: the world has a beginning, the world has no beginning – offer nothing in the way of a handle, no matter how diligently you turn them around and around.

Our antinomies will concern Kant's 'a priori representations'; namely time and space, which we have generally come to think of in historical terms as implicit formal frames that nonetheless vary according to the mode of production. We may presumably, then, learn something about our own mode of production from the ways in which we tend to think of change and permanence, or variety and homogeneity – ways that prove to have as much to do with space as with time.

I

Time is today a function of speed, and evidently perceptible only in terms of its rate or velocity as such: as though the old Bergsonian opposition between measurement and life, clock time and lived time, had dropped out, along with that virtual eternity or slow permanence without which Valéry thought the very idea of a work of art as such was likely to die out (something he seems to have been confirmed in thinking). What emerges then is some conception of change without its opposite; and to say so is then helplessly to witness the two terms of this antinomy folding back into each other, since from the vantage point of change it becomes impossible to distinguish space from time, or object from subject. The eclipse of inner time (and its organ, the 'intimate' time sense) means that we read our subjectivity off the things outside: Proust's old hotel rooms, like old retainers, respectfully reminded him every morning how old he was, and whether he was on vacation or 'at home', and where – that is to say, they told him his name and issued him an identity, like a visiting card on a silver salver. As for habit, memory, recognition, material things do that for us (the way the servants were supposed to do our living, according to Villiers de l'Isle Adam). Subjectivity is an objective matter, and it is enough to change the scenery and the setting, refurnish the rooms, or destroy them in an aerial bombardment for a new subject, a new identity, miraculously to appear on the ruins of the old.

The end of the subject–object dualism, however – for which so many ideologues have yearned for so long – carries with it hidden retroparadoxes, like concealed explosives: Paul Virilio's, for example, in *War and Cinema*, which shows how the seeming speed of the outside world is itself a function of the demands of representation. Not, perhaps, the result of some new subjective idea of velocity that projects itself on to an inert exterior, as in stereotypes of classical idealism, but rather technology versus nature. The apparatus – and very specifically the photographic and filmic one – makes its own demands on reality, which, as in the Gulf War, reality then scrambles to fulfil (like a time-lapse photo in which the photographer himself can be seen breathlessly sliding into place at the end of the row of already posing faces):

[T]he disappearance of the proximity effect in the prosthesis of accelerated travel made it necessary to create a wholly simulated appearance that would restore three-dimensionality to the message in full. Now a holographic prosthesis of the military commander's inertia was to be communicated to the viewer, extending his look in time and space by means of constant dashes, here and there, today and yesterday ... Already evident in the flashback and then in feedback, this miniaturisation of chronological meaning was the direct result of a military technology in which events always unfolded in theoretical time.[1]

Such a 'return of the repressed' (an old-fashioned, now relatively metaphorical name for it to be sure) means that eliminating the subject does not leave us with the object *wie es eigentlich gewesen*, but rather with a multiplicity of simulacra. Virilio's point, like that of so many others today, is that it is the cinema that is the truly centred subject, perhaps indeed the only one: the Deleuzian schizo being only a confused and contradictory idea alongside this apparatus that absorbs the former subject–object pole triumphantly into itself. But it raises the embarrassing secondary question of whether, in that case, there ever was a (centred) subject to begin with: did we ever have to wait? Is boredom a figment of the imagination along with its cousin eternity? Was there a time when things did not seem to change? What did we do before machines? All flesh is grass: and life in the ancient *polis* strikes us at being more fragile and ephemeral than anything in the modern city, even though we ought to be able to remember how many changes this last has undergone. It is as though an illusion of slower permanence accompanies the lived present like an optical projection, masking a change that only becomes visible when it falls outside the temporal frame.

But to put it this way is to measure a gap and to assure ourselves of everything that is radically different from the modernist form-projects and the modernist 'time-senses' in the postmodern dispensation, where the formerly classical has itself been unmasked as sheer fashion, albeit the fashion of a slower, vaster world that took ages to cross by caravan or caravel, and through whose thickened time, as through a viscous element, items descended so slowly as to acquire a patina that seemed to transform their contingencies into the necessities of a meaningful tradition. For a world population, the languages of Periclean Athens can no longer be any more normative than that of other tribal styles (although it is very easy to imagine a cultural United

Nations Security Council operation in which the 'great civilizations' pooled their various classical traditions with a view toward imposing some more generally 'human' classical canon): time thereby also becomes multicultural, and the hitherto airtight realms of demography and of industrial momentum begin to seep into each other, as though there were some analogies between great crowds of people and dizzying rates of speed. Both then spell the end of the modern in some renewed and paradoxical conjunction, as when the new styles seem exhausted by virtue of their very proliferation, while their bearers, the individual creators, prophets, geniuses and seers, suddenly find themselves unwanted owing to sheer population density (if not the realization of the democratic ethos as such).

That the new absolute temporality has everything to do with the urban my references have suggested, without underscoring the requirement in that case of revising traditional notions of the urban as such, in order to accommodate its postnaturality to technologies of communication as well as of production and to mark the decentred, well-nigh global, scale on which what used to be the city is deployed. The modern still had something to do with the arrogance of city people over the provincials, whether this was a provinciality of peasants, other and colonized cultures, or simply the precapitalist past itself: that deeper satisfaction of being *absolument moderne* is dissipated when modern technologies are everywhere, there are no longer any provinces, and even the past comes to seem like an alternative world, rather than an imperfect, primitive stage of this one. Meanwhile, those 'modern' city dwellers or metropolitans of earlier decades themselves came from the country or at least could still register the coexistence of uneven worlds; they could measure change in ways that become impossible once modernization is even relatively completed (and no longer some isolated, unnatural and unnerving process that stands out to the naked eye). It is an unevenness and a coexistence that can also be registered in a sense of loss, as with the slow partial changes and demolitions of Baudelaire's Paris, which almost literally serve as the objective correlative of his experience of passing time: in Proust all this, although apparently more intensely elegiac (and in any case surcharging the text of Baudelaire itself), has already been subjectivized, as though it were the self and its past that were regretted and not its houses (but Proust's language knows better: '*la muraille de l'escalier où je vis monter le reflet de sa bougie, n'existe plus depuis longtemps*';[2] as does his spatial plot construction). Today the very meaning of demolition has been modified, along with that of building: it has become a generalized postnatural process that calls into question the very concept of change itself and the inherited notion of time that accompanied it.

These paradoxes are perhaps easier to dramatize in the philosophical and critical realm, than in the aesthetic one, let alone in urbanism as such. For demolition has surely defined the modern intellectual's vocation ever since the *ancien régime* tended to identify its mission with critique and opposition to established institutions and ideas: what better figure to characterize the strong form of the cultural intellectual from the Enlightenment *philosophes* all the way to Sartre (who has been called the last of the classical intellectuals), if not beyond? It is a figure that has seemed to presuppose an omnipresence of Error, variously defined as superstition, mystification, ignorance, class ideology and philosophical idealism (or 'metaphysics'), in such a way that to remove it by way of the operations of demystification leaves a space in which therapeutic anxiety goes hand in hand with heightened self-consciousness and reflexivity in a variety of senses, if not, indeed, with Truth as such. By attempting to restore, alongside this negative tradition, the intellectual's other mission of the restoration of meaning, Ricoeur sharply dramatized everything the various strands of what he called 'the hermeneutics of suspicion' had in common, from the Enlightenment and its relationship to religion all the way to the destructive relationship to 'Western metaphysics', emphasizing above all the three great formative moments of Marx, Nietzsche and Freud, to which even postmodern intellectuals still owe joint allegiance in some form or another.

What has changed is then perhaps the character of the terrain in which these operations are carried out: just as the transitional period between aristocratic and clerical, *ancien régime* societies and mass-democratic industrial capitalist ones has been much longer and slower than we tend to believe (Arno Mayer suggests that significant remnants of the former survived in Europe until the end of World War Two), so also the objective role of intellectuals to implement modernization's cultural revolution long remained a progressive one. But the process itself often tended to impress observers and participants alike by its self-perpetuating and indeed self-devouring energies. It is not only the Revolution that eats its own children; any number of visions of pure negativity as such do so as well, from Hegel's account of freedom and the Terror to the Frankfurt School's grim theory of the 'dialectic of enlightenment' as an infernal machine, bent on extirpating all traces of transcendence (including critique and negativity itself).

Such visions seem even more relevant for one-dimensional societies like our own, from which the residual, in the forms of habits and practices of other modes of production, has been tendentially eliminated, so that it might be possible to hypothesize a modification or displacement in the very function of ideology-critique itself. This is at least the position of Manfredo Tafuri, who offers a kind of functionalist analysis of the avant-garde intellectual, whose 'anti-institutional phase' essentially involved 'the criticism of outworn values'.[3] The very success of such a mission, however, coterminous with the modernizing struggles of capital itself, 'serves to prepare a clean-swept platform from which to depart in discovery of the new "historic tasks" of intellectual work'.[4] Not surprisingly, Tafuri identifies these new 'modernizing' tasks with rationalization as such: 'what the ideologies of the avant-garde introduced as a proposal for social behaviour was the transformation of traditional ideology into Utopia, as a prefiguration of an abstract final moment of development coincident with a global rationalisation, with a positive realisation of the dialectic'.[5] Tafuri's formulations become less cryptic when one understands that for him Keynesianism is to be understood as a planification, a rationalization, of the future.

Thus seen, demystification in the contemporary period has its own secret 'ruse of history', its own inner function and concealed world-historical mission; namely, by destroying traditional societies (not merely the Church and the old aristocracies but above all the peasants and their modes of agricultural production, their common land and their villages), to sweep the globe clean for the manipulations of the great corporations: to prepare a purely *fungible* present in which space and psyches alike can be processed and remade at will with a 'flexibility' with which the creativity of the ideologues busy coining glowing new adjectives to describe the potentialities of 'post-Fordism' can scarcely keep up. Demolition, under these circumstances, begins to take on new and ominously urbanistic overtones, and to connote the speculations of the developers far more than the older heroic struggles of oppositional intellectuals; while just such objections to and critiques of demolition itself are relegated to a tiresome moralizing and undermine themselves by virtue of their vivid dramatization of outmoded mentalities that are better off being demolished anyhow (*'denn alles, was entsteht/Ist wert, dass es zugrunde geht'*).

These are now media paradoxes, which result from the speed and tempo of the critical process, as well as the way in which all ideological and philosophical positions as such have in the media universe been transformed into their own 'representations' (as Kant might put it) – in other words into images of themselves and caricatures in which identifiable slogans substitute for traditional beliefs (the beliefs having indeed been forced to transform themselves into just such recognizable ideological positions in order to operate in the media marketplace). This is the situation in which it is easier to grasp the progressive value of conservative or residual modes of resistance to the new thing than to evaluate the range of ostensibly left-liberal positions (which, as in Tafuri's model, often functionally prove to be indistinguishable from the structural requirements of the system itself). The diagnosis also projects the mirage of some possible sound barrier, like a telltale line blurring away against the sky; and indeed the obvious question of how much speed the human organism can bear may play its part in naturalist revivals; while the new fact itself does seem to offer a fleeting but vivid dramatization of Engels's old law about the transformation of quantity into quality (or at least of that 'law''s afterimage).

In this form, the paradox from which we must set forth is the equivalence between an unparalleled rate of change on all the levels of social life and an unparalleled standardization of everything – feelings along with consumer goods, language along with built space – that would seem incompatible with such mutability. It is a paradox that can still be conceptualized, but in inverse ratios: of that of modularity, for example, where intensified change is enabled by standardization itself, where prefabricated modules, everywhere from the media to a henceforth standardized private life, from commodified nature to uniformity of equipment, allow miraculous rebuildings to succeed each other at will, as in fractal video. The module would then constitute the new form of the object (the new result of reification) in an informational universe: that Kantian point in which raw material is suddenly organized by categories into an appropriate unit.

But the paradox can also incite us to rethink our conception of change itself. If absolute change in our society is best represented by the rapid turnover in storefronts, prompting the philosophical question as to what has really changed when video stores are replaced by T-shirt shops, then Barthes' structural formulation comes to have much to recommend it, namely, that it is crucial to distinguish between rhythms of change inherent in the system and programmed by it, and a change that replaces one entire system by another one altogether. But that is a point of view that revives paradoxes of Zeno's sort, which derive from the Parmenidean conception of Being itself, which, as it *is* by definition, cannot be thought of as even momentarily becoming, let along failing to be for the slightest instant.

The 'solution' to this particular paradox lies of course in the realization (strongly insisted on by Althusser and his disciples) that each system – better still, every 'mode of production' – produces a temporality that is specific to it: it is only if we adopt a Kantian and ahistorical view of time as some absolute and empty category that the peculiarly repetitive temporality of our own system can become an object of puzzlement and lead to the reformulation of these old logical and ontological paradoxes.

Yet it may not be without its therapeutic effects to continue for one long moment to be mesmerized by the vision attributed to Parmenides, which however little it holds for nature might well be thought to capture a certain truth of our social and historical moment: a gleaming science-fictional stasis in which appearances (simulacra) arise and decay ceaselessly, without the momentous spellbound totality of everything that is ever flickering for the briefest of instants or even momentarily wavering in its ontological prestige.

Here, it is as if the logic of fashion had, accompanying the multifarious penetration of its omnipresent images, begun to bind and identify itself with the social and psychic fabric which tends to make it over into the very logic of our system as a whole. The experience and the value of perpetual change thereby comes to govern language and feelings, fully as much as the buildings and the garments of this particular society, to the point at which even the relative meaning allowed by uneven development (or 'nonsynchronous synchronicity') is no longer comprehensible, and the supreme value of the New and of innovation, as both modernism and modernization grasped it, fades away against a steady stream of momentum and variation that at some outer limit seems stable and motionless.

What then dawns is the realization that no society has ever been so standardized as this one, and that the stream of human, social and historical temporality has never flowed quite so homogeneously. Even the great boredom or ennui of classical modernism required some vantage point or fantasy subject position outside the system; yet our seasons are of the post-natural and post-astronomical television or media variety, triumphantly artificial by way of the power of their National Geographic or Weather Channel images: so that their great rotations – in sports, new model cars, fashion, television, the school year or *rentrée*, etc. – simulate formerly natural rhythms for commercial convenience and reinvent such archaic categories as the week, the month, the year imperceptibly, without any of the freshness and violence of, say, the innovations of the French revolutionary calendar.

What we now begin to feel, therefore – and what begins to emerge as some deeper and more fundamental constitution of postmodernity itself, at least in its temporal dimension – is henceforth, where everything now submits to the perpetual change of fashion and media image, that nothing can change any longer. This is the sense of the revival of that 'end of history' Alexandre Kojève thought he could find in Hegel and Marx, and which he took to mean some ultimate achievement of democratic equality (and the value equivalence of individual economic and juridical subjects) in both American capitalism and Soviet communism, only later identifying a significant variant of it in what he called Japanese '*snobisme*,' but that we can today identify as postmodernity itself (the free play of masks and roles without content or substance). In another sense, of course, this is simply the old 'end of ideology' with a vengeance, and cynically plays on the waning of collective hope in a particularly conservative market climate. But the end of history is also the final form of the temporal paradoxes we have tried to dramatize here: namely that a rhetoric of absolute change (or 'permanent revolution' in some trendy and meretricious new sense) is, for the postmodern, no more satisfactory (but not less so) than the language of absolute identity and unchanging standardization cooked up by the great corporations, whose concept of innovation is best illustrated by the neologism and the logo and their equivalents in the realm of built space, 'life-style' corporate culture, and psychic programming. The persistence of the Same through absolute Difference – the same street with different buildings, the same culture through momentous new sheddings of skin – discredits change, since henceforth the only conceivable radical change would consist in putting an end to change itself. But here the antinomy really does result in the blocking or paralysis of thought, since the impossibility of thinking another system except by way of the cancellation of this one ends up discrediting the utopian imagination itself, which is fantasized as the loss of everything we know experientially, from our libidinal investments to our psychic habits, and in particular the artificial excitements of consumption and fashion.

Parmenidean stasis or Being, to be sure, knows at least one irrevocable event, namely death and the passage of the generations: insofar as the system of Parmenidean simulacrum or illusion is a very recent one, constituted in what we call postmodernity, the temporality of the generations in all their mortal discontinuity is not yet visible in results, except retroactively and as a materialist historiographic imperative. But death itself, as the very violence of absolute change, in the form of the nonimage – not even bodies rotting off stage but rather something persistent like an odour that circulates through the luminous immobility of this world without time – is inescapable and meaningless, since any historical framework that would serve to interpret and position individual deaths (at least for their survivors) has been destroyed. A kind of absolute violence, then, the abstraction of violent death, is something like the dialectical correlative to this world without time or history.

But it is more appropriate to conclude this section with a remark about the relationship of this temporal paradox – absolute change equals stasis – to the dynamics of the new global system itself, for here too we can observe an effacement of the temporalities that seemed to govern an older period of modernity, of modernism and modernization alike. For in that older period, most Third World societies were torn by a penetration of Western modernization that generated over against itself – in all the variety of cultural forms characteristic of those very different societies – a counterposition that could generally be described as traditionalism: the affirmation of a cultural (and sometimes religious) originality that had the power to resist assimilation by Western modernity and was indeed preferable to it. Such traditionalism was of course a construction in its own right, brought into being as it were, by the very activities of the modernizers themselves (in some more limited and specific sense than the one now widely accepted, that all traditions and historical pasts are themselves necessarily invented and constructed). At any rate, what one wants to affirm today is that this second reactive or antimodern term of tradition and traditionalism has everywhere vanished from the reality of the former Third World or colonized societies, where a neotraditionalism (as in certain Chinese revivals of Confucianism, or in religious fundamentalisms) is now rather perceived as a deliberate political and collective choice, in a situation in which little remains of a past that must be completely reinvented.

This is to say that, on the one hand, nothing but the modern henceforth exists in Third World societies; but it is also to correct this statement, on the other, with the qualification that under such circumstances, where only the modern exists, 'modern' must now be rebaptized 'postmodern' (since what we call modern is the consequence of incomplete modernization and must necessarily define itself against a nonmodern residuality that no longer obtains in postmodernity as such – or rather, whose absence defines this last). Here too then, but on a social and historical level, the temporality that modernization promised (in its various capitalist and communist productivist forms) has been eclipsed to the benefit of a new condition in which that older temporality no longer exists, leaving an appearance of random changes that are mere stasis, a disorder after the end of history. Meanwhile, it is as though what used to be characterized as the Third World has entered the interstices of the First one, as the latter also demodernizes and deindustrializes, lending the former colonial otherness something of the centred identity of the former metropolis.

With this extension of the temporal paradox on a global scale something else becomes clear as well, a kind of second paradox or antinomy that begins to make its presence felt behind and perhaps even within the first. Indeed, the repeated spatial characterizations of temporality here – from Proust to storefronts, from urban change to global 'development' – now begin to remind us that if it is so that postmodernity is characterized by some essential spatialization, then everything we have been trying to work out in terms of temporality will necessarily have passed through a spatial matrix to come to expression in the first place. If time has in effect been reduced to the most punctual violence and minimal irrevocable change of an abstract death, then we can perhaps affirm that in the postmodern time has become space anyhow. The foundational antinomy of postmodern description lies then in the fact that this former binary opposition, along with identity and difference themselves, no longer is an opposition as such, and ceaselessly reveals itself to have been at one with its other pole in a rather different way than the old dialectical projection back and forth, the classic dialectical metamorphosis. In order to see what this involves, we now necessarily turn to the other spatial antinomy, which apparently we have been rehearsing all along its temporal version, with a view toward determining whether spatiality has any genuine thematic priority.

II

It is at least certain that the form by which one dimension of the antithesis necessarily expresses itself by way of the figurality of the other, time being required to express itself in spatial terms, is not repeated here; nor is the time–space antithesis symmetrical or reversible in this sense. Space does not seem to require a temporal expression; if it is not what absolutely does without such temporal figurality, then at the very least it might be said that space is what represses temporality and temporal figurality absolutely, to the benefit of other figures and codes. If Difference and Identity are at stake in both the temporal and the spatial antinomy, then the difference pre-eminent in considerations of space is not so much that of change in any temporal understanding of the form, as rather variety and infinity, metonymy and – to reach some more influential and seemingly definitive and all-encompassing version – heterogeneity.

Historically, the adventures of homogeneous and heterogeneous space have most often been told in terms of the quotient of the sacred and of the folds in which it is unevenly invested: as for its alleged opposite number, the profane, however, one supposes that it is a projection backward in time of post-sacred and commercial peoples to imagine that it was itself any single thing or quality (a nonquality, rather); a projection indeed to think that anything like a simple dualism of the profane and the sacred ever existed as such in the first place. For the sacred can be supposed to have meant heterogeneity and multiplicity in the first place: a nonvalue, an excess, something irreducible to system or to thought, to identity, to the degree to which it not merely explodes itself, but its opposite number, positing the spaces for normal village living alongside the chthonic garbage heaps of the *im-monde* (Henri Lefebvre's account, in *The Production of Space*[6]) but also the empty spaces of waste and desert, the sterile voids that punctuate so many naturally expressive landscapes. For by definition there must also have been as many types or kinds of the sacred as there were powers, and one must drain these words of their feeble archaic overtones before we realize that abstractions such as *sacred* or *power* have, in the face of the realities they were meant to designate, about the same expressive force as the abstraction *colour* for the variety of intensities that absorb our gaze.

This also bears on the meaning of landscape, whose secular and painted modern version is a very recent development, as interpreters such as Deleuze or Karatani have so often reminded us. I hesitate to lapse into the fantasies of Romantics like Runge, with his languages of the plants; but they are certainly attractive fantasies, at least until they become socially stabilized in the form of kitsch (with its 'language of flowers'). Such notions of a space that is somehow meaningfully organized and on the very point of speech, a kind of articulated thinking that fails to reach its ultimate translation in propositions or concepts, in messages, ultimately find their justification and theoretical defence in Lévi-Strauss's description, in *La Pensée sauvage*[7], of prephilosophical 'perceptual science'; while their aesthetic reaches at least one kind of climax in the same anthropologist's classic reading of the Pacific Northwest Coast Indian, *La Geste d'Asdiwal*, where the various landscapes, from frozen inland wastes to the river and the coast itself, speak multiple languages (including those of the economic mode of production itself and of the kinship structure) and emit a remarkable range of articulated messages.

This kind of analysis effectively neutralizes the old opposition between the rational and the irrational (and all the satellite oppositions – primitive versus civilized, male versus female, West versus East – that are grounded on it) by locating the dynamics of meaning in texts that precede conceptual abstraction: a multiplicity of levels is thereby at once opened up that can no longer be assimilated to Weberian rationalism, instrumental thought, the reifications and repressions of the narrowly rational or conceptual. It is thereby to be characterized as heterogeneity; and we can go on to describe the sensory articulations of its object, in the mobile landscapes of *Asdiwal*, as heterogeneous space. As Derrida has famously shown, in one of the inaugural documents of what later comes to be called poststructuralism ('Structure, Sign, and Play'[8]), Lévi-Strauss's analysis remains somehow centred around homologous meanings: it fails to reach the ultimately aleatory and undecidable; it persists in clinging for dear life to the very concept of meaning proper; and in a situation that ought to put an end to that concept, it does not even attain the openness of Bakhtinian polyphony or heteroglossia, since there is still a collective agency – the tribe – that speaks through its multiplicities.

But that then becomes the failure of Lévi-Strauss to reach true heterogeneity rather than the historical insufficiency of this latter concept as such, about which Bataille's whole life's work demonstrates that it exists in situation and is, like the surrealism from which it derived and that it repudiates, a strategic reaction against a modern state of things. This leads one to wonder whether heterogeneity can in fact mean anything suitably subversive until homogeneity has historically emerged, to confer upon it the value and the force of a specific oppositional tactic. What has to be described, therefore, is not so much the prestige of such forms of multiplicity and excess that overspill the rational modern mind and rebuke it, as their values as reactions against it whose projection into the past is at best a doubtful and suspicious matter. The prior object of description is rather the gradual colonization of the world by precisely that homogeneity whose tendential conquests it was Bataille's historical mission (as of so many others) to challenge, along with the setting in place of forms of identity that only after the fact allow the anachronistic illusion of heterogeneity and difference to come to seem the logic of what they organized and flattened out.

That process, as far as space is concerned, can surely be identified with some precision: it is the moment in which a Western system of private property in real estate displaces the various systems of land tenure it confronts in the course of its successive enlargements (or, in the European situation itself, from which it gradually emerges for the first time in its own right). Nor does a language of violence – otherwise perfectly appropriate for these supersessions and still observable in settler colonies such as Israel and also in the various 'transitions to capitalism' in Eastern Europe – convey the way in which the substitution of one legal system for another, more customary one is a matter of calculation and elaborate political strategy.[9] The violence was no doubt always implicit in the very conception of ownership as such when applied to the land; it is a peculiarly ambivalent mystery that mortal beings, generations of dying organisms, should have imagined they could somehow 'own' parts of the earth in the first place. The older forms of land tenure (as well as the more recent socialist forms, similarly varied from country to country) at least posited the collectivity as the immortal governor into whose stewardship portions of the soil are given over; nor has it ever been a simple or easy matter to undo these social relationships and replace them with the apparently more obvious and manageable ones based on individualized ownership and a juridical system of equivalent subjects – East Germany in this respect today rather resembling what the American North had to do to the conquered South after the Civil War; while the Israeli settlements often remind one of the brutal displacement of Native American societies in the West of the United States.

The point is, however, that where the thematic opposition of heterogeneity and homogeneity is invoked, it can only be this brutal process that is the ultimate referent: the effects that result from the power of commerce and then capitalism proper – which is to say, sheer number as such, number now shorn and divested of its own magical heterogeneities and reduced to equivalencies – to seize upon a landscape and flatten it out, reorganize it into a grid of identical parcels, and expose it to the dynamic of a market that now reorganizes space in terms of an identical value. The development of capitalism then distributes that value most unevenly indeed, until at length, in its postmodern moment, sheer speculation, as something like the triumph of spirit over matter, the liberation of the form of value from any of its former concrete or earthly content, now reigns supreme and devastates the very cities and countrysides it created in the process of its own earlier development. But all such later forms of abstract violence and homogeneity derive from the initial parcellization, which translates the money form and the logic of commodity production for a market back on to space itself.

Our own period also teaches us that the fundamental contradiction in this reorganization of space, which seeks to stamp
out older and customary forms of collective land tenure (that
then swim back into the modern historical imagination in the
form of religious or anthropological conceptions of 'the sacred'
or of archaic heterogeneity), is to be identified as what we
equally used to call agriculture itself, when that was associated
with a peasantry or even yeoman farmers. In a postmodern
global system, in which the tendency of a hitherto overwhelming
peasant population to drop to some 7 or 8 per cent of the
nation can be observed everywhere in the modernizing fully as
much as in the 'advanced' countries, the relationship between
peasant agriculture and traditional culture has become only too
clear: the latter follows the former into extinction, and all the
great precapitalist cultures prove to have been peasant ones,
except where they were based on slavery. (Meanwhile, as for
what has until today passed for a capitalist culture – a specifically capitalist 'high culture,' that is – it can also be identified as
the way in which a bourgeoisie imitated and aped the traditions
of its aristocratic feudal predecessors, tending to be eclipsed
along with their memory and to give way, along with the older
classical bourgeois class-consciousness itself, to mass culture –
indeed to a specifically American mass culture at that.)

But the very possibility of a new globalization (the expansion
of capital beyond its earlier limits in its second, or 'imperalist',
stage) depended on an agricultural reorganization (sometimes
called the Green Revolution owing to its technological and
specifically chemical and biological innovations) that effectively
made peasants over into farm workers and great estates or
latifundia (as well as village enclaves) over into agribusiness.
Pierre-Philippe Rey has indeed suggested that we understand
the relationship of modes of production to one another as one
of the imbrication or articulation, rather than as one of simple
supersession: in this respect, he suggests the second or 'modern'
moment of capital – the stage of imperialism – retained an older
precapitalist mode of production in agriculture and kept it
intact, exploiting it in tributary fashion, deriving capital by
extensive labour, inhuman hours and conditions, from essentially precapitalist relations.[10] The new multinational stage of

capital is then characterized by the sweeping away of such enclaves and their utter assimilation into capitalism itself, with its wage-labour and working conditions: at this point, agriculture – culturally distinctive and identified in the superstructure as the Other of Nature – now becomes an industry like any other, and the peasants simple workers whose labour is classically commodified in terms of value equivalencies. This is not to say that commodification is evenly distributed over the entire globe or that all areas have been equally modernized or postmodernized; rather, that the tendency toward global commodification is far more visible and imaginable than it was in the modern period, in which tenacious premodern life realities still existed to impede the process. Capital, as Marx showed in the *Grundrisse*, necessarily tends toward the outer limit of a global market that is also its ultimate crisis situation (since no further expansion is then possible); this doctrine is for us today much less abstract than it was in the modern period; it designates a conceptual reality that neither theory nor culture can any longer postpone to some future agenda.

But to say so is to evoke the obliteration of difference on a world scale, and to convey a vision of the irrevocable triumph of spatial homogeneity over whatever heterogeneities might still have been fantasized in terms of global space. I want to stress this as an ideological development, which includes all the ecological fears awakened in our own period (pollution and its accompaniments also standing as a mark of universal commodification and commercialization): for in this situation ideology is not false consciousness but itself a possibility of knowledge, and our constitutive difficulties in imagining a world beyond global standardization are very precisely indices and themselves features of just that standardized reality or being itself.

Such ideological limits, invested with a certain affective terror as a kind of dystopia, are then compensated by other ideological possibilities that come into view when we no longer take the countryside as our vantage point but rather the city and the urban itself. This is of course already an opposition that has left significant traces in the science-fictional or utopian tradition: the antithesis between a pastoral utopia and an urban one, and in particular the apparent supersession in recent years of images of a village or tribal utopia (Ursula Le Guin's *Always Coming Home* of 1985[11] was virtually the last of those) by visions of an unimaginably dense urban reality (therein nonetheless somehow imagined) that is either explicitly placed on the utopian agenda, as in Samuel Delany's 1976 *Trouble on Triton*[12] (or Raymond Williams's prescient forecast that socialism, if it is possible, will not be simpler than all this but far more complicated) or by masquerades under a dystopian appearance whose deeper libidinal excitement, however, is surely profoundly utopian in spirit (as in most current cyberpunk).

Once again, however, we have to deal with the conceptual difficulties in which we are plunged by the disappearance of one of the terms of a formerly functioning binary opposition. The disappearance of Nature – the commodification of the countryside and the capitalization of agriculture itself all over the world – now begins to sap its other term, the formerly urban. Where the world system today tends toward one enormous urban system – as a tendentially ever more complete modernization always promised, a promise which has however been ratified and delivered in an unexpected way by the communications revolution and its new technologies: a development of which the immediately physical visions, nightmares of the 'sprawl' from Boston to Richmond, or the Japanese urban agglomeration, are the merest allegories – the very conception of the city itself and the classically urban loses its significance and no longer seems to offer any precisely delimited objects of study, any specifically differentiated realities. Rather, the urban becomes the social in general, and both of them constitute and lose themselves in a global that is not really their opposite either (as it was in the older dispensation) but something like their outer reach, their prolongation into a new kind of infinity.

Ideologically, what this dissolution of the boundaries of the traditional city and the classically urban enables is a slippage, a displacement, a reinvestment of older urban ideological and libidinal connotations under new conditions. The city always seemed to promise freedom, as in the medieval conception of the urban as the space of escape from the land and from feudal labour and serfdom, from the arbitrary power of the lord: 'city air' from this perspective now becomes the very opposite of

what Marx famously characterized as 'rural idiocy', the narrow-
ness of village manners and customs, the provinciality of the
rural, with its fixed ideas and superstitions and its hatred of
difference. Here, in contrast to the dreary sameness of the
countryside (which is also, however inaccurately, fantasized as
a place of sexual repression), the urban classically promised
variety and adventure, often linked to crime just as the
accompanying visions of pleasure and sexual gratification are
inseparable from transgression and illegality. What happens,
then, when even that countryside, even that essentially provincial reality, disappears, becomes standardized, hears the same
English, sees the same programmes, consumes the same consumer goods, as the former metropolis to which, in the old
days, these same provincials and country people longed to go as
to a fundamental liberation? I think that the missing second
term – provincial boredom, rural idiocy – was preserved, but
simply transferred to a different kind of city and a different
kind of social reality, namely the Second World city and the
social realities of a nonmarket or planned economy. Everyone
remembers the overwhelming power of such Cold War iconog-
raphy, which has perhaps proved even more effective today,
after the end of the Cold War and in the thick of the current
offensive of market propaganda and rhetoric, than it was in a
situation of struggle where visions of terror were more quintessentially operative. Today, however, it is the memory of the
imagined drabness of the classic Second World city – with its
meagre shelves of consumer goods in empty centrals from which
the points of light of advertising are absent, streets from which
small stores and shops are missing, standardization of clothing
fashions (as most emblematically in Maoist China) – that
remains ideologically operative in the campaigns for privatization. Jane Jacob's fundamental identification of a genuine urban
fabric and street life with small business is ceaselessly rehearsed
ideologically, without any reminder that she thought the diagnosis applied fully as much to the North American or capitalist
city in which corporations have equally, but in a different
fashion, driven small business out of existence, and created
canyons of institutional high-rises without any urban personality at all.

This urban degradation, which characterizes the First World, has, however, been transferred to a separate ideological compartment called postmodernism, where it duly takes its place in the arsenal of attacks on modern architecture and its ideals. As for the Second World city, its vision is rather enlisted in the service of a rather different operation, namely to serve as the visual and experiential *analogon* of a world utterly programmed and directed by human intention, a world therefore from which the contingencies of chance – and thereby the promise of adventure and real life, of libidinal gratification – are also excluded. Conscious intention, the plan, collective control, are then fantasized as being at one with repression and renunciation, with instinctual impoverishment: and as in the related postmodern polemic, the absence of ornament from the Second World city – as it were the involuntary enactment of Adolf Loos's program – serves as a grim caricature of the puritanical utopian values of a revolutionary society (just as it had served as that of the equally puritanical utopian values of high modernism in the other campaign that in certain recent theory in the Eastern countries[13] is explicitly linked to this one in an instructive and revealing way).

Only the spatial features of this particular ideological tactic are new: Edmund Burke was of course the first to develop the great anti-revolutionary figure, according to which what people consciously and collectively do can only be destructive and a sign of fatal hubris: that only the slow 'natural' growth of traditions and institutions can be trusted to form a genuinely human world (a deep suspicion of the will and of unconscious intention that then passes over into a certain Romantic tradition in aesthetics). But Burke's pathbreaking attack on the Jacobins was aimed at the middle-class construction and formation of market society itself, about whose commercialism it essentially expressed the fears and anxieties of an older social formation in the process of being superseded. The market theorists today, however, marshal the same fantasies in defence of a market society now supposed itself to be somehow 'natural' and deeply rooted in human nature; they do so against the Promethean efforts of human beings to take collective production into their own hands and, by planning, to control or at least to influence and inflect their own future (something that no longer seems particularly meaningful in a postmodernity in which the very experience of the future as such has come to seem enfeebled, if not deficient).

But this is precisely the ideological and imaginary background against which it is possible to market and to sell the contemporary capitalist city as well-nigh Bakhtinian carnival of heterogeneities, of differences, libidinal excitement and a hyperindividuality that effectively decentres the old individual subject by way of individual hyperconsumption. Now the associations or connotations of provincial misery and renunciation, of petty bourgeois impoverishment, of cultural and libidinal immiseration, systematically reinvested in our images of the urban space of the Second World, are pressed into service as arguments against socialism and planning, against collective ownership and what is fantasized as centralization, at the same time that they serve as powerful stimuli to the peoples of Eastern Europe to plunge into the freedoms of Western consumption. This is no small ideological achievement in view of the difficulties, a priori, in staging the collective control over their destinies by social groups in a negative way and investing those forms of autonomy with all the fears and anxieties, the loathing and libidinal dread, which Freud called counterinvestment or anticathexis and that must constitute the central effect of any successful anti-utopianism.

This is then also the point at which everything most paradoxical about the spatial form of the antinomy under discussion here becomes vivid and inescapable; our conceptual exhibit comes more sharply into view when we begin to ask ourselves how it is possible for the most standardized and uniform social reality in history, by the merest ideological flick of the thumbnail, the most imperceptible of displacements, to emerge as the rich oil-smear sheen of absolute diversity and of the most unimaginable and unclassifiable forms of human freedom. Here homogeneity has become heterogeneity, in a movement complementary to that in which absolute change turned into absolute stasis, and without the slightest modification of a real history that there was thought to be at an end, while here it has seemed finally to realize itself.

5

'End of Art' or 'End of History'?

The debate about the 'end of history', assuming it is still on, seems to have driven out the very memory of its predecessor, the debate about the 'end of art', which was hotly pursued in the sixties, now some thirty years ago, it is strange to think. Both of these debates derive from Hegel and reproduce a characteristic turn in his thinking about history, or in the form of his historical narrative, if you prefer: I trust we are by now far enough along in our consciousness of the narrative structure of historicity that we can forget about hoary old chestnuts about the evils of totalization or teleology. At any rate, the excitement about the Fukuyama/Kojève contribution – welcomed fully as much by a certain Left as by a certain Right – shows that Hegel may not be as old-fashioned as people used to say and think. Here I want to compare these two highly suggestive and symptomatic debates and try to determine what that comparison has to tell us about the historical conjuncture in which we find ourselves. I have consistently argued, over the last few years, that that conjuncture is marked by a dedifferentiation of fields, such that economics has come to overlap with culture: that everything, including commodity production and high and speculative finance, has become cultural; and culture has equally become profoundly economic or commodity oriented. Thus it will not surprise you to learn that conjectures about our current situation can be taken as statements about late capitalism or about the politics of globalization. But maybe that is to get a little ahead of ourselves here.

So let's close our eyes, and by a powerful trance-like effort of the imagination try to think our way back into the halcyon era of the 1960s when the world was still young. The simplest way of approaching the 'end of art' debate can be discerned via a recollection of one of the hottest fashions or crazes of those bygone years, namely the emergence of the so-called happenings, discussed by everyone from Marcuse to the Sunday supplements. I never thought much of happenings myself, and would tend to recontextualize them in the large movement of theatrical innovation generally: for what we call the sixties – which may be said to have begun (slowly) in 1963, with the Beatles and the Vietnam War, and to have ended dramatically somewhere around 1973–75 with the Nixon shock and the oil crisis, and also with what is again derisively known as the 'loss' of Saigon – was amongst other things an extraordinarily rich moment, the richest since the 1920s, in the invention of new kinds of performances and staging of all the canonical playbooks inherited from the cultural past of world literature generally: it suffices to mention the Hallischer Ufer, let alone Schiffbauer Damm, Peter Brook or Grotowski, the Théâtre du soleil, the TNP or Olivier's National Theatre, and the off-Broadway theatre of the New York stage, let alone the production of Beckett and so-called anti-theatre, to conjure back a whole universe of playacting and representational excitement in which, clearly enough, the so-called happenings necessarily take their place.

I hope it will not be misunderstood if I follow a number of historians of the period in suggesting that it was an era of great performances and creative *mise en scène*, rather than one of an original composition and production of new dramas (despite the prestige of the few genuine playwrights like Beckett whose names stud the rosters of the era): new stagings of Shakespeare around the globe, in other words, rather than new and unimaginable Shakespeares on all kinds of unlikely stages of the world-theatre (but let's not waste our time in the amusing exercise of thinking of the names of the exceptions, like Soyenka or Fugard). All I wanted to suggest at this point was that theatrical practice in this period stands at a certain minimal distance from the texts it presupposes as its pretexts and conditions of possibility: happenings would then push this situation to its extreme limit, by claiming to do away with the pretext of the text altogether and offering a spectacle of the sheerest performance as such, which also paradoxically seeks to abolish the boundary and the distinction between fiction and fact, or art and life.

At this point, I must also remind you of what everyone in our kind of society today tries to forget: namely that this was a passionately political period, and that innovations in the arts, and in particular innovations in the theatre, even those of the most aestheticizing and least politically aware performers and directors, were always driven by the firm conviction that theatrical performance was also a form of *praxis*, and that changes in the theatre, however minimal, were also contributions to a general change in life itself, and in the world and the society of which the theatre was both a part and a mirror. In particular, I think it would scarcely be an exaggeration to suggest that the politics of the sixties, all over the world and specifically including the 'wars of national liberation', was defined and constituted as an opposition to the American war in Vietnam, in other words, as a world-wide protest. Theatrical innovation then also staged itself as the symbolic gesture of aesthetic protest, as formal innovation grasped in terms of social and political protest as such, above and beyond the specifically aesthetic and theatrical terms in which the innovation was couched.

Meanwhile, in a narrower sense as well, the very deployment of the theory of the 'end of art' was also political, insofar as it was meant to suggest or to register the profound complicity of the cultural institutions and canons, of the museums and the university system, the state prestige of all the high arts, in the Vietnam War as a defence of Western values: something that also presupposes a high level of investment in official culture and an influential status in society of high culture as an extension of state power. On my view, this is truer today, when nobody cares any more, than it was in those days, particularly in an exceedingly anti-intellectual United States. Hans Haacke is then perhaps a more fitting emblem of that view of things than most of the artists of that period; but the political reminder is at least useful to the degree to which it identifies a left-wing provenance for the theory of the 'end of art', in contrast with the markedly right-wing spirit of the current 'end of history'.

What did Hegel himself mean by the 'end of art' – a phrase he is unlikely to have used himself in quite that sloganeering fashion? The notion of an immanent 'end of art' is in Hegel something like a deduction from the premises of several conceptual schemes or models which are superimposed one upon the other. Indeed, the richness of Hegel's thought – as with any interesting thinker – stems not from the ingenuity or the pertinence or any particular individual concept, but rather from the way in which, in the thinker in question, several distinct systems of concepts coexist and fail to coincide. Imagine models floating above each other as in distinct dimensions: it is not their homologies that prove suggestive or fruitful, but rather the infinitesimal divergences, the imperceptible lack of fit between the levels – extrapolated out into a continuum whose stages range from the pre-choate and the quizzical gap, to the nagging tension and the sharpness of contradiction itself – genuine thinking always taking place within empty places, these voids that suddenly appear between the most powerful conceptual schemes. Thinking is thus not the concept, but the breakdown in the relationships between the individual concepts, isolated in their splendour like so many galactic systems, drifting apart in the empty mind of the world.

Characteristically, Hegel's models or subsystems are all compulsively tidied up into those triplications which the contemporary reader needs to disregard – as a kind of weird and obsessive numerological superstition – in order to make this densely tortuous text[1] interesting for herself. Relevant for us at this point are but two of the famous triadic progressions: that of absolute spirit – or rather the movement towards that absolute of 'objective spirit', as it passes through the three stages of religion, art and philosophy; and that of art itself, as it passes more modestly through the three more local stages of the symbolic, the classical and the romantic ... towards what? Towards the end of art, of course, and the abolition of the aesthetic by itself and under its own internal momentum, the self-transcendence of the aesthetic towards something else, something supposedly better than its own darkened and figural mirror – the splendour and transparency of Hegel's utopian notion of philosophy itself, the historical self-consciousness of an absolute present (which will also turn out to be that self-same allegedly prophetic notion of the so-called 'end of history') – in short, the shaping power of the human collectivity over its own destiny, at which point it founders (for us here and now) into an incomprehensible, unimaginable, utopian temporality beyond what thought can reach.

No doubt other subsystems in Hegel's immense *dictée* – the compulsive graphomanic lifelong transcription of what some daimon of the absolute muttered to him day-in day-out at the very limits of syntax and language itself – could be profitably added to the mix of these superscriptions. But it will be enough today to convince ourselves of the secret and productive discrepancies between these two, that otherwise seem to have so much in common: marching as they do from the only obscurely and unconsciously figural, through the assumption of the sheer autopoiesis of the play of figuration as such, towards the sheer transparency of an end of figuration in the philosophical and the historically self-conscious, in a situation in which thought has expunged the last remnants of figures and tropes from the fading and luminous categories of abstraction itself.

I believe that it is the peculiar emergence of the 'sublime' in the wrong place in these various schemes and progressions that gives us the deeper clue to Hegel's thinking. Let's try to work through them in a flat-footed and deliberately literal, oversimplified and unimaginative fashion. In that case, the first moment of history – religion, pre-Christian religion, or better still, non-Western religion as such – is one in which humanity thinks and is collectively conscious without genuine self-consciousness: or rather, to be a little more precise, since consciousness without self-consciousness is a kind of contradiction in terms – in which humanity is collectively conscious but only unconsciously self-conscious: in short, in which it thinks in images and figures; in which it makes external forms and shapes, the mass and variety of matter as such, think for itself and rear up, deliriously self-fashion itself into the fetish-logic of the great classical religions, very much in the later sense and spirit of Feuerbach and Marx himself. I wish we had time to examine Hegel's remarkably resourceful evocations of Indian ornament and Egyptian hiero-glyph, which return over and over again like *leitmotiven* in Hegel's lifework, and offer the ultimate clues as to his own conception of the figural and figuration as such.

The more familiar version of all this, however, the one you know already from so many carefully controlled contemporary approaches to a single local zone of Hegel's system, is our old friend the pyramid: the mass of matter in which somewhere a little spark of living spirit dwells; that monumental outer shape whose very form – too vast to articulate the differentiations of concrete thinking as such – nonetheless designates, as over some immense distance, the indwelling presence of the form of consciousness itself. Body and spirit no doubt; matter and mind; except that it would be better to say that these barren concep-tual oppositions and dualisms ultimately derive from the dead-end of religious figuration, than that, the other way around, Hegel's notion of the problematical structure of religion repli-cates and reproduces the most banal inherited philosophical stereotype of the tradition.

What happens now, however, is unexpected: instead of the logical and predictable outcome – that matter would simply transcend itself in spirit, that figuration would disengage itself from its material trappings and at once into abstract thought as such – the next step is one in which figuration is as it were distracted in its ultimate mission and destiny and mired even more dangerously within matter and the body itself. It is the moment of the Greeks – of classical art – which scandalously erupts and disrupts the teleology of human history and the movement from Asia to Western Europe, from the great Other of the Eastern religions and empires to the masterful centred self of Western philosophy and capitalist industrial production. The Romans fit that scheme, but not the Greeks, who offer a dangerous and tantalizing, misleading vision of the new and ultimate human age: of a world in which only human measure obtains and the human body itself constitutes the very source and fountainhead of political philosophy; a kind of corporeal humanism in which the secret Pythagorean harmonies of the golden mean suggest a rationality of the human body itself and its proportions, and for the briefest of instants delude us into thinking that the final form of a truly human world and of an achieved philosophy has been reached.

Hegel must denounce the idolatry of this outcome, in order to get history moving again; he must throw a sop to the classical passions of his contemporaries, while gently prodding them to move on, and quietly but insistently reminding them that Christianity still remains on the agenda, along with Tacitus's *Germania*, and breathes a peremptory authority capable of surmounting and overriding all such lingering classical nostalgia.

As for Christianity itself, and the now dominant Germanic fact of Western Europe, it is important to remember that for Hegel and his contemporaries, it is scarcely even to be thought of as a religion any longer: its triadic obsessions and trinitarian logics pass via the Reformation over into the abstractions of German classical philosophy, of the objective idealism of Hegel's own generation, sufficiently trained in dead theological categories and their immanent dialectical movement, to defiguralize all that faint persistent sacred decoration at the speed of the Cartesian *coup de pouce* into the henceforth secular profundities of Fichte, Schelling and Hegel himself. It is the tortured individual body of Christ[2] that will serve as the decompression chamber through which a generation obsessed with Greek bodies disintoxicates itself and passes over into the rather different pleasures and satisfactions of abstraction as such, and what these Germans call the Absolute: the individual body was not really meaningful after all, but rather the human collectivity, with whose apotheosis Marx will complete the Hegelian system, stalled on its way to the end of history by the unexpected regression of the ultramodern Prussian state into despotic and fanatical reaction.

Thus, Christianity seems to dissolve fairly effortlessly into classical German philosophy, just as the Germanic tribal tradition seems to lead directly into modernity itself: if you place Luther and Protestantism squarely in the middle of this historical development, the idea may seem less parochial, let alone chauvinistic. But there is clearly a problem with the final stage of Hegel's tripartite scheme: what he calls the Romantic form of art. It is a formal problem: to begin with, he needs this stage to constitute a dialectical climax to the *Aesthetics*. Whatever kind of historical narrative the dialectic may have been – and it was certainly as fresh and stunningly paradoxical in its day as the competing historical narratives of Derridean supplementarity or Freudian *Nachträglichkeit* in our own – it clearly required the third stage in some satisfying sense as fully to realize the preceding ones as to dissolve them and pass on into something else.

Christianity, again, will provide the hinge on which an unconvincing solution is arranged: for medieval art can now stand as the strong content of the Romantic form, as the most original raw material of this aesthetic modernity; while the medieval nostalgia of the contemporary German Romantics – the Schlegels, whom Hegel hated, the converts who confused Italy with Roman Catholicism, the Nazarene painters and the various exiles southward of the Alps – these weak survivals of a medieval Roman Catholic culture that was genuinely 'Romantic' (or modern, in the broader sense of Hegel's world history) help prove the point by fastening art helplessly to an inescapable medieval and Christian mission, while testifying to the debility of such nostalgic revivals in the present day (let's say 1820 or so) and thereby demonstrating the urgency of a transition into some dialectically new and different era, and the claims of philosophy to replace this sorry aesthetic floundering with something more vigorous and decisive. The ambiguity extends into Hegel's very use of the word Romantic, not generally a positive epithet under his pen: those for whom the German Romantics, and in particular Friedrich Schlegel again, have today come to be seen as precursors of peculiarly contemporary practices and thoughts of our own, will have no great trouble maliciously diagnosing Hegel's distaste for the Romantics as the anxiety of competition and the prescient sense of the dangers offered by Romantic irony and self-consciousness to the sway and claims posed by the dialectic itself.

In any case, whatever reading one chooses to make of Hegel's final stage of art, few historical prognoses have been so disastrously wrong. Whatever the validity of Hegel's feelings about Romanticism, those currents which led on into what has come to be called modernism are thereby surely to be identified with one of the most remarkable flourishings of the arts in all of human history. Whatever the 'end of art' may mean for us, therefore, it was emphatically not on the agenda in Hegel's own time. And, as far as the other part of the prophecy was concerned, the supersession of art by philosophy, he could not have chosen a worse historical moment for this pronouncement either; indeed, if we follow the practice of Hegel and his contemporaries in identifying philosophy with system as such, then few will wish to deny that in that sense, far from being a forerunner of a truly philosophical age, Hegel was rather the last philosopher in the tradition: and this in two senses, by being utterly subsumed and transfigured in and by Marxism as a kind of post-philosophy, and also by having occupied this philosophical terrain so completely as to leave all later purely philosophical efforts (which in our own time have come rather to be identified as theory) to constitute so many local guerrilla raids and anti-philosophical therapies, from Nietzsche to pragmatism, from Wittgenstein to deconstruction.

Yet there is another sense in which Hegel was right and truly prophetic about all this, and it is this secret truth, this moment of truth in the utterly aberrant and seemingly misguided, that we must now try to grasp. 'Philosophy,' said Adorno, in one of his most famous aphorisms, 'philosophy, which once seemed obsolete, lives on because the moment to realise it was missed'. It is true that the 'end of philosophy' did not figure among our official topics here, but Adorno's extraordinary remark offers a richer picture of the 'end' of something than anything we have hitherto confronted: an end which is a realization, which can be missed, and whose omission results in little more than a sorry afterlife and second-best, which is however still essential (the other 'end' of philosophy, as far as Adorno was concerned, the supersession of philosophy by positivism and anti-theory, is for him so pernicious as to call forth 'critical theory' as a way of keeping the negative alive in a period in which praxis, the unity of the negative and the positive, itself seems suspended).

All of which is to say that it was History, rather than Hegel, that was wrong: from this perspective the dissolution of art into philosophy implies a different kind of 'end' of philosophy – its diffusion and expansion into all the realms of social life in such a way that it is no longer a separate discipline but the very air we breathe and the very substance of the public sphere itself and of the collectivity. It ends, in other words, not by becoming nothing, but by becoming everything: the path not taken by History.

Perhaps in that case it is worth asking how, according to Hegel, art itself should have ended in this triumph, which is also another kind of end, of philosophy as such, and which did not happen. 'Just as art', Hegel says,[3] 'has its "before" in nature and the finite spheres of life, so too it has an "after", i.e., a region which in turn transcends art's way of apprehending and representing the Absolute. For art still has a limit in itself and thereby passes over into higher forms of consciousness. This limitation determines, after all, the position which we are accustomed to assign to art in our contemporary life. For us art counts no longer as the highest mode in which truth fashions an existence for itself'; and he goes on to evoke the Islamic and Judaic ban on graven images, along with Plato's critique of art, as the historical motive force for mistrust of figuration which will fulfil itself in the 'end of art'. But Hegel's very language warns us not to take this formulation too literally either, as meaning the utter disappearance of art as such. Indeed, Peter Bürger has written much of interest, speculating on the types of decorative artistic productions (Dutch still lifes, for example) which Hegel thought would survive the 'end of art' and furnish or embellish the lifeworld of a stage of realized philosophy.

Yet the crucial sentence suggests something rather different: 'For us art no longer counts as the highest mode in which truth fashions an existence for itself [*die höchste Weise, in welcher die Wahrheit sich Existenz verschafft*]'. This is the sentence that alerts us to a reversal of Hegel's judgment by History which is as dramatic as the one Adorno's dictum underscored for philosophy itself: for surely what has defined *modernism* in the arts above all is that it laid peremptory claim to a unique mode 'of apprehending and representing the Absolute' and that it was indeed for us or at least wished to be for us par excellence 'the highest mode in which truth claws its way into existence' (to give a somewhat different rendering). Modernism very precisely found its authority in the relativization of the various philosophical codes and languages, in their humiliation by the development of the natural sciences, and in the intensifying critiques of abstraction and instrumental reason inspired by the experiences of the industrial city.

But the ways in which the authority of philosophy was weakened and undermined cannot be said to have simply allowed art to develop and persist alongside it, as some alternative path to an Absolute whose questionable authority remained intact. In this sense Hegel was absolutely right: an event took place, the event he planned to call 'the end of art'. And as a constitutive feature of that event, in fact a certain art ended. What did not conform to Hegel's prognosis was the supersession of art by philosophy itself: rather, a new and different kind of art suddenly appeared to take philosophy's place after the end of the old one, and to usurp all of philosophy's claims to the Absolute, to being the 'highest mode in which truth manages to come into being'. This was the art we call modernism: and it means that in order to account for Hegel's mistake, we need to posit two kinds of art with wholly different functions and claims on truth.

Or rather, we do not need to, because those two types of art had already been theorized and codified in Hegel's day, and we have already commented on the rather suspicious nature of his dealings with the theory in question, which as you will already have guessed is that of the distinction between the Beautiful and the Sublime. I agree with any number of commentators – but perhaps Philippe Lacoue-Labarthe has put it most strongly – that what we call modernism is in the long run to be identified with the Sublime itself. Modernism aspires to the Sublime as to its very essence, which we may call trans-aesthetic, insofar as it lays a claim to the Absolute, that is, it believes that in order to be art at all, art must be something beyond art. Kant's account – a peculiar afterthought and codicil to his more conventional thoughts on Beauty – amounts to an extraordinary premonition of modern art in a period in which little enough else foreshadowed it, and might fruitfully be re-explored for its implications for both the philosophical (he calls it 'moral') and the effective dimensions of the modern generally. That is unfortunately not something we can pursue any further here, where it is rather a somewhat different consequence that must be underscored: namely that the art whose 'end' Hegel foresaw is, in the light of Kant, to be identified as Beauty. It is the Beautiful that comes to an end in this significant event, but what takes its place is finally not philosophy, as Hegel thought, but rather the Sublime itself, or in other words the aesthetic of the modern or the transaesthetic if you prefer. And of course, very much in the spirit of Peter Bürger's suggestion, this supersession is accompanied by a low-level persistence and reproduction of any number of secondary forms of the Beautiful in all the traditional senses; the Beautiful now as decoration, without any claim to truth or to a special relationship with the Absolute.

But if you have been willing to go this far, perhaps you will be prepared to take another step further, or rather a leap, into our own time, or rather our own yesterday, of the 1960s and the happenings, and that particular contemporary 'end of art', to which it is time to return. Now, however, I think that we are in a better position to identify this particular 'end of something': it can only be the end of the modern itself, or in other words the end of the Sublime, the dissolution of art's vocation to reach the Absolute. It should be clear, then, that whatever this particular historical event is, it will scarcely present much similarity to that older and earlier 'end of art' in which philosophy failed to live up to its historic vocation, and in which it was left to the Sublime to supplant the merely Beautiful. The end of the modern, the gradual setting in place of postmodernity over several decades, has been an epochal event in its own right whose changing and shifting evaluations merit some study in themselves.

I was going to say, for example, that this second 'end of art' was scarcely to be imagined as having opened the way to the final realm of philosophy any more than its very different nineteenth-century equivalent had. But if you think of the dissolution of the modern as a lengthy cultural process, which began in the 1960s, and whose 1980s' unveiling as a new gilded age does not perhaps give us its final word either, then other conjectures and historical interpretations seem possible as well. What for example of the emergence of Theory, as that seemed to supplant traditional literature from the 1960s onwards, and to extend across a broad range of disciplines, from philosophy to anthropology, from linguistics to sociology, effacing their boundaries in an immense dedifferentiation and inaugurating that long-postponed moment as well in which a Marxism that had established its credentials as an analysis of political economy finally earned its right to new ones in the analysis of superstructures, of culture and ideology? This grand moment of Theory (which some claim now also to have ended) in fact confirmed Hegel's premonitions by taking as its central theme the dynamics of representation itself: one cannot imagine a classical Hegelian supersession of art by philosophy otherwise than by just such a return of consciousness (and self-consciousness) back on the figuration and the figural dynamics that constitute the aesthetic, in order to dissolve those into the broad daylight and transparency of praxis itself. The 'end of art' of this period, the waning of the modern, was not merely marked by the slow disappearance of all the great *auteurs* who signed modernism in its grandest period from 1910 to 1955; it was also accompanied by the emergence of all those now equally famous names from Lévi-Strauss to Lacan, from Barthes to Derrida and Baudrillard, that adorn the heroic age of Theory itself. The transition was not characterized by an abrupt shifting of gears, in which a preoccupation with the narrative sublime, for example, suddenly gave way jarringly to a return to the study of logical categories: rather Theory emerged from the aesthetic itself, from the culture of the modern, and it is only in the dreary light of the old anti-intellectual distinction between the critical and the creative that the movement from Mayakovsky to Jakobson will seem a downward curve, or that from Brecht to Barthes, or from Joyce to Eco, from Proust to Deleuze.

In these senses, then, and with the significant replacement of the term philosophy by that of theory, perhaps it might be argued, about this particular contemporary 'end of art', that Hegel was not so terribly wrong after all; and that the event in question could at least partially be grasped as a dissolution of figuration at its most intense into a newer form of lucidity which unlike the older philosophical system now attempted to make a place for praxis itself.

If so, however, then the description is only partially correct, and the setting in place of the postmodern also has another dimension to which we have not yet done justice. For Hegel's transitional schema involves the fate of several terms: the function of the Sublime, the modern, of the one half of art, is taken over by Theory; but this also leaves room for the survival of art's other half, namely the Beautiful, which now invests the cultural realm at the moment in which the production of the modern has gradually dried up. This is the other face of postmodernity, the return of Beauty and the decorative, in the place of the older modern Sublime, the abandonment by art of the quest for the Absolute or of truth claims and its redefinition as a source of sheer pleasure and gratification (rather than, as in the modern, of *jouissance*). Both Theory and the Beautiful are constituent elements of that 'end of art' which was the postmodern: but they tend to block each other out in such a way that the seventies appeared to be the age of Theory, where the eighties revealed itself as the moment of garish cultural self-indulgence and consumption (which began indeed to include signed and commodified Theory itself in its lavish feasts).

Art thus, in this new age, seems to have sunk back to the older culinary status it enjoyed before the dominance of the Sublime: yet we must remember that in those days, which are still largely filled with the processes of secularization and with the replacement of a feudal or cultic *ancien régime* culture with a bourgeois one, the field of culture is still shared by even more ancient forms of religious figuration, which have in our own time utterly vanished as such. We must therefore add a significant qualification to this identification to postmodernism with Kant's and Burke's conception of the Beautiful: this has to do with education, the public sphere, and the cybernetic or informational age; and it requires us to underscore a remarkable historic development in our own time, namely the immense expansion of culture and commodification into all these fields – politics and economics, for example – from which it was so rightly differentiated in the daily life of the modern period. The great movement of dedifferentiation of postmodernity has in other words once again effaced these boundaries (and, as has been said, makes the cultural economic at the same time that it turns the economic into so many forms of culture). This is why it seems appropriate to evoke an immense acculturation of daily life and the social generally in our own postmodern moment; and also what justifies prophetic descriptions of our society as the society of the spectacle or of the image – for I would want to argue more generally that this acculturation has taken essentially spatial forms which we tend, crudely and not altogether accurately, to identify as visual. This is not the position generally held, I think, by those who either deplore or celebrate 'an end of art' identified with the end of literature, the canon, or reading as such, and superseded by mass culture in general – a non-Hegelian and moralizing position which generally fails to describe the new moment in a systemic way. But the return of the Beautiful in the postmodern must be seen as just such a systemic dominant: a colonization of reality generally by spatial and visual forms which is at one and the same time a commodification of that same intensively colonized reality on a world-wide scale. Whether the Sublime, and its successor Theory, have that capacity hinted at by Kant, to restore the philosophical component of such postmodernity, and to crack open the commodification implicit in the Beautiful, is a question I have not even begun to explore; but it is a question and a problem which is, I hope, a little different from the alternative we have thought we were faced with until now: namely whether, if you prefer modernism, it is conceivable, let alone possible, to go back to the modern as such, after its dissolution into full postmodernity. And the new question is also a question about Theory itself, and whether it can persist and flourish without simply turning back into an older technical philosophy whose limits and obsolescence were already visible in the nineteenth century.

But now we need to move on to an even more complicated topic – one that turns, not merely on the end of art, but seemingly, on the end of everything; namely the so-called 'end of history' itself. We have unfortunately no time to retrace the fascinating story of this motif: which originates in a certain 'epochality' in Hegel, his sense that a whole new unparalleled era was beginning; which is then readapted by the Russian émigré Alexandre Kojève – an admirer of Stalin and later on an architect of the European Common Market and the European

Economic Community, whose 1930s lectures on Hegel are often credited as the source for what came to be called 'existential Marxism'; finally, the version of 'the idea with which [Francis] Fukuyama startled the world's journalists in the summer of 1989', as Perry Anderson puts it – in short, the notion that at the end of the Cold War capitalism and the market could be declared the final form of human history itself, a notion to which piquancy was added by the position of Fukuyama in George Bush's State Department. Fortunately, however, the history of this concept has been written as definitively as anyone might now wish, in Anderson's book *A Zone of Engagement*,[4] so that we do not have to review the details here, as entertaining as that might be.

Two features of the story need to be retained, however, and both relate to historical materialism. Those conversant with a materialist and dialectical interpretation of history will for one thing not be likely to make the more naive objection to Fukuyama, namely that, in spite of everything, history does go on, there continue to be events and in particular wars, nothing seems to have stopped, everything seems to be getting worse, etc., etc. But insofar as Marx evoked his version of the end of history at all, it was with two qualifications: first, he spoke not of the end of history, but of the end of prehistory; that is to say, of the arrival of a period in which the human collectivity is in control of its own destiny, in which history is a form of collective praxis, and no longer subject to the non-human determinisms either of nature and scarcity, or of the market and money. And, second, he imagined this end of prehistory not in terms of events or individual actions but in terms of systems or better still (his word) *modes* of production. (Nor did he teach the inevitability of any particular outcome; a famous phrase evokes the possibility of 'the mutual ruin of the contending classes' – a rather different end of history, surely – while the equally famous alternative of 'socialism or barbarism' obviously includes a fateful warning and an appeal to human freedom.) Still, the Marxist view, that of the supersession of one mode of production by another, by insisting on radical difference between that kind of systemic event and those events which are more ordinary historical actions or happenings, makes it clear how history would be expected to continue eventfully even after the radical change of socio-economic systems or modes of production themselves.

Oddly enough, however, neither Fukuyama nor Kojève argue for their ends of history in that historical-materialist or systemic way: indeed for people accustomed to the more materialist Hegel of the early Jena economic writings or of the Hegel taken up into Marx himself, they serve as a useful reminder of another basically idealist (if not necessarily conservative) side of Hegel (and perhaps even of existential Marxism), namely that which, via the struggle between master and slave, insists on the motor of history as a struggle for recognition. Kojève's insistence on the Hegelian motif of 'satisfaction' (*Befriedigung*), his consequent (almost Girardian) emphasis on the results of social equality and the end of hierarchy, turn the triumph of capitalism back into social psychology and existentialism rather than the superiority of the mode of production itself. Later theorists combine 'the two motifs that Kojève had opposed as alternatives: no longer a civilisation of either consumption or style, but of their interchangeability – the dance of commodities as *bal masqué* of libidinal intensities'.[5] But Fukuyama's identification of democratic institutions and the market, scarcely an original one even in itself, returns us to social psychology and may stand as a challenge to contemporary or postmodern, late-capitalist Marxism to work up a properly materialist analysis of commodity consumption as well as of the group rivalries of the struggle for recognition – consumerism and ethnic civil wars – which together characterize our own particular era. Marxist theory needs to provide interpretations of all these things – of ideology and class struggle, of culture and the operation of the superstructures – on the vaster scale of contemporary globalization. The spirit of the analyses will have a continuity with the older ones, so triumphantly elaborated at the end of the modern period: but the terms will necessarily be new and fresh, given the novelties of the enlarged capitalist world market which they are designed to explain.

I believe, however, that the historical significance of Fukuyama's essay is not really to be found in Hegel or Kojève, even though I also think we have something to learn from them:

namely, a relationship to our own present which I will call 'epochality' and by way of which we defend the historical meaning and significance of the present moment and the present age against all claims of the past and the future. And this is all the more significant a lesson given the splendours of the preceding period of modernity against which we find it so difficult to defend ourselves, preferring to ward off the unpleasant feeling of being epigones by means of sheer historical amnesia and the stifling of the sense of history itself. To work out a relationship to the modern which neither amounts to a nostalgic call to return to it nor an oedipal denunciation of its repressive insufficiencies – this is a rich mission for our historicity, and success in it might help us to recover some sense of the future as well as of the possibilities of genuine change.

But the usefulness of Fukuyama does not lie in that particular direction, I think: rather it is to be found by juxtaposition with another influential American essay that appeared almost exactly one hundred years earlier, in 1893, and which equally spelled out the end of something. This is to suggest that, despite the appearances, Fukuyama's 'end of history' is not really about Time at all, but rather about Space; and that the anxieties it so powerfully invests and expresses, to which it gives such usable figuration, are not unconscious worries about the future or about Time: they express the feeling of the constriction of Space in the new world system; they bespeak the closing of another and more fundamental frontier in the new world market of globalization and of the transnational corporations. Frederick Jackson Turner's famous essay, 'The Frontier in American History',[6] is thus a better analogy; and the impossibility to imagine a future to which Fukuyama's conception of the 'end of history' gives voice is the result of new and more fundamental spatial limits, not as a result of the end of the Cold War or of the failure of socialism, as rather of the entrance of capitalism into a new third stage and its consequent penetration of as yet uncommodified parts of the world which make it difficult to imagine any further enlargement of the system. As far as socialism is concerned, a different Marx (that of the *Grundrisse* rather than that of *Capital*) always insisted that it would not be on the agenda until the world market had reached its limits and things and labour power became universally commodified. We are today far closer to that situation than in the time of either Marx or Lenin.

But the notion of the 'end of history' also expresses a blockage of the historical imagination, and we need to see more clearly how that is so, and how it ends up seeming to offer only this particular concept as a viable alternative. It seems to me particularly significant that the emergence of late capitalism (or in other words of a third stage of capitalism), along with the consequent collapse of the communist systems in the East, coincided with a generalized and planetary ecological disaster. It is not particularly the rise of the ecological movements that I have in mind here (despite the environmental excesses of Soviet forced modernization, the measures demanded by any consequent ecological movement could surely only be enforced by a strong socialist government); rather, it is the end of a Promethean conception of production that seems to me significant, in the way in which it makes it difficult for people today to continue to imagine development as a conquest of nature. At the moment when the market suffuses the world, in other words, and penetrates the hitherto uncommodified zones of former colonies, further development becomes unthinkable on account of a general (and quite justified) turn away from the older heroic forms of productivity and extraction. At the moment, in other words, when the limits of the globe are reached, notions of intensive development become impossible to contemplate; the end of expansion and old-fashioned imperialism is not accompanied by any viable alternative of internal development.

Meanwhile, the second feature of the new situation that blocks our imagination of the future, lies in its sheer systematicity: in the way in which, with the cybernetic and informational revolutions and their consequences for marketing and finance, the entire world is suddenly sewn up into a total system from which no one can secede. It is enough to think of Samir Amin's suggestive term 'delinking' – opting out of the world system – to measure the resistance of our imaginations to this possibility.

These two blocks, then – the taboo on Prometheanism and on the value of intensive development and industrialization; the impossibility of imagining a secession from the new world system and a political and social, as well as economic, delinking from it – these spatial dilemmas are what immobilize our imaginative picture of global space today, and conjure up as their sequel the vision that Fukuyama calls the 'end of history', and the final triumph of the market as such. Turner's pronouncement about the closing of the frontier still offered the possibility of an imperialist expansion beyond the borders of the now saturated continental United States; Fukuyama's prophecy expresses the impossibility of imagining an equivalent for that safety valve, nor even of an intensive turn back inside the system either, and this is why it was so powerful an ideologeme, an ideological expression and representation of our current dilemmas. How the various 'ends of art' are now to be co-ordinated philosophically and theoretically with this new 'closing' of the global frontier of capitalism is our more fundamental question, and the horizon of all literary and cultural study in our time. This, with which I now have to end, is where we ought to begin.

6

Transformations of the
Image in Postmodernity

I

Postmodernity has most often been characterized as the end of something (by myself as well as by so many other people): nor is it surprising, when we have to do with the emergence of a whole new mode of living the quotidian, that random indices of change should be seized upon and theorized, in the place of the as yet absent full form. I remember Immanuel Wallerstein, in discussion, inviting us to consider what a bunch of monkish dons might have imagined, in fourteenth-century Oxford, as the lineaments of a high capitalism of the then far future. It is true that we have to do here, not with some new mode of production as such, but rather with a dialectical mutation of a capitalist system already long in place (profit, commodity production, boom and bust, wage labour); and to that degree the tracing of internal narrative lines, the detection of this or that still faintly drawn subplot – such as the one here sketched in, having to do with the destiny of the visual or the image – may not be the most unsatisfactory way of proceeding.

Yet we must also register, not without a certain ruefulness, the return, in the postmodern, of any number of older things we thought we had seen the end of, for good. Let's spend our time on the bad new things, Brecht joyously recommended, and let the good old things bury themselves: yet the passion and the praxis of actuality evidently proves less usable when the very sense of what constitutes actuality becomes confused and aimless. At which point, a certain programmatic 'postmodernism' can help out by reassuring us that the Brechtian new was just a subset of that more general modernist telos of innovation, 'making it new' and the Novum, which we are supposed to have unmasked and indicted in our new avatar. The Brechtian new would then, today, turn out to be just another of those 'good old things' he suggested we do away with.

Still, what is presently returning would not seem to offer any of the intellectual excitement of the old modern novelty or the new postmodern kind either. The market, to begin with, whose rediscovery can surely not be much more stimulating than the reinvention of the wheel. (I've argued elsewhere[1] that what people imagine to be their enthusiasm for this good old thing is most often a mask and cover for the untheorized excitations of a genuinely new cybernetic technology.) But in the conceptual revival of the market and its dynamics, in reality we confront a more general resurrection of philosophy itself, in all its most outmoded academic and disciplinary forms. Even Richard Rorty seems to have forgotten that it was he himself who wrote the death certificate of this 'field' with his comprehensive demonstration of the way in which 'philosophy' constructed a spurious and retroactive history and tradition for itself out of its henceforth timeless themes and problems.[2]

So it is that 'theory''s dissolution of the old philosophical disciplines now seems to have been but a passing moment. Now philosophy and its branches are back in force: with ethics, first of all, as though Nietzsche, Marx and Freud had never existed: Nietzsche, with his once shattering discovery of the aggressivity that seethed through all the old ethical injunctions; Freud, with his disarticulation of the conscious subject and its rationalizations, and the glimpse of the forces that informed and inhabited it without its knowledge; Marx, finally, by flinging all the old individual ethical categories up on to a new dialectical and collective level, in such a way that what used to look like the ethical must now be grasped as the ideological. For ethics is irredeemably locked into categories of the individual, when not in fact of individualism as such: the situations in which it seems to hold sway are necessarily those of homogeneous relations within a single social class. But only those whose thinking has been irreparably damaged by empiricism can imagine that to pronounce the end of ethics (beyond good and evil!) is tantamount to recommending wholesale violence and the Dostoyevskian 'anything goes', rather than a sober historical judgment on the inadequacy of certain mental categories.

The revival of ethics also knows its more modish poststructuralist variant, the return to the 'subject'. There is to be sure no little embarrassment in the sounding of the new theme, whose novelty stems largely from its correction of the earlier symmetrical doxa of the 'death of the subject', with the resultant implication that the immense intellectual achievements of 'poststructuralism' generally (to use that irritating shorthand designation) as well as of theory may now be admitted to have been rolled back (along with Marxism or the sixties). But the notions of 'responsibility' that have accompanied this revival of the subject belong back in ethics where they came from; while the other meaning of the death of the subject – namely the end of individualism and of the entrepreneurial capitalism that gave rise to it – might better have spurred us on into new explorations of collective and institutional subjectivity: for Marx was right, after all, whatever they say, and no human society has ever been so collective in its structures than this one, where the Althusserian state and ideological state apparatuses reign supreme, like high rises in any contemporary city, and the apparent renewal of interest in 'subjectivity' betrays its more secret motives by an utter disinterest in the psychoanalytic developments (mostly Lacanian) that ought to have centrally attracted its attention and aroused its curiosity. But those things still lie behind the iron curtain of Theory; and do not seem particularly accessible to philosophical and disciplinary classification of the older sort.

Nietzsche has of course been subjected to innumerable rewritings in the last years; Freud himself has been the target of unaccountably passionate denunciations; but it is evidently the discrediting of Marx – his life's work supposedly 'disproven' by the deterioration of any number of state socialisms that appealed to his authority – which has seem to go hand in hand with the elaborations of this or that conception of postmodernism or postmodernity (although not in my own work, I hope it is unnecessary to add). It is therefore into the vacuum left by the new taboos on Marx that the most significant and symptomatic revival of a philosophical discipline has been able to insinuate itself; I mean the return of political philosophy itself. 'Political science' was never much more than an empirical and operational field during the long night of the modern (or Marxian) period, its theoretical heights all borrowed from sociology, its practical endeavours all in one way or another infeodated to statistics, its historical great texts gathering dust in the upheavals of a revolutionary and an ideological age for which they seemed to have little relevance. Now these last re-emerge into the light of academic day, and seem once again to speak to the age of big business with a wisdom usefully committed to moderation. As though Locke or Rousseau, Hobbes or Carl Schmitt all had as their central ambition to make a contribution to the development of something called political science! Or even to that as yet non-existent thing rebaptized political philosophy! Today professionally scanned for useful material on the current four c's of the ideological reequipment of late capitalism – contracts, constitutions, citizenship and civil society – the classic texts, like so many well-worn vagrants newly bathed, shaven and dressed up in respectable new clothes, find themselves reinstated on the syllabus, no doubt with suitable bewilderment. For us they were rich and contradictory texts, with unequalled lessons on the problems and antinomies of representation; now they are authorities, whose prestige derives from a fundamental category mistake. Indeed, some of the most creative innovations in the anti-communist arsenal – I think, for example, of Wittfogel's *Oriental Despotism* – drew their force from an assimilation of the forms of state socialism to precapitalist – essentially feudal – structures: all these seemingly modern 'totalitarianisms' were thus argued to be little more than ancient 'despotic' tyrannies of a whole range of archaic types. But such poetic characterizations make for conceptual and historical confusion when it comes to analysing what has pleasantly come to be known as the 'transition to capitalism': and it is precisely under cover of such confusion that the appeal to the classics of political theory can be made plausible.

For those classics all addressed a problem and a situation which is no longer our own, namely the emergence of bourgeois society and institutions from an overwhelmingly feudal universe. The conception of 'civil society' for example, does not designate some timeless value, which the Nongovernmental Organisations (NGOs) of our own world system somehow reincarnate like the periodic visitations of the hidden god in a benighted humanity: rather, 'civil society' amounts to an attempt to theorize the modes of secularization available within the structures of European feudal society, that is, within the European *ancien régime*. It has no relevance for modern societies, and indeed the great political theorists are themselves to be historically resituated as thinkers of the bourgeois revolution as such. But the bourgeois revolution failed; what happened instead of it was industrial capitalism: which is no doubt to say, as Marx did, that these thinkers attempted to invent political solutions for what were essentially economic problems. And this is also the sense in which one may say, with Habermas, if one likes, that the bourgeois revolution was an 'unfinished project' (or perhaps one should rather say, as Gandhi did on a related occasion, and about the positive and progressive face to be put on Western civilization, that 'it would be a good idea'). Unfortunately, any overview of the contemporary world which takes stock of its possibilities within a global framework is likely to conclude that the bourgeois project will remain forever unfinished, and that we need another one.

But this is also the moment to observe a peculiar intellectual development: namely that the current proliferation of work of all kinds on postmodernism and postmodernity has inspired a return or revival in its own right and specific to it: the renewal of discussions of modernity as such. It might plausibly be thought, or argued indeed, that it is only after this is over and done with that it can adequately be assessed and understood; but this is not at all the position of these postmodern defenders of modernity, who see it in our own future as something still to be achieved and worthy of being achieved, at the very moment in which so many other intellectuals are celebrating its timely passing. The confusion between modernism and modernity is often at stake here, and I will come back to modernism itself in a moment. Otherwise, most of the newer works on that old thing called modernity raise the banner of the various philosophical themes I have enumerated above: the subject, ethics, constitutions, individual responsibility and, to be sure, last but not least, philosophy itself. The difference lies in the historical period being revived: if political philosophy aimed at resurrecting the thinkers of the first bourgeois revolutions, in the seventeenth and eighteenth centuries, these renewed theories of 'modernity' wish to resurrect the conceptual baggage of capitalism's second moment, the age of monopoly and industrialization, substituting Max Weber for Locke or Kant. But this is intellectual progress in appearance only. The language of modernization brings an enrichment to the older conceptualizations of bourgeois society and capitalism (that is to say, its complex substitutions bring new contradictions usefully to the surface); but it is also the language of an ideology, or of several of them; and it abuses the new problems any notion of postmodernity necessarily raises by using this last as the pretext of returning to modernity itself, in order this time 'to get it right'.

Yet, paradoxically, the new return to an older problematic of the modern and of modernity is not really to be grasped as an attack on that of postmodernity: it is itself postmodern, and this is the deeper significance of all the multiple returns and revivals we have been speaking of here. The political determinants of such returns, and of the return of academic philosophy itself, should already have been apparent, in the intellectual aimlessness of a late capitalism universally triumphant but without legitimation, and whose older apologias were all thoroughly discredited and undermined in the now heroic era of ideological struggle. If all that is now past, why not go back to the 'values' and certainties once in place? Why not indeed? Nor would one particularly wish to resurrect another successful formula, however tempting, and characterize the recurrence of once tragic intellectual struggles as farce, since so much of it is too tiresome to offer the joyous liberation of folly (while the rest of it is dangerous enough to promise real enough tragedies to come).

But the theory of postmodernism has a concept particularly apt for resolving this dilemma and it is that of pastiche. The newer work, which seems to rebuke the frivolities of the postmodern by returning to the truly serious older texts of a more wholesome past, is itself postmodern in the sense in which it offers the merest pastiche of those older texts: postmodern pastiches of an older ethics and an older philosophy, pastiches of the older 'political theories', pastiches of the theories of modernity – the blank and non-parodic reprise of older discourse and older conceptuality, the performing of the older philosophical moves as though they still had a content, the ritual resolution of 'problems' that have themselves long since become simulacra, the somnambulistic speech of a subject long since historically extinct. In all this, even repetition itself, in earlier times a vital instinct, is an irrelevant concept, since it is repetition which is here merely represented (rather than being repeated 'for the first time'). Indeed, in this spirit of a somewhat newer development than those ancient ones, for which 'we are spoken by language' and it is some nonpersonal instance which uses us as its vehicle for expression, it might be fairer to say that what was mistaken for language turned out to be the institutions: it is the institutions which are now speaking through us in the form of pastiche, and rehearsing the dead letter of older thoughts in a simulation of reaction.

At any rate, we will shortly be able to verify this evaluation of the 'return' of modernity theory in a specific instance, indeed in that of an academic philosophical subdiscipline not yet mentioned above, namely aesthetics. For the current postmodern age seems also to be experiencing a general return to the aesthetic as such, at the very moment, paradoxically, when the trans-aesthetic claims of modern art seem completely discredited and a bewildering variety of styles and mixtures of all kinds flows through consumer society under its new postmodern dispensation. The older aesthetic traditions were rarely prescient enough to theorize these new works, many of them incorporating new communications and cybernetic technology (film was already developed enough to produce several proposals for a specifically filmic aesthetics, but video, far more generally used and influential, came too late for that kind of theoretical codification). Meanwhile, the discrediting of the older modernist idea of 'progress' – the telos leading to new technical discoveries and new formal innovations – spells the end of evolutionary time in the arts and augurs a new kind of spatial proliferation of artistic modes which can no longer be valorized in the older modernist ways. Finally, the general breakdown of the divisions between the older disciplines and specializations – in this case, the collapse of the once fiercely defended border between high art and mass culture (let alone daily life) – leaves traditional analyses of the 'specificity' of the aesthetic, of the nature or artistic experience as such, of the autonomy of the work as a space somehow beyond the practical and the scientific realms, in much uncertainty, as though somehow the very nature of reception and consumption (perhaps even the production) of art in our time had undergone some fundamental mutation, leaving the older paradigms irrelevant or at least outmoded. Indeed, we shall see shortly that in a culture so overwhelmingly dominated by the visual and the image as ours has become, the very notion of aesthetic experience is either too little or too much: for in that sense, aesthetic experience is now everywhere and saturates social and daily life in general; but it is this very expansion of culture (in the larger or perhaps the nobler sense) which has rendered the very notion of an individual art work problematic and the premise of aesthetic judgment something of a misnomer. The crisis in reading is, of course, the locus of these new uncertainties and the arguments they generate. The return to the aesthetic may well find its rationale in the expansion of culture, and particularly of image culture, and its greater diffusion throughout the social: still, plausible context does not exempt a strategic reaction from criticism, and we will make a few objections to this particular ideological move later on. Yet a general rhetoric about the need and value of art today and of aesthetic experience in general is far from justifying a wholesale revival of aesthetics as a philosophical discipline, about which it would be important to argue, not only that it is singularly ill equipped to deal with the aesthetic dimension of postmodernity, but that it was already significantly problematized and undermined during the preceding period of modernism.

It is an argument that could be reduced and concentrated in the following proposition: what distinguishes modernism in general is not the experimentation with inherited forms or the invention of new ones – or at least it is not that 'outward and visible sign' which captures modernism's essence. Modernism constitutes, above all, the feeling that the aesthetic can only fully be realized and embodied where it is something more than the merely aesthetic. But if you are willing to entertain this idea of an art that in its very inner movement seeks to transcend itself as art (as Adorno thought, and without it being particularly important to determine the direction of that self-transcendence, whether religious or political), then it becomes at least minimally clear that a philosophical aesthetics will always necessarily miss the fundamentals of the modernist work or the modernist mode of production. For it will be able to describe everything about the work of art and its functions and effects, save what transcends all those things and constitutes the work as modernist in the first place. (If the aesthetics in question then seeks itself to assign an extra- or trans-aesthetic direction to the modernist work, then we are in the sheerest ideology or metaphysics; we would not have needed modernism in the first place, if philosophy had been able to solve those riddles and assign those transcendental values in a secular and commercial modern society.)

I want therefore to assert, not that there have not been extraordinary texts produced within the framework of a philosophical discipline called aesthetics, but rather that what gives those texts their power – from Kant's Third *Critique* all the way to Adorno's *Aesthetic Theory* – is the way in which they blow up the field in which they sought to work, in which they undermine the very framework which justified their project. In Kant, this can be seen in the unaccountable eruption of a theory of the sublime at the end of a standard treatise on beauty, which already had achieved and codified everything that philosophical aesthetics necessarily takes as its programme. But suddenly this unexpected supplement, which Kant musters all his ingenuity to reintegrate into his conception of a philosophical 'critique', yet which somehow cannot be fully mastered, opens up the space for more historical forces that, as yet unrealized, but now liberated for the first time, make a mockery of such systems. I have suggested elsewhere[3] (I am not the only one to do so) that what Kant calls the sublime will be the very space of modernism in the largest sense, which finds its first groping embodiments in

Romanticism and then its fuller deployment in the later nine-teenth century and its sequels. As for Adorno, his remarkable (and unfinished, posthumous) speculations take their force from the way in which his keen sense of the historicity of art forms problematizes the attempt to codify and systematize the 'features' of the aesthetic at every point. In this sense, Adorno's aesthetics can be seen as a quintessentially 'modernist' text in its own right, with everything paradoxical and energetic about the contradiction between the aesthetic and the historical 'end' of aesthetics that it does not cease to exasperate. Hegel mean-while was supremely able to have it both ways, constructing an aesthetics whose very conception of possibility was a frame in which aesthetics as such was seen to have a historical end (the famous 'end of art' with which his *Aesthetik* necessarily con-cludes, thereby abolishing itself).

In that case, this new form of philosophical aesthetics, beyond the philosophical system as such – this self-cancelling and undermining aesthetics, which now at a second power struggles with itself and the limits of its own concepts – can be expected to be coterminous with the modern movement itself. It will therefore not be surprising that with the end of that movement and the end of modernism itself (if not of the modern), the older 'unfinished' project of a properly philosophical aesthetics and its subdiscipline should re-emerge. But we have not yet grasped the reasons for this re-emergence, or its significance and it is this inquiry that I want to pursue in the following essay, in some beginning and speculative fashion, yet not without the hope that this historical investigation of the role of aesthetics in the postmodern, and what it finds to tell us about the 'return' of aesthetics today, or rather the emergence of the various pas-tiches of a traditional philosophical aesthetics in recent years, will shed some light on all those other 'returns' enumerated above – political philosophy, religion, ethics and even the old theories of modernity itself in full 'postmodernism'! But I want to come at all this from an angle and not head-on, so the discussion of contemporary aesthetic texts will be preceded by speculation about the transformations of the visual dimension of contemporary culture, and only after that the return of older kinds of aesthetic effects and pleasures inventoried in the area of contemporary film-making, itself a kind of strange and transitional no-man's-land in which an older modernist aesthetic, akin to the modern novel, coexists and overlaps with a flood of newer and more 'postmodern' visual stimuli.

II

The history of vision and the visible in our time has been told in a number of versions, the most recent being Martin Jay's encyclopaedic *Downcast Eyes*,[4] and Jonathan Crary's *Techniques of the Observer*,[5] behind which stand rich developments in contemporary film theory. I want to tell this story in a different way, a project which demands two initial comments. The first is that it would be misguided to think that any single historical narrative of this kind is true or correct: the various alternative stories are ways of staging or representing material which is not intrinsically representable in its own right. The second has to do with the use of new philosophical or theoretical concepts as evidence for the emergence of new kinds of perception: the premise here is that what has not yet been articulated in social language does not yet exist in some fuller historical sense; or if you prefer, that the emergence of new formulations announces the active presence of a new experience.

It is a story I mean to tell in three stages: in the beginning was the Look, which appears as a philosophical theme in its own right, dramatically and as though for the first time, in the *Being and Nothingness* (1944) of Jean-Paul Sartre. Indeed, the Look can be taken as virtually his major philosophical innovation, indebted only for its inner conceptual content to the Hegelian master–slave struggle that Alexandre Kojève had reinscribed on the philosophical agenda in the late 1930s, and owing nothing whatsoever to that Heideggerian existentialism of which Sartre has so often been said to be derivative. Indeed, at a time when the matter of Heidegger's Nazism has again come up for much debate, it is perplexing to note that a search for fascist motifs and structures in his philosophy has neglected to scrutinize his feeble theory of the Other (called the *Mitsein*, the being-with-others), in which everything conflictual in my relations with other people is either smothered under the indistinction of what is elsewhere blandly called 'intersubjectivity' or else sublimated into the possibility of some heightened fascist or nationalist sense of community. The extraordinary conceptual innovation of the Sartrean Look is to be grasped against this weakness in the Heideggerian system, and its productivity measured against the *Critique of Dialectical Reason* which will later on develop out of it (but which we will not consider here[6]).

The Look is what posits my immediate relationship to other people; but it does so by way of an unexpected reversal in which the experience of being looked at becomes primary and my own look a secondary reaction. The ancient philosophical false problem of the existence of other people ('que vois-je de cette fenêtre,' asks Descartes famously in the *Discourse on Method*, 'sinon des chapeaux et des manteaux, qui peuvent couvrir des spectres ou des hommes feints qui ne se remuent que par ressorts?') is thus at one stroke 'solved' and displaced or abolished by the shame and pride with which the Other's look at me confirms his own existence as a trauma that transcends my own. Yet the Look is at the same time reversible; by returning it, I can attempt to place the Other in a similar position. It thereby becomes the very medium through which the Hegelian struggle for recognition is concretely waged; while the master–slave positions now open my relations with other people up into a perpetual alternation which only the dialectical shift to the collective level can transform. In Sartre, then, the great theme of the Look is bound up with the problematic of 'thingification', or reification in its literal sense, as the becoming object, the making over of the visible – and most dramatically of the visible subject – into the object of the gaze.

Any number of political and aesthetic currents now flow from this first formulation: a new politics of decolonization and race, for example, in Frantz Fanon; a new feminism, in Simone de Beauvoir; and, in a kind of reactive reversal, a new aesthetics of the body and its visible or painterly flesh, in Merleau-Ponty. To resume this first moment overhastily, it would seem appropriate to describe it in terms of that protopolitical phenomenon called domination, insofar as the fact of objectification is grasped as that to which the Other (or myself) must necessarily submit. To make other people over into things by way of the Look thus becomes the primal source of a domination and a subjection which can only be overcome by looking back or 'returning the gaze': in Fanon's terms, by the latter's therapeutic violence. Perhaps then, in honour of Fanon, and also of de Beauvoir, we may call this first moment that of the colonial or colonizing gaze, of visibility as colonization. On this conception, the Look is essentially asymmetrical: it cannot offer the Third World the occasion of productive appropriation, but must rather be radically reversed, as when Alejo Carpentier turns European surrealism inside out and decrees its Third World equivalent ('lo real maravilloso') to be the primary phenomenon of which surrealism becomes little more than a wish-fulfilment or a form of cultural envy.[7] Magic realism thus comes first; surrealism is rewritten as a weak European attempt to fashion its own version in a social order in which the reality in question must remain imaginary. This is then the moment in which the Third World, seen as Caliban by the First, *assumes* and *chooses* that identity for itself (to use characteristically Sartrean verbs). Yet this aggressive affirmation of visibility necessarily remains reactive: it cannot overcome the contradiction betrayed by the fact that the identity thereby chosen in Sartrean 'shame and pride' is still that conferred on Caliban by Prospero and by the First World colonizer, by European culture itself. The violence of the riposte, therefore, does nothing to alter the terms of the problem and the situation from which it springs. Europe remains the place of the universal, while Caliban's art affirms a host of merely local specificities.

Michel Foucault's appropriation of the themes of Otherness and reification, beginning with his *Madness and Civilization* and developing idiosyncratically throughout his career, can now be seen as a second moment in our process: the moment of its bureaucratization. Foucault's attempt to translate epistemological analysis into a politics of domination, and to conjoin knowledge and power so intimately as to make them henceforth inseparable, now transforms the Look into an instrument of measurement. The visible thereby becomes the bureaucratic gaze, which everywhere seeks out the measurability of the henceforth reified Other and its henceforth reified world.

This move involves a basic redistribution of emphases, if not a complete inversion, of the earlier Sartrean model of the Look: since here it is the fact of being visible for a henceforth absent look, of the sheer vulnerability to the Look and its measurements, which is generalized, to the point at which the individual act of looking itself is no longer required. Being looked at becomes a state of universal subjection that can be separated out from the event of any specific individual gaze.

> Traditionally, power is what can be seen, what displays and manifests itself, and it paradoxically finds the very principle of its power in the movement by which this last is deployed ... In [this new disciplinary world] it is power's subjects that are required to be seen. Their illumination secures the hold of the power exercised upon them. It is the fact of being seen uninterruptedly, of always being able to be seen, which maintains the disciplinary individual in his subjection. Examination, observation, is then the technique whereby power, instead of emitting the sign of its force, instead of imposing its own mark on its subjects, seizes them in an objectifying mechanism ... The [medical] examination stands as the ceremony of this objectivisation.[8]

The ambiguity of Foucault's multiple positions, but also the consequences of his work generally, is at one with the ambiguity of a rhetoric of the exclusively political, or in other words of domination alone, and which excludes economic structures. A rhetoric of power which omits or shuts out any complementary notion of liberation or utopia feeds back into a Hobbesian notion of the evils of human nature whether it wants to or not. It is certain that Foucault's positions, however incoherent, struck a responsive note in the anti-authoritarian politics which emerged from the 1960s, and which modulated without great difficulty into a feminist politics critical of patriarchal authority and hierarchy on the one hand, or an anarchist politics hostile to institutions and the state generally. Today, with a critical revaluation of notions of subversion, transgression and negativity or critique underway everywhere (a re-examination in which Foucault's own paradoxical denunciation of the notion of repression, in the *History of Sexuality*, volume I, played no small role), Foucault's work may seem more classbound and less politically productive than it once was.

I make these overhasty judgments on Foucault's positions because it seems to me they offer a clarification of the new role of the Look and of visibility in his work, while reinforcing my assertion that the vision in Foucault is more generally bureaucratic, and thus paradoxically less political than it was in the Sartrean moment, which did dramatically posit a moment of liberation, however mythical. The identification of knowledge with power, of the epistemological with the politics of domination, tends to dissolve the political itself as a separate instance or possibility of praxis, and by making all forms of knowledge and measurement over into forms of discipline, control and domination, in effect evacuates the more narrowly political altogether.

Another way of saying so is that the new regime fatally and tendentially excludes agency as such from the process of visual domination, which becomes an impersonal (and an irreversible) one. In the Sartre–Fanon moment, agency is no doubt at first passive: I register the colonial situation by way of the sheer oppression of being seen. Individual colonists or oppressors need no longer be present, no doubt; but my very visible being testifies to their existence, in a new kind of 'ontological proof'. It is a position very consistent with the situation of colonization as such, where, unlike what so often obtains in domestic or class politics, it is scarcely necessary to argue for the existence of the apparatus of colonial domination or that of the colonizers themselves, and when the 'war of national liberation' imposes itself as a self-evident need and an unavoidable 'solution'. A different, radically modified reign of visibility can thereby be imagined – the utopia for my own collectivity, as that is appropriated by my act of resistance: it can still give rise to a utopian space, as opposed to the Foucauldian heterotopia, whose unrelated and radically distinct corners and folds rise from a generalized yet inaccessible spatiality (reflected in Foucault's own characteristically spatial style). So it is that, from the very outset, Aimé Césaire's 'return' to a ruined and colonized 'native land' generates a space beyond it:

Beat it, I said to him, you cop, you lousy pig, beat it, I detest the flunkies of order and the cockchafers of hope. Beat it, evil grigri, you bedbug of a petty monk. Then I turned toward paradises lost for him and his kin, calmer than the face of a woman telling lies, and there, rocked by the flux of a never exhausted thought I nourished the wind, I unlaced the monsters and heard rise, from the other side of disaster, a river of turtledoves and savannah clover which I carry forever in my depths height-deep as the twentieth floor of the most arrogant houses and as a guard against the putrefying force of crepuscular surroundings, surveyed night and day by a cursed venereal sun.[9]

What is at stake in such visions is to be sure a utopia of separatism, a cultural nationalist space swept free of the colonial gaze, in a secessionist (and as we would say today, ethnic) vision easier to sustain and defend during the imperialist period than after decolonization and the accompanying globalization.

Yet it is precisely just such a possibility of Otherness, of a transfiguration of the visible space of domination, which is lost in Foucault, or in modernization theory generally, where archaic social relations are thrown irrevocably into a distant and irretrievable past by the now universal forces of rationalization and calculation. For this new Foucauldian process, a very different kind of literary language seems the appropriate emblem, one locked into the visible and measurable universe without alternative.

This is the paranoiac enumeration of Alain Robbe-Grillet's 'new novel', or 'roman du regard', whose visual data betray only an unformulable underside which marks them as symptoms that must forever remain indeterminable. Detail here no longer awakens the interpretative lust of Dali's 'paranoiac-critical' method, where the very grain of gold sand, the individual beads of perspiration on the limp watches, promise an impending revelation. In Robbe-Grillet, for all the catastrophic temporality of the accumulated sentences, it is something closer to obsessional neurosis that declares itself, mindless compulsions not unrelated to workaholic efficiency, in which an absent subject desperately attempts to distract itself by way of sheer rote measurement and enumeration, as pre-eminently in his one tropical or 'colonial' novel, *La Jalousie*:

In front of him, on the other bank, stretches a trapezoidal plot, curvilinear on the water's edge, all of whose banana trees have been harvested at a relatively recent date. It is easy to count its stock, where trees chopped for the cuttings have left a short stump terminated by a disk-shaped scar, white or yellowish depending on its freshness. A line-by-line count yields the following, from left to right: twenty-three, twenty-two, twenty-one, twenty, twenty, etc.[10]

Such pages can seem a virtual parody of the Foucauldian theory to the degree to which they seem to express not the supreme omnipresence of the power or the measuring eye, but rather its impotent delirium, its victimization by its own exorbitant power. Yet they convey something of the nightmarish feeling Foucault's own evocations of absolute visibility have often been seen to have for his readers; and they also underscore the peculiar dissociation – in Foucault as well as in Robbe-Grillet – of the sensory and the formerly conceptual, still felt to be active somewhere, impersonally, behind the now denuded sense perception itself.

It is a dissociation also associated, but in a very different way from either of these writers, with what came to be called conceptual art: where a tangible object seemed to offer no toehold for a thinking that continued to turn around it, in endless circles of paradox and categorical self-cancellation. There is no metaphysical or political kinship between conceptual art and the visual theories and practices I have been discussing here: yet its mention usefully dramatizes a moment in the becoming universal of visibility in which the abstract mind seems unable to find its niche or function in this unexpected primacy of a sense once subordinate to it. Conceptual art also foregrounds the significance of the enigmatic and no-longer-mediatory object itself, as a place of transit (like Descartes' pineal gland) between an impersonal visibility and the equally impersonal and disembodied forces of a universal rationalization and bureaucratization.

The true breakthrough in this second moment, which will prepare and enable a very different third stage, can take place when the enigmatic object itself is replaced by a technological one, and in particular by mediatic technology. Now the silent object itself can once again speak, indeed visibility will find itself transformed into a whole new speech, with momentous consequences for the previous systems. It is a potential transformation whose dimensions can be read in the very ambiguities of the word 'image', which had not yet seemed appropriate for the acts of vision celebrated either in Sartre or in Foucault, but which now suddenly (as in Guy Debord's great book, *The Society of the Spectacle*, where it is announced that 'the image is the final form of commodity reification') imposes itself everywhere, at the same time that it insistently begins to designate a technological origin. This is then the paradoxical outcome of the Foucauldian moment of the bureaucratic eye, which, in the very process of revealing the intimate connection between seeing and measurement or knowledge, suddenly turns out to posit the media as such (and in retrospect the now only too familiar Foucauldian emblem of the panopticon reveals itself as a first form of the media as well). For in our time, it is technology and the media which are the true bearers of the epistemological function: whence a mutation in cultural production in which traditional forms give way to mixed-media experiments, and photography, film and television all begin to seep into the visual work of art (and the other arts as well) and to colonize it, generating high-tech hybrids of all kinds, from installations to computer art.

But at this point, the Foucauldian moment begins to give way to a third stage, which it is appropriate to identify with postmodernity as such. Everything that was paranoid about Foucault's total system or Robbe-Grillet's compulsive enumerations vanishes away, to make room for a euphoria of high technology proper, a celebratory affirmation of some post-McLuhanite vision of culture transmogrified by computers and cyberspace. Now suddenly a hitherto baleful universal visibility that seemed to brook no utopian alternative is welcomed and revelled in for its own sake: this is the true moment of image society, in which human subjects henceforth exposed (according to Paul Willis) to bombardments of up to a thousand images a day (at the same time that their formerly private lives are thoroughly viewed and scrutinized, itemized, measured and enumerated, in data banks) begin to live a very different relationship to space and time, to existential experience as well as cultural consumption.

It seems to me that in this new situation the reflexivity implied by the mixed-media or technological works of art is of very brief duration indeed. For, as I've argued elsewhere,[11] in this new stage the very sphere of culture itself has expanded, becoming coterminous with market society in such a way that the cultural is no longer limited to its earlier, traditional or experimental forms, but is consumed throughout daily life itself, in shopping, in professional activities, in the various often televisual forms of leisure, in production for the market and in the consumption of those market products, indeed in the most secret folds and corners of the quotidian. Social space is now completely saturated with the culture of the image; the utopian space of the Sartrean reversal, the Foucauldian heterotopias of the unclassed and unclassifiable, all have been triumphantly penetrated and colonized, the authentic and the unsaid, *in-vu*, *non-dit*, inexpressible, alike, fully translated into the visible and the culturally familiar.

The closed space of the aesthetic is thereby also opened up to its henceforth fully culturalized context: whence the critical attacks of the postmodernists on antiquated notions of the 'autonomy of the work of art' and the 'autonomy of the aesthetic' that persisted through the modernist period, or better still, that served as its philosophical cornerstone. Indeed, in a strict philosophical sense, this end of the modern must also spell the end of the aesthetic itself, or of aesthetics in general: for where the latter suffuses everything, where the sphere of culture expands to the point where everything becomes in one way or another acculturated, the traditional distinctiveness or 'specificity' of the aesthetic (and even of culture as such) is necessarily blurred or lost altogether.

The return of the aesthetic, however, has (as has earlier been observed) seemed to go hand in hand with the equally widely trumpeted end of the political in the postmodern era. This paradox demands a dialectical explanation, which has to do with the end of artistic autonomy, of the work of art and of its frame. For once one no longer scrutinizes individual works as such, for their form and inner organization, the tour of the museum calls forth aleatory perceptions, in which glints of colour are collected from this or that surface in passing, fragments of form consumed in Benjaminian distraction, and as though laterally, out of the corner of the eye, textures acknowledged, densities navigated in an unmappable way with space assembling and disassembling itself oneirically around you. Under these conditions aesthetic attention finds itself transferred to the life of perception as such, abandoning the former object that organized it and returning into subjectivity, where it seems to offer a random and yet wide-ranging sampling of sensations, affectabilities and irritations of sense data and stimulations of all sorts and kinds. This is not a recovery of the body in any active and independent way, but rather its transformation into a passive and mobile field of 'enregistrement' in which tangible portions of the world are taken up and dropped again in the permanent inconsistency of a mesmerizing sensorium.

It is this new life of postmodern sensation which has been appealed to as evidence for a renewal of the aesthetic, a conceptual fiction or allusion then transferred back to accounts of newer works that most fittingly serve as pretexts for its shimmering play and exercise. Here the former aesthetic is celebrated in terms of something like an intensification, a heightening upwards or downwards, of perceptual experience: among which can be ranged interesting speculations on the 'sublime' (which has known a new 'postmodern' revival of its own, in a radically modified role than the one it played in modernism), on the simulacrum and the 'uncanny' – now taken less as specifically aesthetic modalities than as local 'intensités', accidents in the continuum of postcontemporary life, breaks and gaps in the perceptual system of late capitalism. Nor is it a question of 'repudiating' this new system of experience, let alone of calling essentially moral condemnation down on it in the name of some value from the past. *Hic Rhodus, hic salta!* as Marx liked to say; this is our world and our raw material, the only kind with which we can work. Only it would be better to look at it without illusions, and get some clarity and precision about what confronts us. Current revivals of the aesthetic have not wanted to do that, but rather to stage an elaborate apology of the tradition and to elaborate complex arguments about its continuing relevance. We will look at some of those now.

III

The works I have in mind are mostly European, and of very high intellectual quality, which puts to shame reactionary American operations like Hilton Kramer's *New Criterion*. That the 'return to the aesthetic' they propose also has political implications in a rather different European context is unquestionable, for, as with the Kramer journal, they all breathe relief at the end of the sixties, and beyond that, of the Cold War itself, with its obligatory ideological struggles. But they come out of traditions in which reflection on the aesthetic has been philosophically central, and not, as in the anti-intellectualism of American culture, a marginal hobby at best. Thus, Karl-Heinz Bohrer seeks to recover an authentic Nietzschean perception in his extraordinary book, *Plötzlichkeit*,[12] which argues for an existence of aesthetic experience outside historical time, and for the irrelevance of historical thinking in this area, thus turning Adorno against himself, and expertly retrieving the non-historical parts of Heidegger (and even more notoriously in another book, of Ernst Jünger).

Thus, these works tend to associate the recovery of the aesthetic with the recovery of great modernism itself; and their arguments thus attempt to validate Jean-François Lyotard's impertinent proposition that 'postmodernism' does not follow modernism but *precedes* it and prepares its re-emergence and some new and historically unexpected flowering of what was once the New of high modern art. I want to show, however, that it is a rather different 'return' that is at stake here, however deceptive the appearances.

In France, the vital source of the modern and its aesthetic and philosophical theorization does not lie in philosophical texts, but rather in Baudelaire, coiner of the very word 'modernity', whose poetic practice as well as his theory lends an imperishable resonance and gravity to the word modern (in all the European languages). It is thus as a return to Baudelaire that Antoine

Compagnon stages his exemplary theoretical move, in a splendid theoretical performance, in which the conventional narratives of modernist literary history are reversed. *The Five Paradoxes of Modernity*[13] is laid out in bravura Hegelian form, in which the five features of the title become five distinct moments in the historical progression from the first intuition of the modern in Baudelaire all the way to the confused pluralism of the postmodern, in which, however, Compagnon reserves the right to discern the glimmering of a rebirth of some more authentic return to Baudelaire and to the spirit of the original 'modernism'.

His five themes or moments are the following: 'the superstition of the new, the religion of the future, the theoretical (or theoreticist) obsession, the appeal to mass culture, and the passion of subversion [by which the critical and negative features of contemporary 'theory' are meant]'.[14] One is tempted to read this progression – clearly a gradual degradation – as something like an anti-modernist argument: but this is to reckon without a dialectic of authenticity and perversion, in which, for example, the authentic modernities of Baudelaire and Nietzsche are deformed and their lessons gradually lost. If the position is antimodernist, then, it must also be characterized as being equally antipostmodern, for this last is seen as a superficial, media and decorative production and a fundamentally frivolous moment in the history of art (and even of architecture). The dialectical twist here lies in the way in which the historic mission of the postmodern is said to consist in discrediting the more noxious aspects and developments of the modern itself (as that is conventionally understood). Here then, less prophetically than Lyotard, but more plausibly and ingeniously, Compagnon secures the hope that the postmodern moment may yet pave the way for the return of a more authentic and genuinely modernist aesthetic.

Another crucial dialectical mechanism in Compagnon's argument turns on the phenomenon of the avant-garde which, with Peter Bürger, he wishes radically to distinguish from 'normal-paradigmatic' art production: thus the great and isolated modern writers and artists (who follow the example of Baudelaire himself) are to be sharply differentiated from those avant-garde movements whose full form is almost universally identified with the surrealists. But where for Bürger the avant-gardes mark the moment in which art breaks through to a self-consciousness about its own activity and a critique of its sustaining institutions, for Compagnon the avant-garde simply spells a falling off from art itself and a deterioration into that politics of intellectuals which is substituted for it. This is a rather traditional aestheticist view (Adorno shared it, for example) as well as a self-fulfilling and unfalsifiable proposition, for it suffices to enumerate those orthodox surrealist poets and painters to whom Compagnon is prepared to deny all aesthetic merit, and then to subtract the great exceptions – Masson, for example, or Max Ernst – whose achievements are then explained by their having abandoned avant-garde politics for a return to genuine art as such.

At any rate, such distinctions now allow the critic to distinguish between the authenticity of a truly aesthetic production, from Baudelaire himself and Cézanne all the way to Beckett and Dubuffet, and that inauthentic appropriation of art for other purposes, which will be documented by Compagnon's five themes and stages.

The crucial operation in the first moment is the way in which Baudelaire's first institutions of a relationship of art to the present is degraded into a conception of the merely New. A most ambiguous passage from Baudelaire's 'Painter of Everyday Life' is adduced to secure this vital distinction, a passage in which the poet-theorist describes a truly modern art as one which would somehow combine the fleeting reality of the ephemeral historical instant with an equal commitment to the eternal and changeless realm of form: which would in other words (those of Baudelaire himself) 'draw the eternal out of the transitory', with the implication that it is the modern painter who finds the eternal in the transitory in the first place. 'Modernity', declares Baudelaire famously, 'is the transitory, the fleeting, the contingent, the one half of art, whose other half is the eternal and the immutable'. It is therefore a misunderstanding – but one with momentous consequences – to think that artistic modernity is here defined only by the transitory or the 'new' as such: it is rather to be grasped, following

Baudelaire, as the invention and conquest of a certain 'presence to the world'[15] and its artists 'do not seek the new but the present' as such. This is the point at which Compagnon's analysis intersects with Bohrer's (mentioned above), where temporal 'suddenness' (*Plötzlichkeit*) designates just such a presence to the world which cannot be interpreted as a merely historical innovation, even though it may express a kind of 'timeless' Heideggerian historicity. I believe that this kind of argument overlooks the question of the social and historical preconditions for the emergence of such a 'modern' presence to the world, which the other part of the argument presumed to be a novelty of Baudelaire's society, unavailable in that form to earlier historical moments of cultural and social organization. Even the possibility of getting out of history (if it exists) remains a historical one; and it is as though both Bohrer and Compagnon need to forget the historical limits of their discussions of the modern, in order not to open up their 'timeless' aesthetic to the sheerest classicism.

Yet once this initial disjunction between the present and the New is granted, the inevitable stages of a decline, the progressive decadence of an inauthentic modernism, follow logically enough. For the New, and the break it stages with tradition, now quickly unmasks itself as a commitment, not to the present but to the *future*. It thereby generates spurious narratives about the development of art in general, in which the discredited bourgeois value of progress is secretly or not so secretly installed in the aesthetic realm. There emerges thereby what Compagnon rightly calls the 'orthodox narrative of the modern tradition', exemplified in Clement Greenberg and rehearsed in the latter's relations with a post-war North American abstract expressionism (with no reference to the historical necessity of Greenberg's theoretical work, to forge an American teleological myth in order to break the hold of European and in particular of Parisian art institutions in the period of the Marshall Plan).[16] Compagnon's critique of Greenberg here rejoins much of contemporary anti-historicism, with its dissatisfaction with the potted meta-narratives of old and new history manuals and its assimilation of analyses in terms of innovation to the various older genetic and evolutionary accounts. But Compagnon's diagnosis adds the covert apologia for contemporary schools to this wholesale distrust of the historical in art history: 'The orthodox narrative is always written in function of the climax it steers for – this is its teleological aspect – and serves to legitimate a contemporary art that wants however to look as though it had broken with tradition – this is its apologetic one.'[17]

But now such narratives seem to demand a conceptual content and a thematization to expound them in slogans and lend them an ideological rationale: this is now the function of the avant-garde as such, where the mirage of the future finds support in the sheer polemic violence of their avant-garde mission, in spokespeople like Breton and his followers. There was, Compagnon asserts in what is perhaps his boldest 'paradox', no theory in Cézanne or Baudelaire: 'they did not consider themselves either revolutionaries or theoreticians'.[18] This is a swerve which allows Compagnon to associate his polemic for aesthetics with the current reaction against theory as such, in France as well as in the US. Here the word theory tacitly encompasses everything from radicalism to philosophical speculation, from Marxism to poststructuralism, from literary theory to 'Critical Theory', from sociology to philosophies of history: everything, in short, which today prevents the university work of the humanities from deteriorating into a sandbox operation devoted to harmless and decorative eternal values and formalisms (probably not what Baudelaire meant by 'the eternal and the immutable', as I will show later on).

Two features of Compagnon's diagnosis are plausible and need to be retained: the first is his assertion of a link between theoretical legitimation (by way of the manifesto, for example) and the reduction of artistic production to a 'method', or in other words to a few isolated features or procedures,[19] which could then serve as the theme for aesthetic propaganda and be identified as somehow truly revolutionary (whether in the artistic or the political sense, it scarcely matters). But this impoverishment of sheer procedure and technique would then go a long way towards accounting for the one-dimensionality imputed to avant-garde art.

Then, in terms of reception, one can evoke the way in which

this kind of art 'remains inseparable from the intellectual discourse which justified it theoretically':[20] here what is posited is not only that avant-garde art comes after the theoretical apologia for it, but also that it finds itself thereby transformed into a mere example of the theory. But I think that Compagnon also suggests here a new kind of reception in which the sensory, the formerly aesthetic, is somehow mingled with the ideational or the theoretical: it would be very interesting to develop a phenomenology of such mingled reactions (indeed, the conceptual art referred to above gives us one distinct variety); yet as with the initial defences of theory generally against empiricism, it is not plausible that there can be imagined to exist forms of reception which are purely sensory or even purely aesthetic. Meanwhile, we have learned to be suspicious of the very idea of the 'pure' or the 'purified' as a norm to be defended and reinforced in its own right.

The last two chapters are more schematic and also more ambiguous, for they quickly bring us down to modern times and at length to postmodernism itself. The first of these suggests that the new acknowledgement of mass culture (let us say, pop art) amounts simply to the coming to consciousness and awakening of a profoundly inauthentic art to its own deep complicity with the market system as such and to the commodity form: the logic rather resembles that of blaming the victim, particularly when one remembers the way in which Peter Bürger grasped such reflexivity as a positive moment in the coming to consciousness in modern art of its own conditions of production. Adorno thought, indeed, that the very specificity of modern art lay in its confrontation with the commodity form, albeit on the mode of resisting it and reappropriating its essential reification. But the interpretation allows Compagnon a discreet participation in another contemporary North-American cultural-political debate, namely the assault of the conservatives on the dangers of so-called Cultural Studies. What else can he mean by his ambiguous rhetorical question: 'Does not the illness of modern art, indeed its very curse, lie in the obligation it has always felt to pose aesthetic questions in cultural terms?'[21]

Theory then reappears in the final chapter, in which the final stage of the decadence of the modern is identified with the rhetoric of subversion and critique, this last now also seen as the final form of the 'orthodox narrative' denounced above. Theory thus seems to make two cameo appearances in this story: the first under the guise of the avant-garde manifesto, in which some artistic production (albeit spurious) nonetheless continued to take place; and finally here, in full postmodernity, in which (as one imagines) literature and art have definitively been assigned a second place, if not a purely supernumerary function (it may be permitted to hear echoes here of the standard conservative complaint that our students read Derrida instead of Proust, when, indeed, they read anything at all). But subversion and critique accompanied modern art throughout its lifespan, and can certainly be found in Baudelaire's horror of the bourgeoisie. To introduce the motif so late in the game is to court the ridicule of Hilton Kramer's assertion that the modernist artists were always the 'loyal opposition' of capitalism. The accompanying denunciation of the vested interest of radical intellectuals in such values (i.e. subversion and critique) is of little more interest than the other face of the proposition which would identify the classic *ressentiment* of conservative intellectuals deprived of their rightful place in a still essentially liberal cultural establishment: both observations have their truth, but it ill behoves an intellectual to make them.

Yet, as has already been suggested, this sorry tale has an at least potentially happy ending: particularly since postmodernism arrived on the scene armed with a repudiation of the modernist teleology as such, and can thus be read as the negation of precisely some of the very features associated by Compagnon, not with true modernism, but with the avant-garde: 'The historical avant-gardes, nihilist and futurist, always guided by some theory or other, believed that artistic development had a meaning; but the pop art of the 1960s, and then the complete aesthetic permissiveness of the [19]70s, have freed art from the imperative to innovate'.[22] So now at last the fetishism of the New, the narrative obsession with the future, the infeodation of art theory itself, can be definitely abandoned: 'postmodern consciousness now allows us to reinterpret the modern tradition, without seeing it as a kind of historical conveyor belt, and the great adventure of the New'.[23]

The postmodern has thus for Compagnon and others at least one imaginably positive function: to cleanse the modern tradition of its anti- or trans-aesthetic motives, to purify it of whatever was protopolitical or historical, or even collective, in it, to return artistic production to the disinterested aesthetic activity that a certain bourgeois tradition (but not that of the artists themselves) always attributed to it. The other, more progressive features of the postmodern – its populism and pluralizing democratization, its commitment to the ethnic and the plebeian, and to feminism, its anti-authoritarianism and anti-elitism, its profound anarchism, precisely its anti-bourgeois features – these must of course drop out of the picture. Once they have done so, however, the outlines of a whole new aestheticism, a new return to traditional conceptions of the beautiful (as those survive residually even in Baudelaire himself) become visible.

But before taking this final step, it would seem helpful to juxtapose Compagnon's contemporary analysis (which we will finally, and despite his own judgments on the matter, have to class as an essentially postmodern text) with one of the authentic, if belated, dinosaurs of the modern movement, André Malraux's *Voices of Silence*, which still makes ultimate claims on the metaphysical nature of modern art (and art in general), in ways utterly inconsistent with postmodern theory and values. It is certain that the ineradicable 'humanism' of Malraux's work ('la force et l'honneur d'être homme') as well as the solemnity of its rhetoric, are not calculated to appeal to a contemporary public. On the other hand, Malraux's pan-aestheticism, his comprehensive and global assimilation of human art since the cave paintings into the new 'imaginary museum' of some world civilization, go well beyond any of the contemporary 'returns to the aesthetic', which are staged, as in Compagnon and Bohrer, under the sign of some resurrected high modernism. The role this last plays in Malraux, however, is far more complex (and it might well also be objected that more contemporary art – abstract expressionism itself, let alone pop art and its sequels – where they are mentioned at all, are simply in Malraux assimilated to the modern paradigm: which is to say that nothing can be found here to correspond to what will later on become the postmodern).

But this very expansion of the corpus of what now counts for us as art (and Malraux's theory of the metamorphosis of forms secures the 'modern' transformation into 'works of art' for us of cultic and religious items that precede any conception of secular art as such) makes for theoretical problems in Malraux's argument which have no equivalent in the contemporary aesthetic treatises mentioned above. In particular, besides the assimilation of older pre-aesthetic forms into the Western secular categories, there is also the issue, central for him ideologically, of the metaphysical spirit of such pre-Western cultures (and the religions around which they were organized): above all, what is at stake is the distinction between cultures which affirm human life (from the first smiles of the seventh-century Greek Kouroi) and those (like that of the Aztecs, or even the Christianity of the tortured deity) which deny it, and betray a nihilistic impulse apparently at odds with the humanistic principles of the 'imaginary museum'.

Besides this problem of value as such, there are specific features of Malraux's own modernism which seem inconsistent with his scheme, or irrelevant to it (and which are not at all thematized in Compagnon's account of the modern). First and foremost among these is the conviction of the quintessential modernity of the machine or of modern technology: a fascination Malraux shared with many of his modernist contemporaries, from the futurists to Brecht, delighting in the machine age, and celebrating the airplane and the photograph, the tank and the motorcar, the radio and aerial or panoramic perspective. Indeed, I believe it could be plausibly argued that the modernist Novum conjoins the Bohrer/Compagnon's 'presence to the world' with a technological excitement alien to them, and an excitement of the machine which imprints the sheer aesthetic innovations of the modern as a secret model or prototype (and I think that this could even be demonstrated in indirect ways for those modern writers like Proust who seem for the most part innocent of technological enthusiasms in their content). It would, however, be crucial to insist on the historical specificity of this particular modernist technology, resulting from the second or industrial stage of capitalism, and quite different in its effects from the cybernetic and atomic technology of post-modernity, despite seemingly analogous infatuations.

The technological paradigm, meanwhile – already present in Baudelaire himself, but omitted from Compagnon's ideal stage of the latter's authentic modernity – persists into Malraux's late, Gaullist and aestheticist, period, and can be observed to be ingeniously woven into the argument and indeed the very conceptual fabric of *The Voices of Silence*. For one thing, as the immense first chapter of this book demonstrates, the very proposition of some new 'imaginary museum' has as its fundamental precondition the existence of photography as a new technological medium. But this initial technological prerequisite is then interiorized and assimilated into the very content of Malraux's historical narrative, not merely in the familiar sense of the competition between photograph and painting in the nineteenth century, but above all in the transformation of the former into the new narrative art of cinema – whose emergence and existence has been crucial to the practice as well as the theory of Malraux – and to which the torch of a hitherto narrative painting will now be passed, with decisive consequences for the art we consider to be modern: 'the first characteristic of modern art is not to tell a story'.[24]

From this characteristically negative and positive dialectic the specificity of an at first Western and European modernist art will be deduced, which must now take its place alongside the 'humanist' and nihilist premodern arts as a further complication of Malraux's central theoretical problem: now not only this opposition must be resolved in order to welcome the nonsecular 'arts' of other cultures and religions into the 'imaginary museum', but the very opposition between sacred and secular, between thousands of years of cult objects and this peculiarly modern practice, in which painting takes itself as its own deepest subject matter, and stages a radical and seemingly unbridgeable rupture with all the arts of the past. But so do the world's religions: thereby adding the fact of ineradicable historical discontinuities to Malraux's theoretical difficulties.

It is by the way of the notion of the 'Absolute' that Malraux cuts across these various knots: the Absolute considered, very much as in *La Condition humaine*, as any authentic confrontation by human beings with their own finitude and death. This transhistorical conception of the Absolute thus squares the circle that leads from nihilism to whatever fragile humanism, for both are modes of confrontation with death, and indeed their confluence was already foreshadowed in Perken's significant remark (in the early *Voie royale*), that 'il y a aussi quelque chose de . . . satisfaisant dans l'écrasement de la vie . . .'. At the same time a secular 'modernism' or modern art can now also be added to this list of the great absolutes; and if I have dwelt at such length on this still impressive work, it was to arrive at this point at which a paradigmatic modernist aestheticism necessarily completes itself with a trans-aesthetic dimension. Malraux's 'Absolute' then confirms Adorno's remark – 'where art is experienced purely aesthetically, it fails to be fully experienced even aesthetically'[25] – and rebukes those contemporary returns to the aesthetic which seek to purify the latter by eradicating everything extra-aesthetic in the works they celebrate.

But it is also a point that could be made by way of a different kind of terminology: for it seems to me that Malraux's aesthetic conception of the Absolute is also to be assimilated to the notion of the Sublime, as that gradually became the fundamental motor impulse of modernism from the romantic period onwards. The function of the Sublime, it will be recalled, was to displace those merely decorative forms classified under the opposing rubric of Beauty, whose properties are the central concern of traditional aesthetics and traditional artistic production. In that case, however, not only are the 'returns' to the modern and to 'pure' or authentic aesthetics unmasked as so many forms of Beauty, rather than as contemporary versions of the modernist Sublime; but the aesthetics of postmodernism generally can be characterized in just such a way, as the displacement of various modernist claims to 'sublimity' by more modest and decorative practices in which sensory beauty is once again the heart of the matter. This is what I will try to show in a concluding section.

IV

We will now explore the visual consequences of this 'return of the aesthetic' in the image production of contemporary film, where the lure of Beauty and the ideology of aestheticism seems to play a renewed, if historically modified, role. I want to examine an English filmmaker (Derek Jarman), an African one (Souleymane Cissé) and a Mexican (Paul Leduc), before looking at some recent European high-cultural successes and once again examining the vexed question of contemporary historical films (which I have elsewhere called 'nostalgia films'). The premise has nothing to do with individual influences, but rather with the mediation of a common situation to which all these directors react in one way or another, and which is diffused and transmitted by an international film festival culture, which constitutes the level of globalization in film production today (as that seeks to oppose and to pose alternatives to an equally global US commercial film exporting system).

Derek Jarman's most widely distributed film, *Caravaggio* (1986), is in many ways supremely representative, in its content as well as in its form, of the *painterly* strategy, in which, as in Godard's *Passion* (1982), the well-known but still electrifying paintings alternate with tableaux of the living bodies of actors imitating them, in the guise of posing for them. The separation of form and content implicit in the posing of a pre-existent tableau by actors reconfirms and strengthens the simulacrum-qualities of the filmic image itself, by restoring some 'real world' of which this is but the visionary staging in an aleatory image.

The succession of such images – a fog-blue room holding a motionless figure in purple, bodies with a corpse-like pallor adjoining the folds of a brilliant red garment, the spilling of a jug in pieces, or a dish of oranges, smoke filtering through a classic low-life tavern, or a religious procession, or a knife-duel among toughs – these stunning shots, which frame each other by their very alternation and bring each other into being, produce each other by their very contrast, are in their formal logic deeply static. They do not merely burden the plot – such as it is – they turn it inside out, and make the biographical sequence of actions and events into a mere pretext for the visuals. This is inscribed within the film as a kind of boredom – the boredom of the models, the boredom of the hangers-on in the painter's studio, drowsing and waiting endlessly for the painter to decide on an angle or a tint of colour-contrast; it is inscribed, even more deeply, in the painter's life, which is itself little more than a marking time and a waiting between acts of the painting of a canvas which are somehow essentially outside of human time or praxis. But nothing is more paradoxical when we have to do with this particular painter, whose notorious life is virtually a paradigm of adventure and of crisis, the beaux-arts' equivalent of Villon or Genet! Boredom is here finally the sign of the withdrawal from history, of which classical plot now becomes the allegory. Even sexuality and violence – elsewhere the very staples of an essentially visual mass-cultural pornography – are emptied out by the painterly gaze, the aesthetic fetishism of this immense world-weariness. Indeed, a supplement of boredom is the price the viewer is asked to pay, as a kind of devotion to 'art' as such, to the reappearance of a virtual religion of the image on the other side of countercultural marginality (and in another sense, no doubt, the spectator is inscribed in this film allegorically in the person of the mute and slow-witted companion-servant of the painter).

But I have not mentioned the most striking feature of this work, namely its magic-realist anachronisms, as when we hear a train in the background of a lovers' bed, watch a Renaissance protagonist work on his motorcycle, a prince of the church peck away at his old-fashioned typewriter, observe a scene acted out in a cavernous garage in front of an old roadster, or watch court figures in silken finery calculate something on a portable adding machine. These are all, it will be noted, the technologies of an expanded conception of the media as such, encompassing both transportation and communication: densely crystallized and then projected into the painterly past in the form of discrete gadgets, these tell-tale objects stand as the symptom for the deeper complex of impulses at work here, foregrounding the relationship between aesthetics and technology in the postmodern, and unmasking the dialectical link between this conception of beauty and the high-tech structure of late capitalism. Jarman[26] thereby demystifies the very different nature of mystique of a Tarkovsky, about whom I've suggested in another place[27] that his breathtaking reinvention of the natural elements on the wide screen – sodden marshes, rain, blazing flames – are themselves mere inversions of the advanced technology that permits their reproduction: they are thus in the truest sense simulacra, and one is tempted to turn to a film from a very different tradition to seek their estrangement and demystification. I am thinking of the American SF film *Soylent Green* (Richard Fleischer, 1973), with its mesmerizing euthanasia sequence, in which the citizens of a dead and barren, polluted and overpopulated planet, from which clean air and water, and all plant life, have been effaced, are encouraged in one last high-tech ritual to go to their deaths consuming enormous National Geographic holographs of a natural beauty that had ceased to exist on Earth a century before.

But one can also imagine a very different image production from this one, and it is this that seems to me to mark the turn of the Malian filmmaker Souleymane Cissé away from social realism to the extraordinary visual and mythic narrative of *Yeelen* (*The Light*, 1987), a film which has stunned audiences all over the world by its visual splendour and by the power of its fable, in which a bad ogre-like father, endowed with frightening magical powers and capable of documenting the assertions of anthropologists that the original shamans were technically paranoid schizophrenics, implacably hunts down his son, who equally seeks his own share of the magic, and confronts him in an ultimate duel in which they destroy each other along with the organic world itself, in a final atomic blast that leaves nothing but desert. The monitory dénouement, with its ecological overtones, clearly asserts a certain contemporary intention; while the mythic vehicle allows the power of the image to invest directly in the narrative in virtually the reverse of what happens in Jarman, and to stage a plot whose very characters have become vessels for natural forces and elements. It is a very remarkable experience, indeed; but it is also, particularly following on Cissé's social films describing the crises and state repression of contemporary Third World society, a peculiarly aestheticizing one in all the senses in which we have used this word. I hope it is not puritanical of a Western viewer to say so, but I feel a certain perplexity about this work which I am at least reassured to find that my African friends share. Myths are pseudo-narratives which can have no conclusion and no genuine contemporary content; the atomic flash at the end of this one is rather the symptom of impoverishment and the acknowledgement of a certain ideological defeat or failure: but where the recourse to myth in the modernist period (Thomas Mann, T. S. Eliot's essay on *Ulysses*) provided the possibility of substituting one kind of narrative for another, whose closure presented structural difficulties, this more postmodern 'mythic' procedure can better be grasped as the pretext for substituting an image for the otherwise unresolvable narrative contradiction.

A rather different light is shed on this problem of the legitimation of the image by the films of the Mexican director Paul Leduc, and in particular his extraordinary *Latino Bar* (1990). This film eschews all mythic motivation, and yet foregrounds the image as such even more absolutely insofar as, despite a 'total flow' of popular music in its soundtrack, it does without all dialogue, thereby less approximating the operatic version of MTV practised by Jarman than returning in some original and idiosyncratic fashion to the dynamics of silent films as such. Yet the sequence of shots does not, as in the greatest silent films of the tradition, confront us with the labour and the emergence of some primal narrativity from out of the specific sign-system and wordless impoverished stills of the photographic image. Rather, it stunningly reinvents itself on two dialectically distinct registers: on the one hand, a simple and even stereotypical narrative of love and jealousy, violence and struggle, set in a complex spatial labyrinth of booths, huts and taverns on a pier in Maracaibo, a narrative which needs no words; and on the other, a system of colour distinct either from the dynamics of sheer black-and-white or the garish effects of modern technicolour (as exemplified by the other films under discussion here). *Latino Bar* is rather expressed and articulated in a system of darkened and virtual colour, whose only imaginable equivalent might be the tinting occasionally experimented with during the silent era. The image, now liberated from the complex temporalities of a plot you need to read and decipher, to reconstruct at every point, begins to call for a different kind of visual attention, its depths and tenebrosities projecting something like a visual hermeneutic which the eye scans for ever deeper layers of meaning.

We can, I think, detect here a subterranean return of the

sacred of an altogether different kind than what was posited in
Yeelen, for as the camera approaches elements of the pier's
installations and then draws back from them again, what the
image offers is nothing less than the altars of the *candomble* or
the *santeria*, with their profusion of gaudy devotional bric-à-
brac intertwined with vegetal masses and floral decoration. The
filmic image of Leduc thus imitates the elements of traditional
filmic narrative in much the same way that the altar of *candomble* imitates the 'high' or official religion of the Christian altar,
secretly decentring and destabilizing a Eurocentric hierarchy
organized around the axis of a central sacred painting or
sculpture – a centring and centred representation – and offering
at the outer limit some archaic chance at a pre-theocentric
inversion and liberation of libidinal energies.

Leduc is an all the more useful reference point for us in this
context, owing to his better known film portrait of Frida Kahlo
(*Frida*, 1984), a work insensibly infiltrated and colonized by an
omnipresent postmodern decoration (which symbolically enacts
the reappropriation of Frida by the cultural politics of contemporary social movements). This is then a work which exemplifies
some new type of postmodern documentary whose formal
originality is comparable to that of the 'new historicism' or the
new ethnography with respect to older cultural histories or
older anthropological reports. In all these formal mutations, an
aesthetic attention and motivation is substituted for older
'rational' interpretation, even though it is an aesthetic of tex-
tuality rather than one of sheer style and appearance (as in the
aesthetic historicism of the late nineteenth century). Other films
that can document this new kind of form might include Isaac
Julian's work, and *Daughters of the Dust* (Julie Dash, 1990).

I now want briefly to follow traces of the new aesthetic of
Beauty through some lower-level contemporary film genres or
types of production. The predominance in commercial cinema
of so-called action films, save for the occasional lyric filler, is
not implicated here, even though what can descriptively (and
non-morally) be called sex-and-violence porn does offer something of a grim caricature of current aesthetic notions of an
absolute present in time. For these films offer, in a powerful
reduction to the sheer present of sex or violence, intensities

which can be read as a compensation for the weakening of any sense of narrative time: the older plots, which still developed and flexed the spectator's local memory, have seemingly been replaced by an endless string of narrative pretexts in which only the experiences available in the sheer viewing present can be entertained.

Yet, precisely this enfeeblement of narrative time – now projected on to narrative history itself – is also one of the determinants of what I have called nostalgia film, a misnomer to the degree to which the term suggests that genuine nostalgia – the passionate longing of the exile in time, the alienation of contemporaries bereft of older historical plenitudes – is still available in postmodernity. The latter is, however, anything but alienated in that older modernist sense: its relationship to the past is that of a consumer adding another rare object to the collection, or another flavour to the international banquet: the postmodern nostalgia film is then very precisely such a consumable set of images, marked very often by music, fashion, hairstyles and vehicles or motorcars (for it is difficult for the form to accommodate periods more distant than the modern era itself). In such films the very style of a period is the content and they substitute a fashion-plate of the age in question for its events, thus producing a kind of generational periodization of a stereotypical kind which is, as we shall see, not without its impact on their capacity to function as narratives. I don't want to be understood as dismissing the often high quality of these reconstructions, which include *The Godfather* (for the late forties and fifties), followed by any number of versions of the twenties and thirties that take the Mafia for their vehicle – including a number of interesting experiments in television series (*Crime Story*, for example). Artefacts like these are indisputably experimental work in new forms of historical representation and raise the most interesting philosophical questions about the representation of history generally: for that very reason judgments on the new forms are not ways of marking merely personal successes or failures but rather judgments one passes on the age itself and its capacity to generate form.

In this respect, I would suggest that the most interesting test case for nostalgia films might be staged within the work of a single auteur; I'm thinking of the Cuban filmmaker Humberto Solas to whom we owe two distinct representations of the Machado dictatorship, first in the second episode of his classic *Lucia* (1969), and then in his later film *The Opportunist* (*Un hombre de éxito*, 1986), which to be sure spans a longer period and brings us up to the Revolution itself. The Machado episode in *Lucia* is constructed according to what I am tempted to characterize as a well-nigh *symboliste* aesthetic: an aesthetic of absence, whose point of view is the woman rather than the man, contiguity to great or violent events rather than their head-on representation, what Jakobson would surely have called a metonymic rather than a metaphoric approach to the historical object. This episode, which touches on a fundamental moment of Cuban history, is then a model of stylistic restraint and understatement and a filmic narrative of great delicacy. *The Opportunist* on the other hand makes a brassy head-on onslaught on the same historical object, trying to represent all the best-known features and events of the period directly. It thereby becomes degraded to a mere illustration of those same events, whose knowledge has to precede its own illustration. This is indeed on my view the most pertinent a priori formal observation to nostalgia film as such: since it is necessarily based on the recognition by the viewer of pre-existing historical stereotypes, including the various styles of the period, it is thereby reduced to the mere narrative confirmation of those same stereotypes. It can do little more than offer the most predictable testimony about their features (learned from history manuals and pre-existing collective attitudes and references); it cannot contradict the stereotypes of the period without falling into gratuitous and purely individual singlarity. It does not, in other words, know that rich dialectic of the unique and the iterative, the typical and the individual, that made up the older historical art, as Lukács and others have characterized it for us. Nostalgia film is historicist rather than historical, which explains why it must necessarily displace its centre of interest on to the visual as such and substitute breathtaking images for anything like the older filmic storytelling; and indeed, I think that it is axiomatic that attention to the image as such breaks narrative and is incompatible with a more purely narrative attention. It is an argument I would be tempted to extend on into the opposition between black-and-white and colour (which in fact characterizes Solas's two films), and to generalize as a no doubt extravagant hypothesis about the incompatibility of colour with narrative as such. But I will not go quite so far here, and will content myself with a rather different observation on the two works, namely that, while modernism may be an improbable characterization of *Lucia*, it is certain that its three episodes juxtapose their three modes of production by way of the mediation or three distinct aesthetics or styles. History in *Lucia* is thus also conveyed indirectly by way of a message of the form itself: which in *The Opportunist* is simply taken for granted as an unproblematical and relatively transparent representational language. At any rate, I conclude this discussion of commercial film by suggesting that their postmodernity consists at least in part in the way in which they package the past as a commodity and offer it to the viewer as an object of purely aesthetic consumption; and something like this can also be said, I believe, for most of the other objects of current visual production today, whether in film, advertising or MTV.

This is the point at which I would also like to read into the record the deplorable recrudescence of works of art about art and artists in the most recent years of the postmodern era: works which also testify to a hint of nostalgia, but in this case a nostalgia for art itself and for aesthetics, for the art about art of the modernist period itself, which is fantasized as being non- or a-political. In fact, modernism, the great modernists, were all profoundly utopian in the sense of being committed to the fateful premonition of momentous impending transformations of the Self or the World: what I would call essentially proto-political experiences. Meanwhile it must also be added in the present context that their art-novels, their inveterate self-referentiality, always turned on language as such, and on the poetic as the mode by which those transformations were made. In that sense, Heidegger was the last modernist, and the difference, the distance, between his utopian meditations on language and current postmodern art about art is that language no longer occupies any privileged position in the postmodern, which is rather focused on decoration, on the visual arts and on music now understood itself in a decorative space-filling way (rock and its headsets on the one hand, precapitalist or baroque and earlier music on the other), rather than on the grandiose ambitions of modern bourgeois music as such, from Wagner to Schönberg.

I take as my text for such a hypothesis the typical and very successful embodiment of neo-aestheticism in Alain Corneau's *Tous les matins du monde* (1992): a film about the rivalry between two eighteenth-century composers – one an opportunist and a charlatan, the other a true creator and virtually a mystical seer in his aesthetic withdrawal from the world. The opportunist disciple takes advantage of his master's daughter to steal the latter's music and artistic secrets, and then sells out to the king's court, becoming a famous, wealthy and powerful figure, who nonetheless acknowledges and regrets the genuine, the 'real' music of his patron. It is a 'beautiful' film, but one which, unlike *Caravaggio*, disguises consumption as art, and gives us a pseudo-historical set of images for its own purpose, which are certainly not those of historiography. The historical setting indeed is used as a set of signals: the great musician is a Jansenist, which gives us the sign for French classicism, the court to which his pupil sells out is the corrupt *ancien régime* court against which the French Revolution was made. These combined signals allow us to read a protest against a decadent elite which is, however, not registered in political but rather in artistic terms. Meanwhile the rigours and asceticism of Jansenism – a kind of vague and general equivalent of English puritanism – allow the film to affirm the values of renunciation, while the beauty of images and the music, and the sexual freedoms with which the film is dusted, indicate nonetheless the pleasures of renunciation, renunciation as a kind of aesthetic gratification. The film is coded nationally, as a French contribution to the international film market, elegant, signifying what we call high culture, marking a retreat from Americanization and rampant consumer culture, from the grosser manifestations of contemporary business and market society, while still participating in a dignified way in this last as a distinct European option. The film is therefore a high-class consumer good, offered under the guise of art and aesthetics, as a distinctly European export. Its beauty is regressive and vacuous, and comes as all the more useful for my present purposes in that Corneau is very conscious of the symbolic and indeed political nature of his gesture here. He has said in a recent interview: 'we now have behind us thirty years of heated discussions about the relationship between politics and art ... today the vision of creative people is changing ... it is the very notion of engaged or committed art that is in the process of disintegrating ... In some deeper sense, however, the artist still remains the same. Isolated, caught in institutions that are too vast for him, a minority, the artist remains a pathological case; he produces a strange kind of content ... We have to revise our history ... [Even] the New Wave was not the leftist movement it has been taken for. Bazin was a practising Catholic ...' etc., etc.[28] These thoughts underscore the function of art as a substitute for politics and the work of art about art, or the movie about the artist as being essentially a reaction formation. That it can take very distinguished forms indeed can be witnessed by Kieslówski's production, in particular *Blue* (1993) and *The Double Life of Véronique* (1991). But these films themselves lead us on into another dimension of the new aestheticism, which is religion itself, or if you prefer the Gorecki-3rd-Symphony syndrome. *Tous les matins du monde* already solemnly underscored the religiose if not exactly the religious features of the new aestheticism. Kieslówski now deconceals the more intimate connections between these new visions of art and some new religious or mystical turn, whose traces one can find all over the new Europe, beginning as far back, if you like, as Godard's *Je vous salue Marie* (1985). (Godard always had an extraordinary sense of new trends and ideas in the air, and his new films are in addition textbook examples of aestheticism at least as far as classical music is concerned.) I am tempted to characterize these simulacra of religion as nostalgia products, very much along the lines of the aesthetic nostalgia we have been discussing here. Both are, on my view, substitutes for genuine content in the strong sense in which Hegel and after him Lukács used that word. Where prudence suggests a turn away from the concrete view of the social – real content – which is always bound up with the protopolitical, at that point other forms of pseudo-content have to take its place. The work still has to pretend to be about something. Yesterday, a turn away from the world meant a turn towards the self: a turn away from Marxism meant a turn towards psychoanalysis: in that case, the Real was still somehow present, if only as an aching throb, an open wound. Today, even psychoanalysis and desire must be shunned as being too modern, and as requiring an assessment of late capitalism that the postmodern subject cannot tolerate. What offers itself as a substitute is then art and religion, pseudo-aestheticism in the form we have examined it here and its ghostly afterimages in the slow rotation of the religion of art into the art of religion.

V

The final point I want to make has to do with beauty itself. In a period in which the 'Decadence' is itself undergoing some very interesting revaluations, it only seems appropriate in the present context to recall beauty's subversive role in a society marred by nascent commodification. The fin de siècle, from Morris to Wilde, deployed beauty as a political weapon against a complacent materialist Victorian bourgeois society and dramatized its negative power as what rebukes commerce and money, and what generates a longing for personal and social transformation in the heart of an ugly industrial society. Why then can we not allow for similar genuinely proto-political functions today, and at least leave the door open for an equally subversive deployment of the kinds of beauty and art-religions I have been enumerating? It is a question that allows us to measure the immense distance between the situation of modernism and that of the postmoderns (or ourselves), and between tendential and incomplete commodification and that on a global scale, in which the last remaining enclaves – the Unconscious and Nature, or cultural and aesthetic production and agriculture – have now been assimilated into commodity production. In a previous era, art was a realm beyond commodification, in which a certain freedom was still available; in late modernism, in

Adorno and Horkheimer's Culture Industry essay, there were still zones of art exempt from the commodifications of commercial culture (for them, essentially Hollywood). Surely what characterizes postmodernity in the cultural area is the supersession of everything outside of commercial culture, its absorption of all forms of art high and low, along with image production itself. The image is the commodity today, and that is why it is vain to expect a negation of the logic of commodity production from it, that is why, finally, all beauty today is meretricious and the appeal to it by contemporary pseudo-aestheticism is an ideological manoeuvre and not a creative resource.

Culture and Finance Capital

I want here to report on a book which has not yet received the attention it deserves, partly no doubt because it is substantial and difficult to digest, but also I think, because it purports to be a history of capitalism, whereas, I think, its secret originality is to have given us a new structural understanding of features of capitalism not yet fully elucidated. Giovanni Arrighi's *The Long Twentieth Century*[1] is remarkable, among many other things, for producing a problem we did not know we had, in the very process of crystallizing a solution to it: the problem of finance capital. No doubt it swarmed around our heads in the form of vague perplexities, quizzicalities that never paused long enough to become real questions: Why monetarism? Why are investment and the stock market getting more attention than an industrial production that seems on the point of disappearing anyway? How can you have profit without production in the first place? Where does all this excessive speculation come from? Does the new form of the city (including postmodern architecture) have anything to do with a mutation in the very dynamic of land values (ground rent)? Why should land speculation and the stock market come to the fore as dominant sectors in advanced societies, where 'advanced' certainly has something to do with technology but presumably ought to have something to do with production as well? All of these nagging questions were also secret doubts, about the Marxian model of production, as well as about the turn of history in the 1980s, stimulated by the Reaganite/Thatcherite tax cuts. We seemed to be returning to the most fundamental form of class struggle, one so basic that it spelled the end of all those Western-Marxist and theoretical subtleties that the Cold War had called forth.

Indeed, during the long period of the Cold War and of Western Marxism – a period one really needs to date from 1917 – a complex analysis of ideology needed to be developed in order to unmask the persistent substitutions of incommensurate dimensions, the passing off of political arguments in the place of economic ones, the appeal to alleged traditions – freedom and democracy, God, manichaeism, the values of the West and of the Judaeo-Christian or Roman-Christian heritage – as answers to new and unpredictable social experiments; in order, as well, to accommodate the new conceptions of the operations of the unconscious discovered by Freud and presumably also at work in the layering of social ideology.

In those days, the theory of ideology constituted the better mousetrap: and every self-respecting theorist felt the obligation to invent a new one, to ephemeral acclaim and momentarily attracting a horde of curious spectators always ready to move on to the next model at a moment's notice, even when that next model meant revamping the very name of ideology itself and substituting episteme, metaphysics, practices, or whatever.

But today many of these complexities seem to have disappeared, and, faced with the Reagan–Kemp and Thatcher utopias of immense investments and increases in production to come, based on the deregulation and privatization and the obligatory opening of markets everywhere, the problems of ideological analysis seem enormously simplified, and the ideologies themselves far more transparent. Now that, following master thinkers like Hayek, it has become customary to identify political freedom with market freedom, the motivations behind ideology no longer seem to need an elaborate machinery of decoding and hermeneutic reinterpretation; and the guiding thread of all contemporary politics seems much easier to grasp: namely, that the rich want their taxes lowered. This means that an older vulgar Marxism may once again be more relevant to our situation than the newer models; but it also poses more objective problems about money itself which had seemed less relevant in the Cold War period.

The rich were certainly doing something with all this new

income that no longer needed to be wasted on social services: but it did not seem to go into new factories, but rather to get invested in the stock market. Whence a second perplexity. The Soviets used to joke about the miracle of their system, whose edifice seemed comparable only to those houses kept standing by the swarm of termites eating away inside them. But some of us had the same feeling about the United States: after the disappearance (or brutal downsizing) of heavy industry, the only thing that seemed to keep it going (besides the two prodigious American industries of food and entertainment) was the stock market. How was this possible, and where did the money keep coming from? And if money itself rested on so fragile a basis, why did 'fiscal responsibility' matter so much in the first place, and on what was the very logic of monetarism itself grounded?

Yet the dawning suspicion that we were in a new period of finance capitalism was not given much theoretical encouragement or nourishment by the tradition. One old book, Hilferding's *Finance Capital* of 1910,[2] seemed to give a historical answer to an economic and structural question: the techniques of the great German trusts of the pre-World War One period, their relations with the banks and eventually the *Flottenbau*, and so forth – the answer seemed to lie in the concept of monopoly, and Lenin appropriated it in this sense for his 1916 pamphlet on *Imperialism: the Highest Stage of Capitalism*, which also seemed to do away with finance capital by changing its name and displacing it on to the power relations and competition between the great capitalist states. But these 'highest stages' now lie well in our own past; imperialism is gone, replaced by neo-colonialism and globalization; the great international financial centres do not (yet) seem the locus of ferocious competition between the nations of the capitalist First World, despite a few complaints about the Bundesbank and its interest policies; imperial Germany meanwhile has been replaced by a Federal Republic which may or may not be more powerful than its predecessor but which is now part of an allegedly united Europe. So these historical descriptions do not seem to do us much good; and here the teleological ('highest stage') does seem fully to merit all the opprobrium called down upon it in recent years.

But where the economist could only give us empirical history,[3] it remained for a historical narrative to give us the structural and economic theory we needed to solve this conundrum: finance capital has to be something like a stage, in the way it distinguishes itself from other moments of the development of capitalism. Arrighi's luminous insight was that this peculiar kind of telos need not lie in a straight line, but might well organize itself in a spiral (a figure which also avoids the mythical overtones of the various cyclical visions).

It is a picture that unites various traditional requirements: capitalism's movement must be seen as discontinuous but expansive. With each crisis, it mutates into a larger sphere of activity and a wider field of penetration, of control, investment and transformation: this doctrine, most forcefully argued by Ernest Mandel in his great book *Late Capitalism*, has the merit of accounting for capitalism's resilience, which Marx himself already posited in the *Grundrisse* (but which is less evident in *Capital* itself), and which has repeatedly unsettled left prognostications (immediately after two World Wars, and then again in the 1980s and 1990s). But the objection to Mandel's positions has turned on the latent teleology of his slogan 'late capitalism', as though this were the last stage conceivable, or as though the process were some uniform historical progression. (My own use of the term is meant as a homage to Mandel, and not particularly as a prophetic forecast; Lenin does say 'highest', as we have seen, while Hilferding, more prudently, simply calls it the 'jüngste', the latest or most recent, which is obviously preferable.)

The cyclical scheme now allows us to co-ordinate these features: if we position discontinuity not only in time but also in space, and if we add back in the historian's perspective, which clearly enough needs to reckon in the national situations and the uniquely idiosyncratic developments within the national states, let alone within the greater regional groupings (Third versus First Worlds, for example), then the local teleologies of the capitalist process can be reconciled with its own spasmodic historical developments and mutations as those leap from geographical space to space.

Thus, the system is better seen as a kind of virus (not Arrighi's figure), and its development as something like an epidemic (better still, a rash of epidemics, an epidemic of epidemics). The system has its own logic, which powerfully undermines and destroys the logic of more traditional or pre-capitalist societies and economies: Deleuze calls this an axiomatic, as opposed to the older precapitalist, tribal or imperial codes. But epidemics sometimes play themselves out, like a fire for want of oxygen; and they also leap to new and more propitious settings, in which the preconditions are favourable to renewed development. (I hasten to add that Arrighi's complex political and economic articulation of these paradoxical turns, whereby winners lose and losers sometimes win, is far more dialectical than my figures suggest.)

Thus, in the new scheme of *The Long Twentieth Century*, capitalism has known any number of false starts and fresh starts; any number of new beginnings, on an ever larger scale. Bookkeeping in Renaissance Italy, the nascent commerce of the great city states – all this is evidently a Petri dish of modest proportions which does not allow the new thing much in the way of scope, but which offers a still relatively restricted and sheltered environment. The political form, here, the city state itself, stands as an obstacle and a limit to development, although it should not be extrapolated into some more general thesis about the way in which form (the political) restricts content (the economic). Then the process leaps over into Spain, where Arrighi's great insight lies in the analysis of this moment as an essentially symbiotic form: we knew that Spain had an early form of capitalism, of course, which was disastrously undermined by the conquest of the New World and the fleets of silver. But Arrighi stresses the way in which Spanish capitalism is to be understood in close functional and symbiotic relationship to Genoa, which financed the Empire and which was thus a full participant in the new moment. It is a kind of dialectical link to the earlier Italian city-state moment, which will not be reproduced in the later discontinuous history, unless one is also willing to posit a kind of propagation by rivalry and negation: the way in which the enemy is led to take on your own development, to match it, to succeed where you fell short.

For such is the next moment, the leap to Holland and the

Dutch, to a system more resolutely based on the commercialization of the ocean and the waterways. After that, the story becomes more familiar: the limits of the Dutch system pave the way for a more successful English development along the same lines. The United States becomes the centre of capitalist development in the twentieth century; and Arrighi leaves a question mark, fraught with doubts, about the capacity of Japan to constitute yet another cycle and another stage, to replace an American hegemony in full internal contradiction. At this point, perhaps, Arrighi's model has touched the limits of its own representativity, and the complex realities of contemporary globalization perhaps now demand something else of a wholly different synchronic mode.

Yet we have not yet come to the most exciting feature of Arrighi's history, namely the internal stages of the cycle itself, the way in which capitalist development in each of these moments replicates itself and reproduces a series of three moments (this may be taken to be the local teleological content of his new 'universal history').

These are modelled on the famous formula of *Capital*: M-C-M', in which money is transformed into capital, which now generates supplementary money, in an expanding dialectic of accumulation. The first phase of the tripartite process has to do with trade which in one way or another, and often by way of the violence and brutality of primitive accumulation, brings into being a quantity of money for eventual capitalization. In the second classic moment, then, that money becomes capital, and is invested in agriculture and manufacture: it is territorialized, and transforms its associated area into a centre of production. But this second stage knows internal limits: those that weigh on production, distribution and consumption alike; a 'falling rate or profit' endemic to the second stage in general: 'profits are still high, but it is a condition for their maintenance that they should not be invested in further expansion'.[4]

At this point, the third stage begins, which is the moment that primarily interests us here. Arrighi's treatment of this the recurrent moment of a cyclical finance capitalism is inspired by Braudel's remark that 'the stage of financial expansion' is always 'a sign of autumn'.[5] Speculation, the withdrawal of profits from the home industries, the increasingly feverish search, not so much for new markets (these are also saturated) as for the new kind of profits available in financial transactions themselves and as such – these are the ways in which capitalism now reacts to and compensates for the closing of its productive moment. Capital itself becomes free-floating. It separates from the 'concrete context' of its productive geography. Money becomes in a second sense and to a second degree abstract (it always was abstract in the first and basic sense): as though somehow in the national moment money still had a content – it was cotton money, or wheat money, textile money, railway money and the like. Now, like the butterfly stirring within the chrysalis, it separates itself off from that concrete breeding ground and prepares to take flight. We know today only too well (but Arrighi shows us that this contemporary knowledge of ours only replicates the bitter experience of the dead, of disemployed workers in the older moments of capitalism, of local merchants as well, of the dying cities also) that the term is literal. We know that there exists such a thing as capital flight: the disinvestment, the pondered or hasty moving on to greener pastures and higher rates of investment return, and of cheaper labour. Now this free-floating capital, on its frantic search for more profitable investments (a process prophetically described for the US as long ago as Baran and Sweezy's *Monopoly Capital* of 1965) will begin to live its life in a new context; no longer in the factories and the spaces of extraction and production, but on the floor of the stock market, jostling for more intense profitability, but not as one industry competing with another branch, nor even one productive technology against another more advanced one in the same line of manufacturing, but rather in the form of speculation itself: spectres of value, as Derrida might put it, vying against each other in a vast world-wide disembodied phantasmagoria. This is of course the moment of finance capital as such, and it now becomes clear how on Arrighi's extraordinary analysis finance capital is not only a kind of 'highest stage', but the highest and last stage of every moment of capital itself, as in its cycles it exhausts its returns in the new national and international capitalist zone, and seeks to die and be reborn in some 'higher' incarnation, a vaster and immeasurably more productive one, in which it is fated to live through again the three fundamental stages of its implantation, its productive development, and its financial or speculative final stage.

All of which, as I suggested above, might be dramatically heightened, for our own period, by a reminder of the results of the cybernetic 'revolution', the intensification of communications technology to the point at which capital transfers today abolishes space and time and can be virtually instantaneously effectuated from one national zone to another. The results of these lightning-like movements of immense quantities of money around the globe are incalculable, yet already have clearly produced new kinds of political blockage and also new and unrepresentable symptoms in late-capitalist everyday life.

For the problem of abstraction – of which this one of finance capital is a part – must also be grasped in its cultural expressions. Real abstractions in an older period – the effects of money and number in the big cities of nineteenth-century industrial capitalism, the very phenomena analysed by Hilferding and culturally diagnosed by Georg Simmel in his path-breaking essay 'Metropolis and Mental Life' – had as one significant offshoot the emergence of what we call modernism in all the arts. In this sense, modernism faithfully – even 'realistically' – reproduced and represented the increasing abstraction and deterritorialization of Lenin's 'imperialist stage'. Today, what is called postmodernity articulates the symptomatology of yet another stage of abstraction, qualitatively and structurally distinct from that one, which the preceding pages have drawn on Arrighi to characterize as our own moment of finance capitalism: the finance-capital moment of globalized society, the abstractions brought with it by cybernetic technology (which it is a misnomer to call 'post-industrial' except as a way of distinguishing its dynamic from the older, 'productive' moment). Thus any comprehensive new theory of finance capitalism will need to reach out into the expanded realm of cultural production to map its effects: indeed mass cultural production and consumption themselves – at one with globalization and the new information technology – are as profoundly economic as the other productive areas of late capitalism, and as fully integrated into the latter's generalized commodity system.

Now I want to speculate on the potential uses of this new theory for cultural and literary interpretation, and in particular for the understanding of the historical or structural sequence of realism, modernism and postmodernism, which has interested many of us in recent years. For better or for worse, only the first of these – realism – has been the object of much serious attention and analysis in the Marxist tradition, the attacks on modernism being on the whole largely negative and contrastive, although not without their occasional local suggestivity (particularly in the work of Lukács). I want to show how Arrighi's work now puts us in a position to frame a better and more global theory of these three cultural stages or moments, it being understood that the analysis will be staged on the level of the mode of production (or in brief, that of the economic) rather than on that of social classes, a level of interpretation which, as I argued in *The Political Unconscious*,[6] we need to separate from the economic frame in order to avoid category mistakes. I hasten to add that the political level, the level of social classes, is an indispensable part of interpretation, whether historical or aesthetic, but it is not part of our work here. Arrighi's work gives us themes and materials to work with in this area; and it is worth vulgarizing that work by suggesting that it offers us a new, or perhaps we should simply say a more complex and satisfying, account of the role of money in these processes.

Indeed, the classical political thinkers of the period, from Hobbes to Locke, and including the Scottish Enlightenment, all identified money far more clearly than we do as the central novelty, the central mystery, at the heart of the transition to modernity, taken in its largest sense as capitalist society (and not merely in narrower cultural terms). In his classic work,[7] C. B. MacPherson has shown how Locke's vision of history turns on the transition to a money economy, while the ambiguous richness of Locke's ideological solution was predicated on the positioning of money in both places, in the modernity that follows the social contract of civilized society, but also in the state of nature itself. Money, MacPherson demonstrates, is what allows Locke his extraordinary dual and superimposed systems, of nature and of history, of equality and of class conflict at the same time; or, if you prefer, the peculiar nature of money is what allows Locke to operate as a philosopher of human nature and as a historical analyst of social and economic change simultaneously.

Money has continued to play this kind of role in the traditions of a Marxian analysis of culture, where it is less often a purely economic category than a social one. In other words, Marxist literary criticism – to limit ourselves to that – has less often tried to analyse its objects in terms of capital and value, in terms of the system of capitalism itself, than it has in terms of class, and most often of one class in particular, namely the bourgeoisie. This is obviously something of a paradox: one would have expected an engagement of the literary critics with the very centre of Marx's work, the structural account of the historic originality of capitalism – but such efforts seem to have involved too many mediations (no doubt in the spirit in which Oscar Wilde complained that socialism required too many evenings). It was thus much simpler to establish the more direct mediation of a merchant and business class, with its emergent class culture, alongside the forms and texts themselves. Money enters the picture here insofar as only exchange, merchant activity and the like, and later on nascent capitalism, determine the coming into being of some historically original burgher or city merchant, bourgeois class life. (Meanwhile, the aesthetic dilemmas of modern times are for Marxism almost exclusively linked to the problem of imagining some equivalent and parallel class culture and art for that other emergent group which is the industrial working class.)

This means that Marxian cultural theory has almost exclusively turned on the question of realism, insofar as that is associated with a bourgeois class culture; and for the most part (with some famous and signal exceptions) its analyses of modernism have taken a negative and critical form: how and why does the latter deviate from the realistic path? (It is true that in the hands of a Lukács, this kind of question can produce enlightening and sometimes significant results.) At any rate, I would like briefly to illustrate this traditional Marxian focus on realism by way of Arnold Hauser's *Social History of Art*. I refer

145

you, for example, to the moment in which Hauser notes the naturalistic tendencies in the Egyptian art of the Middle Kingdom at the moment of Ikhnaton's abortive revolution. These tendencies stand out sharply against the hieratic tradition so familiar to us, and therefore suggest the influence of new factors. Indeed, if one persists in a much older anthropological and philosophical tradition for which it is religion that is determinate of the spirit of a given society, Ikhnaton's abortive attempt to substitute monotheism would probably be explanation enough. Hauser rightly feels that the religious determination requires a further social determination in its turn, and unsurprisingly proposes a heightened influence of commerce and money on social life and on the emergence of new kinds of social relations. But there is a hidden mediation here, which Hauser does not articulate: and that is the matter of the history of perception as such and the emergence of new kinds of perceptions.

Herein lies the unorthodox kernel of these orthodox explanations: for it is tacitly assumed that with the emergence of exchange value a new interest in the physical properties of objects comes into being. Their equivalence by way of the money form (which in standard Marxian economics is grasped as the supersession of concrete use and function by an essentially idealistic and abstract 'fetishism of commodities') here rather leads to a more realistic interest in the body of the world and in the new and more lively human relationships developed by trade. The merchants and their consumers need to take a keener interest in the sensory nature of their wares as well as in the psychological and characterological traits of their interlocutors; and all this may be supposed to develop new kinds of perceptions, both physical and social – new kinds of seeing, new types of behaviour – and in the long run create the conditions in which more realistic art forms are not only possible but desirable, and encouraged by their new publics.

It is an epochal explanation or account, which will not be satisfying for anyone seeking to scrutinize the individual text; the proposition is also subject to radical and unexpected dialectical reversals in the later stages; above all, except for the obviously suggestive implications for plot and character, the relevance of the account for language itself is less clear. It would be abusive to assimilate the one great theoretician of the relations between realism and language, Erich Auerbach, to this schema, even though a notion of expanding social democratization tactfully underpins Auerbach's work and informs an insistence on the transfer of popular language to writing, which is, however, by no means his central argument. For this is no Wordsworthian emphasis on plain speech and speakers, but rather, I would like to suggest, an immense *Bildungsroman* whose protagonist is Syntax itself, as it develops throughout the Western European languages. He does not cite Mallarmé:

> Quel pivot, j'entends, dans ces contrastes,
> à l'intelligibilité? Il faut une garantie –
> La Syntaxe (!)[8]

Yet the adventures of syntax down the ages, from Homer to Proust, is the deeper narrative of *Mimesis*: the gradual unlimbering of hierarchical sentence structure, and the differential evolution of the incidental clauses of the new sentence in such a way that each can now register a hitherto unperceived local complexity of the Real – this is the great narrative and teleological thread of Auerbach's history, whose multiple determinants remain to be worked out, but clearly include many of the social features already mentioned.

It should also be noted that in both these theories of realism, the new artistic and perceptual categories are grasped as being absolutely and fundamentally linked to modernity (if not yet modernism) of which, however, here realism can be seen as a kind of first stage. They also include the great modernist topos of the break and the Novum: for whether it is with the older hieratic conventions of a formulaic art, or the cumbersome inherited syntax of a previous literary period, both insist on the necessarily subversive and critical, destructive, character of their realisms, which must clear away a useless and jumbled monumentality in order to develop their new experimental instruments and laboratories.

This is the point at which, without false modesty, I want to register the two contributions I have felt able to make to some as yet unformulated and properly Marxian theory of modernism. The first of these proposes a dialectical theory of the paradox we have just encountered: namely realism as modernism, or a realism which is so fundamentally a part of modernity that it demands description in some of the ways we have traditionally reserved for modernism itself – the break, the Novum, the emergence of new perceptions, and the like. What I proposed was to see these historically distinct, and seemingly incompatible modes of realism and modernism, as so many stages in a dialectic of reification, which seizes on the properties and the subjectivities, the institutions and the forms, of an older pre-capitalist life world, in order to strip them of their hierarchical or religious content. Realism and secularization are a first Enlightenment moment in that process: what is dialectical about it comes as something like a leap and an overturn from quantity into quality. With the intensification of the forces of reification, and their suffusion through ever greater zones of social life (including individual subjectivity), it is as though the force that generated the first realism now turns against it and devours it in its turn. The ideological and social preconditions of realism – its naive belief in a stable social reality, for example – are now themselves unmasked, demystified and discredited; and modernist forms – generated by the very same pressure of reification – take their place. And in this narrative, the supersession of modernism by the postmodern is predictably enough read in the same way as a further intensification of the forces of reification, which now has utterly unexpected and dialectical results for the now hegemonic modernisms themselves.

As for my other contribution, it posited a specific formal process in the modern which seemed to me much less significantly influential in either realism or postmodernism, but which can be linked dialectically to both. For this 'theory' of modernist formal processes I wanted to follow Lukács (and others) in seeing modernist reification in terms of analysis, decomposition, but above all of internal differentiation. Thus, in the course of hypothesizing modernism in various contexts, I also found it interesting and productive to see this particular process in terms of 'autonomization', of the becoming independent and self-sufficient of what were formerly parts of a whole. It is something that can be observed in the chapters and sub-episodes in *Ulysses*, and also in the Proustian sentence. I wanted to establish a kinship here, not so much with the sciences (as is customarily done when people talk about the sources of modernity) as rather with the labour process itself: and here the great phenomenon of Taylorization (contemporaneous with modernism) slowly imposes itself; a division of labour (theorized as long ago as Adam Smith) now becoming a method of mass production in its own right, by way of the separation of different stages and their reorganization around principles of 'efficiency' (to use the ideological word for it). Harry Braverman's classic *Labor and Monopoly Capital*[9] remains the cornerstone of any approach to that labour process, and seems to me full of suggestions for the cultural and structural analysis of modernism as such.

But now, in what some people like to call post-Fordism, this particular logic no longer seems to obtain; just as in the cultural sphere, forms of abstraction which in the modern period seemed ugly, dissonant, scandalous, indecent or repulsive, have also entered the mainstream of cultural consumption (in the largest sense, from advertising to commodity styling, from visual decoration to artistic production) and no longer shock anyone; rather, our entire system of commodity production and consumption today is based on those older, once anti-social modernist, forms. Nor does the conventional notion of abstraction seem very appropriate in the postmodern context; and yet, as Arrighi teaches us, nothing is quite so abstract as the finance capital which underpins and sustains postmodernity as such.

At the same time, it also seems clear that if autonomization – the becoming independent of the parts or fragments – characterizes the modern, it is still very much with us in postmodernity: the Europeans were the first, for example, to be struck by the rapidity of the editing and the sequence of shots that characterized classical American film – it is a process that has everywhere intensified in television editing, where an advertisement lasting only half a minute can today include an extraordinary number of distinct shots or images, without in the least provoking the modernist estrangement and bewilderment of the work of a great modernist independent filmmaker like Stan Brakhage, for example. So a process and a logic of extreme fragmentation still seems to obtain here, but without any of its earlier effects. Is one then to imagine, with Deleuze, that we here confront a 'recoding' of hitherto decoded or axiomatic materials – something he posits as an operation inseparable from late capitalism, whose intolerable axiomatics are everywhere locally turned back into private gardens, private religions, vestiges of older or even archaic local coding systems? This is, however, an interpretation that raises embarrassing questions: and, in particular, how different this opposition Deleuze and Guattari develop between the axiomatic and the code really is from classical existentialism – the loss of meaning everywhere in the modern world, followed by the attempt locally to re-endow it, either by regressing to religion or making an absolute out of the private and the contingent.

What also militates against the concept of 'recoding' here is that it is not a local but a general process: the languages of postmodernity are universal, in the sense in which they are media languages. They are thus very different from the solitary obsessions and private thematic hobbies of the great moderns, which selectively achieved their universalization, indeed their very socialization, only through a process of collective commentary and canonization. Unless entertainment and visual consumption are to be thought of as essentially religious practices, then, the notion of recoding seems to lose its force here. Put another (more existential) way, it can be said that the scandal of the death of god and the end of religion and metaphysics placed the moderns in a situation of anxiety and crisis, which now seems to have been fully absorbed by a more fully humanized and socialized, culturalized society: its voids have been saturated and neutralized, not by new values, but by the visual culture of consumerism as such. So the anxieties of the absurd, to take only one example, are themselves recaptured and recontained by a new and postmodern cultural logic, which offers them for consumption fully as much as its other seemingly more anodyne exhibits.

It is thus to this new break that we must turn our attention, and it is in its theorization that Arrighi's analysis of finance capitalism makes a signal contribution, which I first propose to examine in terms of the category of abstraction itself and in particular of that peculiar form of abstraction which is money itself. Worringer's pathbreaking essay on abstraction[10] linked it to distinct cultural impulses, and finally drew its force from the intensifying assimilation, into the West's 'imaginary museum', of more ancient and non-figurative visual materials, which he associates with a kind of death drive. But the crucial intervention for our purposes is Georg Simmel's great essay, 'Metropolis and Mental Life', in which the processes of the new industrial city, very much including the abstract flows of money, determine a whole new and more abstract way of thinking and perceiving, radically different from the object world of the older merchant cities and countryside. What is at stake here is dialectical transformation of the effects of exchange value and monetary equivalence: if the latter had once announced and provoked a new interest in the properties of objects, now, in this new stage, equivalence has as its result a withdrawal from older notions of stable substances and their unifying identifications. Thus, if all these objects have become equivalent as commodities, if money has levelled their intrinsic differences as individual things, one may now purchase as it were their various, henceforth semi-autonomous, qualities or perceptual features; and both colour and shape free themselves from their former vehicles and come to live independent existences as fields of perception and as artistic raw materials. This is then a first stage, but only a first one, in the onset of an abstraction which becomes identified as aesthetic modernism, but which in hindsight should be limited to the historical period of the second stage of capitalist industrialization – that of oil and electricity, that of the combustion engine and the new velocities and technologies of the motorcar, the steamship liner and the flying machine – in the decades immediately preceding and following the turn of the century.

But before continuing this dialectical narrative, we need to return to Arrighi for a moment. We have already spoken of the imaginative way in which Arrighi exfoliates Marx's famous formula, M-C-M', into a supple and cyclical historical narrative. Marx began, as will be remembered, with an inversion of another formula, C-M-C, which characterizes commerce as such: 'the simple circulation of commodities begins with a sale and ends with a purchase'. The merchant sells C and with the

M(oney) received, buys another C: 'the whole process begins when money is received in return for commodities, and comes to an end when money is given up in return for commodities'. It is not, as one can readily imagine, a very profitable trajectory, except in those instances between trading regions in which very special commodities such as salt or spice can be transformed into money as exceptions to the general law of equivalence. Besides this, as has already been said, the centrality of the physical commodites themselves determines a kind of perceptual attention, along with the philosphical categories of the substance, that can only lead to a more realistic aesthetic.

It is, however, the other formula that interests us, for that reversal of this one, which has now become M-C-M, will be the dialectical space in which commerce (or if you prefer merchant capital) is transformed into capital *tout court*. I abridge Marx's explanation (in chapter 4 of *Capital*, Volume I), and merely observe the gradual imposition of the prime on the second M: the moment in which the focus of the operation is no longer on the commodity but on money, and in which its impulse now lies in the investment of money in commodity production, not for its own sake, but to increase the return of M, now M': in other words, the transformation of riches into capital itself, the autonomization of the process of capital accumulation, which asserts its own logic over that of the production and consumption of goods as such, as well as over the individual entrepreneur and the individual worker.

Now I want to introduce a Deleuzian neologism which is this time very relevant (his most famous and successful, I believe) and which seems to me dramatically to enhance our sense of what is at stake in this momentous transformation: this is the word 'deterritorialization', and I think it will immensely clarify the meaning of Arrighi's story. It is a term which has been very widely used for all kinds of different phenomena; but I wish to assert that its first and as it were foundational meaning lies in this very emergence of capitalism itself, as any patient reconstruction of the central role of Marx in the Deleuze–Guattari *Capitalism and Schizophrenia* would demonstrate.[11] The first and most fateful deterritorialization is then this one, in which what Deleuze and Guattari call the axiomatic of capitalism decodes the terms of the older precapitalist coding systems and 'liberates' them for new and more functional combinations. The resonance of the new terms can be measured against an altogether more frivolous and even more successful current media word, 'decontextualization': a term which not improperly suggests that anything wrenched out of its original context (if you can imagine one) will always be recontextualized in new areas and situations. But deterritorialization is far more absolute than that (although its results can indeed be recaptured and even occasionally 'recoded' in new historical situations): for it rather implies a new ontological and free-floating state, one in which the content (to revert to Hegelian language) has definitively been suppressed in favour of the form, in which the inherent nature of the product becomes insignificant, a mere marketing pretext, while the goal of production no longer lies in any specific market, any specific set of consumers or social and individual needs, but rather in its transformation into that element which by definition has no content or territory and indeed no use-value as such, namely money. So it is that in any specific region of production, as Arrighi shows us, there comes a moment in which the logic of capitalism – faced with the saturation of local and even foreign markets – determines an abandonment of that kind of specific production, along with its factories and trained workforce, and, leaving them behind in ruins, takes its flight to other more profitable ventures.

Or, rather, that moment is a dual one: and it is in this demonstration of the two stages of deterritorialization that I see Arrighi's most fundamental originality, and also his most suggestive contribution for cultural analysis today. For one moment is a deterritorialization in which capital shifts to other and more profitable forms of production, often enough in new geographical regions. Another is the grimmer conjuncture, in which the capital of an entire centre or region abandons production altogether in order to seek maximization in those non-productive spaces, which, as we have seen, are those of speculation, the money market, and finance capital in general. Of course, here the word 'deterritorialization' can celebrate its own kinds of ironies: for one of the privileged forms of speculation today is that of land and city space: the new postmodern informational or global cities (as they have been called) thus result very specifically from the ultimate deterritorialization, that of territory as such – the becoming abstract of land and the earth, the transformation of the very background or context of commodity exchange into a commodity in its own right. Land speculation is therefore one face of a process whose other one lies in the ultimate deterritorialization of globalization itself,[12] where it would be a great mistake to imagine something like 'the globe' as yet a new and larger space replacing the older national or imperial ones. Globalization is rather a kind of cyberspace in which money capital has reached its ultimate dematerialization, as messages which pass instantaneously from one nodal point to another across the former globe, the former material world.

I now want to offer some speculations as to the way in which this new logic of finance capital – its radically new forms of abstraction, in particular, which are sharply to be distinguished from those of modernism as such – can be observed to operate in cultural production today, or in what people have come to call postmodernity. What is wanted is an account of abstraction in which the new deterritorialized postmodern contents are to an older modernist autonomization as global financial speculation is to an older kind of banking and credit; or as the stock market frenzies of the eighties are to the Great Depression. I don't particularly want to introduce the theme of the gold standard here, which fatally tends to suggest a really solid and tangible kind of value as opposed to various forms of paper and plastic (or information on your computer). Or perhaps, the theme of gold would become relevant again only to the degree that it was also grasped as an artificial and contradictory system in its own right. What we want to be able to theorize is a modification in the very nature of cultural tokens, and the systems they operate in. If modernism is a kind of cancelled realism, as I have suggested, one which segments and differentiates some initial mimetic starting point, then it might be likened to a largely accepted paper money, whose inflationary ups and downs suddenly leads to the introduction of new and historically original financial and speculative instruments and vehicles.

It is a point of historical change which I want to examine in terms of the fragment and its destiny throughout these various cultural moments. The rhetoric of the fragment has been with us since the dawn of what will later retroactively be identified as modernism, namely with the Schlegels. It will be understood that I think it is something of a misnomer, since the image contents in question are the result, not of breakage, incompletion or extreme wear or tear, but rather of analysis ('to divide each of the difficulties I want to examine into as many smaller parts as possible and as needed in order to solve them' – Descartes). But the word is convenient for want of a better one, and I'll go on using it in this brief discussion. I want to begin by recalling Ken Russell's seemingly jocular remark, that in the twenty-first century, all fiction films will last no longer than fifteen minutes apiece: the implication being that in a Late Show culture like our own, the elaborate preparations we used to require in order to apprehend a series of images as a story of some kind will be, for whatever reason, unnecessary. But actually I think this can be documented by our own experience. Everyone who still visits movie theatres has become aware of the way in which intensified competition by the film industry for now inveterate television viewers has led to a transformation in the very structure of the preview. The latter has had to be developed and expanded, becoming a far more comprehensive teaser for the film in store for us. Now the preview is obliged, not merely to exhibit a few images of the stars and a few samples of the high points, but virtually to recapitulate all the plot's twists and turns, and to preview the entire plot in advance. At length, the inveterate viewer of these enforced coming attractions (five or six of them preceding every feature presentation, and replacing the older kinds of shorts) is led to make a momentous discovery: namely, that the preview is really all you need. You no longer need to see the 'full' two-hour version (unless the object is to kill time, which it so often is). Nor is this something that has to do with the quality of the film (although it may have something to do with the quality of the preview, the better ones being cunningly arranged in such a way that the story they seem to tell is not the same as the 'real story' in the 'real film'). Nor does this new development have much to do with knowing the plot or the story – for, in any case, in contemporary action film, the former story has become little more than a pretext on which to suspend a perpetual present of thrills and explosions. It is thus the images of these which is provided in the seemingly brief anthology of shots and highlights offered by the preview, and they are fully satisfying in themselves, without the benefit of the laborious threads and connections of the former plot. At that point it would seem that the preview, as a structure and a work in its own right, bears something of the same relationship to its supposed final product as those novelized films, written after the fact of the movie and published later on as a kind of xeroxed reminder, is to the filmic original it replicates. The difference is that, in the case of the feature film and its book version, we have to do with completed narrative structures of a similar type, structures both equally antiquated by these new developments. Whereas the preview is a new form, a new kind of minimalism, whose generic satisfactions are distinct from the older kind. It would thus seem that Ken Russell was imperfectly prophetic in his forecast: not in the twenty-first century, but already in this one; and not fifteen minutes, but only two or three!

Of course, what he had in mind was something rather different, for he was evoking MTV, whose imaginative representations of music in visual analogues find their immediate predecessors less in Disney and in music animation than in television commercials as such, which can, at their best, achieve an aesthetic quality of great intensity. Thus, in a sequence purporting to celebrate the transportation conglomerate Norfolk Southern, there erupts upon the screen a horse in full career, shot from below in such a way that its distended body in flight spans swiftly scudding clouds against an omnipresent sky; the sky itself, by metonymy, comes to stand for a movement whose ominous menace is not the least mystery of this visual artifact and seeps into the metamorphoses that follow immediately upon it: the horse now together with its background evolving into an Arcimbaldo assemblage of gadget parts that gallop through an early-industrial background, before entering a mine shaft in which, in the style of Giacometti or Dubuffet, it becomes a mineralized mass of limbs, a form of 'inorganic life' (Deleuze) that strangely echoes the rock surface behind it, before returning to the organic as a composite being made up of corn ears and kernels – Arcimbaldo again! – that races across a field of grain to reach a final metamorphosis as wooden assemblage of joints and prostheses traversing a wood of stripped and smooth tree trunks: the whole sequence no doubt activating some system of the senses at the same time that it emits messages about its cargoes, from the industrial to the agricultural in some peculiar reversal of the normal evolutionary chronology from agriculture and extraction to heavy industry. What kind of a perpetual present is this, and how to disentwine an attention to the persistencies of the Same from that shock of visual difference alone entitled to certify temporal novelty? Metamorphosis – as violent and convulsive, yet static, variation – certainly offers a means of holding on to the thread of narrative time while allowing us to disregard it and to consume a visual plenitude in the present instant; yet it also stands as the abstract monetary container, the empty universal tirelessly refilled with new and shifting content. Yet that content is little more than a fullness of images and stereotypes: the creative transformation not of riches into dead leaves, but rather of banalities into elegant visuals self-consciously offered for the eye's consumption. This particular commercial advertisement, it is worth noting, is regularly screened during an hour-long programme of financial news, where, unlike the accompanying automobile and hotel promotions, it is clearly meant to designate an investment opportunity – investment of images promoting investment of capital.

But it also seems appropriate to turn in a more familiar direction and to juxtapose an explicitly aesthetic practice of the fragment with some emergent postmodern one. It thus seems instructive to contrast the full currency of Buñuel's surrealist films, *An Andalusian Dog* (1928) or *The Golden Age* (1930), or of the very different experimental film-making of Stan Brakhage's *Dog Star Man* (1965), with the junk bonds of Derek Jarman's epic *Last of England* (1987).

As a matter of fact, we ought to note in passing that Jarman also expressed the same formal interest in the innovations of MTV as Russell, but, unlike him, deplored the temporal restrictions of the new mode and dreamed of immense epic-length deployment of this image language, something he was to put into practice in just such a work as this ninety-minute film from 1987 (the longer films by Buñuel and Brakhage run some sixty-two and seventy-five minutes respectively, but it is the comparative quality of their interminabilities that is here in question). Yet, even in the modern, the practice of the fragment resulted in two distinct and antithetical tendencies or strategies: the minimalism of a Webern or a Beckett on the one hand, as opposed to the infinite temporal expansion of Mahler or Proust. Here, in what some people call the postmodern, we might want to juxtapose the brevity of the Russell conception of MTV with the epic temptations of a Jarman or the literal interminability of a text like *Gravity's Rainbow*.

But what I want to bring out, for this speculative discussion of the cultural impact of finance capital, is a rather different property of such image-fragments. It seems appropriate to characterize those of Buñuel, working at the very centre of the classical modern movement, as a practice of the symptom. Deleuze has indeed thus brilliantly described them, in his only apparently idiosyncratic classification of Buñuel (along with Stroheim) under what he calls naturalism: 'The naturalist image, *l'image-pulsion* (the image as drive or libido), knows in fact two kinds of signs: symptoms and idols or fetishes'.[13] The image-fragments in Buñuel are thus forever incomplete, markers of incomprehensible psychic catastrophe, abrupt upshoulderings, obsessions and eruptions, the symptom in its pure form as an incomprehensible language which cannot be translated into any other. Brakhage's practice is completely different from this one, as befits a different historical period and also virtually a different medium, that of experimental film (which I have elsewhere suggested is to be inserted into a kind of ideal genealogy of experimental video rather than of mainstream cinema). This could be described, in analogy with music, as a deployment of quarter tones, of analytic segments of the image which are somehow visually incomplete to eyes still trained for and habituated to our Western visual languages: something like an art of the phoneme rather than of the morpheme or the syllable. Both of these practices, however, share the will to confront us with the structurally incomplete, which, however, dialectically affirms its constitutive relationship with an absence, with something else that is not given and perhaps never can be.

In Jarman's *Last of England*, however, about which words like surrealist have loosely been bandied, what we really confront is the commonplace, the cliché. A feeling tone is certainly developed here: the impotent rage of its punk heroes smiting about themselves with lead pipes, the disgust with the royal family and with traditional trappings of an official English life: but these feelings are themselves clichés and disembodied ones at that. One can certainly speak of the death of the subject here, if by that is meant the substitution for some agonizing personal subjectivity (as in Buñuel) or some organizing aesthetic direction (as in Brakhage) a Flaubertian autonomous life of banal media entities floating through the empty public realm of a galactic Objective Spirit. But everything here is impersonal on the mode of the stereotype, including the rage itself; the most familiar and hackneyed features of a dystopian future: terrorists, canned music classical and popular, along with Hitler's speeches, a predictable parody of the royal wedding, all of this is processed by a painterly eye in order to generate mesmerizing sequences which alternate between black-and-white and colour for purely visual reasons. The narrative or pseudo-narrative segments are certainly longer than anything in Buñuel or Brakhage, yet they sometimes alternate and oscillate, overprint each other as in *Dog Star Man*, while generating an oneiric feeling which is a kind of cliché in its own right and radically different from the obsessive precision of a Buñuel.

How to account for these qualitative differences, which surely themselves imply structural ones? I find myself reverting to Roland Barthes' extraordinary insights in *Mythologies*: Jarman's fragments are meaningful or intelligible, Buñuel's or Brakhage's are not. Barthes' great dictum, that in the contemporary world there is an incompatibility between meaning and experience or the existential, was richly exercised in his *Mythologies*, which denounce the excess of meaning in clichés and ideologies, and the nausea that sheer meaning brings with itself. Authentic language- or image-practice then tries to keep faith with some more fundamental contingency or meaninglessness – a proposition that holds either from an existential or a semiotic perspective. Barthes meanwhile tried to account for the overdose of meaning in the stereotypical by way of the notion of connotation as a kind of second-degree meaning built up provisionally on more literal ones. It is a theoretical tool he was later to abandon, but that we have every interest in revisiting, particularly in the present context.

For I want to suggest that in the modern moment, of both Buñuel and Brakhage, the play of autonomized fragments remains meaningless: the Buñuel symptom is no doubt meaningful as such, but only at a distance and not for us, meaningful no doubt as another side of the carpet we will never see. Brakhage's descent into the fractional states of the image is also meaningless, although in a different way. But Jarman's total flow is only too meaningful, for in him the fragments have been re-endowed with a cultural and mediatic meaning; and here I think we need a concept of the renarrativization of these fragments to complement Barthes' diagnosis of connotation at an earlier stage of mass culture.[14] What happens here is that each former fragment of a narrative, that was once incomprehensible without the narrative context as a whole, has now become capable of emitting a complete narrative message in its own right. It has become autonomous, but not in the formal sense I attributed to modernist processes, and rather in its newly acquired capacity to soak up content and to project it in a kind of instant reflex. Whence the vanishing away of affect in the postmodern: the situation of contingency or meaninglessness, of alienation, has been superseded by this cultural renarrativization of the broken pieces of the image world.

What does all this have to do with finance capital, you may well want to inquire? Modernist abstraction, I believe, is less a function of capital accumulation as such, than rather of money itself in a situation of capital accumulation. Money is here both abstract (making everything equivalent) and empty and uninteresting, since its interest lies outside itself: it is thus incomplete like the modernist images I have been evoking, it directs attention elsewhere, beyond itself, towards what is supposed to complete (and also abolish) it, namely production and value. It knows a semi-autonomy, certainly, but not a full autonomy in which it would constitute a language or a dimension in its own right. But that is precisely what finance capital brings into being: a play of monetary entities which needs neither production (as capital does) nor consumption (as money does): which supremely, like cyberspace, can live on its own internal metabolism and circulate without any reference to an older type of content. But so do the narrativized image-fragments of a stereotypical postmodern language: suggesting a new cultural realm or dimension which is independent of the former real world, not because, as in the modern (or even the romantic) period, culture withdrew from that real world into an autonomous space of art, but rather because the real world has already been suffused with it and colonized by it, so that it has no outside in terms of which it could be found lacking. Stereotypes are never lacking in that sense, and neither is the total flow of the circuits of financial speculation. That each of these also steers unwittingly towards a crash I must leave for another book and another time.

The Brick and the Balloon: Architecture, Idealism and Land Speculation

I want to think aloud about a fundamental theoretical problem – the relationship between urbanism and architecture – which, alongside its own intrinsic interest and urgency, raises a number of theoretical issues of significance to me, although not necess-arily to all of you. So I need to ask for some provisional interest in those issues, and in my own work in relationship to them, in order to reach the point of being able to formulate some more general urban and architectural problems. For instance, an investigation of the dynamics of abstraction in postmodern cultural production, and in particular of the radical difference between that structural role of abstraction in postmodernism and the kinds of abstractions at work in what we now call modernism, or, if you prefer, the various modernisms, has led me to reexamine the money form – the fundamental source of all abstraction – and to ask whether the very structure of money and its mode of circulation has not been substantially modified in recent years, or in other words during the brief period some of us still refer to as postmodernity. That is, of course, to raise again the question of finance capital and its importance in our own time, and to raise formal questions about the relationships between its peculiar and specialized abstractions and those to be found in cultural texts. I think everyone will agree that finance capital, along with globalization, is one of the distinctive features of late capitalism, or in other words of the distinctive state of things today.

But it is precisely this line of inquiry which, reoriented in the direction of architecture itself, suggests the further development I want to pursue here. For in the realm of the spatial, there does seem to exist something like an equivalent of finance capital, indeed a phenomenon intimately related to it, and that is land speculation: something which may have found its field of endeavour in the countryside in bygone years – in the seizure of native American lands, in the acquisition of immense tracts by the railroads, in the development of suburban areas, alongside the privatization of natural resources – but which in our time is a preeminently urban phenomenon (not least because everything is becoming urban) and has returned to the big cities, or to what is left of them, to seek its fortunes. What is then the relationship, if any, between the distinctive form land speculation has taken today and those equally distinctive forms we find in postmodern architecture (now using that term in a general and chronological, hopefully rather neutral, sense)?

It has often been observed that the emblematic significance of architecture today, and also its formal originality, lies in its immediacy to the social, in the 'seam it shares with the economic': and this is a rather different immediacy than even that experienced by other expensive art forms, such as cinema and theatre, which are certainly also dependent on investments. But this very immediacy presents theoretical dangers, which are actually themselves fairly well known. It does not seem preposterous to assert, for example, that land speculation and the new demand for increased construction open up a space in which a new architectural style can emerge: but, to use the time-honoured epithet, it equally seems 'reductive' to explain the new style in terms of the new kinds of investment. It is said that this kind of reductionism fails to respect the specificity, the autonomy or semi-autonomy, of the aesthetic level and its intrinsic dynamics. In fact, it is objected, bald assertions of this kind never seem to descend into the detail of the styles they thereby stigmatize; they are able to neglect formal analysis, having as it were discredited its very principle in advance.

One might then attempt to enrich and complexify this

163

interpretation (of 'the origins of postmodernism') by introducing the matter of new technologies and showing how they dictated a new style at the same time that they responded more adequately to the aims of the investments. This is then to insert a 'mediation' between the economic level and the aesthetic one; and it can begin to give an idea of why, for the immediacy of an assertion about economic determination, we would do better to elaborate a series of mediations between the economic and the aesthetic; in other words, of why we need a revitalized conception of the mediation as such. The concept of mediation is posited on the existence of what I have referred to as a 'level', or in other words (those of Niklas Luhmann) a differentiated social function, a realm or zone within the social that has developed to the point at which it is governed internally by its own intrinsic laws and dynamics. I want to call such a realm 'semi-autonomous', because it is clear that it is still somehow part of the social totality, as the term *function* suggests; my own term is deliberately ambiguous or ambivalent, in order to suggest a two-way street, in which one can either emphasize the relative independence, the relative autonomy, of the area in question, or else, the other way round, insist on its functionality and its ultimate place in the whole: at least by way of its consequences for the whole, if not its 'function', understood as a kind of material interest and slavish or subservient motivation. So, to use a few of Luhmann's more obvious examples, the political is a distinct 'level', because, since Machiavelli and since the emergence of the modern state under Richelieu, politics is a semi-autonomous realm in modern societies, with its own mechanisms and procedures, its own personnel, its own history and traditions, or 'precedents', and so forth. But this does not imply that the political level does not have manifold consequences for what lies outside it. The same can be said for the realm of law, the legal or juridical level, which might in many ways be said to be the model and exemplar of just such a specialized and semi-autonomous domain. Those of us who do cultural work will no doubt also want to insist on a certain semi-autonomy of the aesthetic or the cultural (even though the relationship between those two alternate formulations is today once again a very contested topic indeed): the laws of storytell-

ing, even for television series, are surely not immediately redu-
cible to the institutions of parliamentary democracy, let alone
the operations of the stock market.

And what about that – the stock market itself? It is certain
that the emergence of the market, and of the theory of the
market, from the eighteenth century onwards, has formed the
economy over into a semi-autonomous level, if it was not one
before. As for money and land, well, those are precisely the
phenomena that will concern us here, and which will allow us
to test the usefulness of both the concept of mediation and its
related idea, the semi-autonomous instance or level: it being
understood in advance that neither money nor land can constitute such a level in its own right, since both are clearly functional
elements within that more fundamental system or sub-system
which is the market and the economy.

Any discussion of money as a mediation needs to confront
the work of Georg Simmel, whose massive *Philosophy of Money*
(1900) pioneered what we would today call a phenomenological
analysis of this peculiar reality. Simmel's subterranean influence
on a variety of twentieth-century thought currents is incalculable, partly because he resisted coining his complex thinking into
an identifiable system; meanwhile, the complicated articulations
of what is essentially a non-Hegelian or decentred dialectic are
often smothered by his heavy prose. A new account of his life
work would be an indispensable preliminary stage in the
discussion I want to stage here:[1] to be sure, Simmel bracketed
the economic structures themselves, but is very suggestive for
the ways in which the phenomenological as well as the cultural
effects of finance capital might be described and explored.
Clearly, this is not the moment for any such full-dress study,
and so I will limit myself to a few remarks on his seminal essay,
'Metropolis and Mental Life', in which money also plays a
central role.[2]

It is fundamentally an account of the increasing abstraction
of modern life, and most particularly of urban life (in the Berlin
of the late nineteenth century): abstraction is, to be sure,
precisely my topic, and still one very much with us, sometimes
under different names (Anthony Gidden's key term *disembed-
ding*, for example, says very much the same thing while directing

us to other features of the process). And in Simmel's essay, abstraction takes on a remarkable multiplicity of forms, from the experience of time to some new distance in personal relations; from what he calls 'intellectualism' to new kinds of freedom; from indifference and the 'blasé' to new anxieties, value crises and those big-city crowds so dear to Baudelaire and Walter Benjamin. It would be an oversimplification to conclude that for Simmel money is the cause of all these new phenomena: not only does the big city triangulate this matter, but in our present context surely the concept of mediation is a more satisfactory one. In any case, Simmel's essay places us on the threshold of a theory of modern aesthetic forms and of their abstraction from older logics of perception and production; but it also places us on the threshold of the emergence of abstraction within money itself, namely what we now call finance capital.[3] And within the Benjaminian collage of phenomena that makes up the essay's texture we also find the following fateful sentence: discussing the new internal dynamics of abstraction, the way in which, like capital itself, it begins to expand under its own moment, Simmel tells us this: 'This may be illustrated by the fact that within the city the "unearned increment" of ground rent, through a mere increase in traffic, brings to its owner profits which are self-generating.'[4] It is enough: these are the connections we have been looking for; now let us retrace our steps and begin again with the possible kinships between modern or postmodern architectural form and the self-multiplying exploitations of the space of the great industrial cities.

I have been particularly interested, in this respect, in a badly organized and repetitive book, which, like a good detective story, has an exciting narrative to tell and has all the excitement of discovery and revelation: this is *The Assassination of New York*, by Robert Fitch, and it will offer the occasion not merely to confront the urban with the architectural, but also to assess the function of land speculation and to compare the explanatory value of various theories (and the place of mediations in them). Put baldly, as he himself does fairly often, Fitch conceives of the 'assassination' of New York as the process whereby – deliberately – production is driven out of the city in order to make way for business office space (finance, insurance, real estate): the policy is supposed to revitalize the city and promote new growth, and its failure is documented by the astonishing percentage of floor space left vacant and unrented (so-called see-through buildings). Fitch's theoretical authority here seems to be Jane Jacobs, whose doctrine about the relationship of small business to the flourishing neighbourhood he enhances by positing the equally necessary relationship between small business (shops and the like) and small industry (of the garment district type). His is a radical rather than a Marxian analysis, which aims to promote activism and partisanship; he therefore lashes out at a variety of theoretical targets, which include certain Marxisms and certain postmodernisms along with the official ideologies of the city planners themselves; and it is these polemics (or rather, these denunciations) which will mainly interest us here. Making allowances for a characteristically American anti-intellectualism and anti-academic stance, it seems evident enough that Fitch's primary theoretical target is the doctrine of historical inevitability, in whatever form it is to be found: no doubt on the grounds that it demoralizes and depoliticizes those who begin believing in it and makes political mobilization and resistance much more difficult, if not altogether impossible. This is a plausible and pertinent position, but finally all conceptions of long-range trends and of a meaningful logic of capitalism become identified with this 'inevitabilist' ideology, and this in turn rebounds onto the very forms of praxis Fitch wishes to promote, as we shall see.

But let's begin all over again at the beginning. What is first to be shown is not only that New York has undergone a massive restructuration in which 750,000 manufacturing jobs have disappeared, and in which the ratio of manufacturing to office work (his acronym is FIRE: finance, insurance, real estate) has been modified from 2:1 before the war to 1:2 today,[5] but also that this change (not inevitable! not in the 'logic of capital'!) was the result of a deliberate policy on the part of New York's power structure. It was, in other words, the result of what is today widely and loosely called 'conspiracy', something for which the evidence is very suggestive indeed. It lies in the absolute congruence between the unrealized 1928 zoning plan for the metropolitan area and the current state of things: the removal of manufacturing posited there has been realized here, the implantation of office buildings foreseen there has here come to pass; and Fitch supplements all this with lavish quotes from the planners of yesteryear and those of the recent past. For example this, from an influential businessman and political figure of the 1920s:

> Some of the poorest people live in conveniently located slums on high-priced land. On patrician Fifth Avenue, Tiffany and Woolworth, cheek by jowl, offer jewels and jimcracks from substantially identical sites. Childs' restaurants thrive and multiply where Delmonico's withered and died. A stone's throw from the stock exchange the air is filled with the aroma of roasting coffee; a few hundred feet from Times Square with the stench of slaughter houses. In the very heart of this 'commercial' city, on Manhattan Island south of 59th Street, the inspectors in 1922 found nearly 420,000 workers employed in factories. Such a situation outrages one's sense of order. Everything seems misplaced. One yearns to rearrange things to put things where they belong.[6]

Such statements clearly reinforce the proposition that the aim of getting rid of the garment district and the port of New York was a conscious one, elaborated in a number of strategies over the fifty-year period between the late 1920s and the 1980s which were finally successful, entailing in the process the deterioration of the city in its present form. One does not particularly have to argue about the evaluation of the result, but the motivation behind this 'conspiracy' does now need to be set in place. Unsurprisingly it has to do with land speculation and the stunning appreciation of land values which results from the 'liberation' of real estate from its occupancy of various kinds of small businesses and manufacture. 'There is a nearly 1000 percent spread between the rent received for factory space and the rent landlords get for class A office space. Simply by changing the land use, one's capital could increase in value many times. Presently, a long-term U.S. bond yields something on the order of 6 percent.'[7]

Behind this more general 'conspiratorial' explanation, there lies, as we shall see, a more specific and local conspiracy whose investigators will be named in time. But this particular explanation, on this level of generality, in fact tends to confirm a more properly Marxian notion of the 'logic of capital', and in particular of the causal relationship of such immediate real estate developments to a (relatively cyclical) notion of the moment of finance capital, which interests me in the present context. Save for one exception, which will be identified in the second conspiracy theory, and which will be touched on later, Fitch is not interested in the cultural level of these developments, or in the kind of architecture or architectural style which might accompany a deployment of finance capital. These are presumably superstructural epiphenomena which it is customary to dismiss in debunking analyses of this kind, or which such analyses tend to see as a kind of cultural and ideological smokescreen for the real processes (in other words, an implicit apology for them). We'll come back to this central problem of the relationship between art or culture and the economy later on.

For the moment, what needs to be observed is that concepts of 'trends' or the inevitability of the logic of capital do not give a complete or even an adequate picture of the Marxian view of these processes: what is missing is the crucial idea of contradiction. For the very notion of trends in investment, capital flight, the movement of finance capital away from manufacturing and into land speculation, is inseparable from the contradictions that produce these uneven investment possibilities across the field, but also, and above all, from the impossibility of resolving them. This is in fact exactly what Fitch shows with his impressive statistics about vacancy rates in the new speculative construction of white-collar office buildings: the redeployment of investments in that direction also solves nothing, having destroyed the viable city fabric that would have produced new returns (and increasing employment) in those spaces in the first place. There could obviously be a narrative satisfaction in this outcome, too ('the wages of sin'); but clearly enough, from Fitch's point of view, the prospect of inevitable contradictions – which might enhance a rather different conception of the possibilities of political action – is equally incompatible with the kind of activism he has in mind.

At this stage, we already have several levels of abstraction: at the most rarefied end, a conception of the preponderance of finance capital today, which Giovanni Arrighi has usefully redefined for us as a moment in the historical development of capital as such.[8] Arrighi posits, indeed, three stages – first, the investment-seeking implantation of capital in a new region; then, the productive development of that region in terms of industry and manufacture; and finally, a deterritorialization of the capital in heavy industry in order for it to seek its reproduction and multiplication in financial speculation – after which this same capital takes flight to a new region and the cycle begins again. Arrighi finds his point of departure in a phrase of Fernand Braudel – 'the stage of financial expansion is always a sign of autumn' – and thus inscribes his analysis of finance capital on a spiral, rather than, in some static and structural fashion, as a permanent and relatively stable feature of 'capitalism' everywhere. To think otherwise is to relegate the most striking economic developments of the Reagan–Thatcher era (developments which are also cultural ones, as I want to argue) to the realm of sheer illusion and epiphenomena; or to consider them, as Fitch seems to do here, as the merest and most noxious by-products of a conspiracy whose conditions of possibility remain unexplained. The shift from investments in production to speculation on the stock market, the globalization of finance and – what concerns us especially here – the new level of a frenzied engagement with real estate values: these are realities with fundamental consequences for social life today (as the rest of Fitch's book so dramatically demonstrates for the admittedly very special case of New York City); and the effort to theorize those new developments is very far from being an academic matter.

But with this in mind, we may turn to Fitch's other basic polemic target, which he tends to associate with Daniel Bell's old idea of a 'postindustrial' society, a social order in which the classic dynamics of capitalism have been displaced, and perhaps even replaced, by the primacy of science and technology, itself now offering a different kind of explanation of the alleged shift from a production to a service economy. The critique here is thus focused on two not necessarily related hypotheses. The one posits a well-nigh structural mutation of the economy away from heavy industry and in the direction of an unaccountably massive service sector: it thereby offers ideological support to the elite New York planners who wish to deindustrialize New York and can therefore find aid and comfort in the notion of the historical inevitability of the 'end' of production in its older sense. But the commodification of services can also be accounted for in a Marxian framework (and was so explained, prophetically, as long ago as Harry Braverman's great book, *Labor and Monopoly Capital*, in 1974); I won't pursue that point any further here, particularly since the development Fitch has principally in mind concerns office workers in business high-rises more specifically than the service industries.

The second idea he associates with that of Bell's putative 'postindustrial society' has to do with globalization and the cybernetic revolution, in the process taking sideswipes at some very eminent contemporary accounts of the new global or informational city (by Manual Castells and Saskia Sassen in particular).[9] But surely the emphasis on the new communications technologies need not imply a commitment to Bell's notorious hypothesis of a change in the mode of production itself. The replacement of water power by gas and later on by electricity involved momentous mutations in the spatial dynamics of capitalism, as well as in the nature of daily life, the structure of the labour process and the very constitution of the social fabric: but the system remained capitalist. It is true that a whole variegated ideology of the communicational and the cybernetic has emerged in recent years, and that it merits theoretical challenge, ideological analysis and critique, and sometimes even outright deconstruction. On the other hand, the account of capital developed by Marx and by so many others since his day can perfectly well accommodate the changes in question; and indeed the dialectic itself has as its most vital philosophical function to coordinate two aspects or faces of history which we otherwise seem ill-equipped to think: namely, identity and difference all at once, the way in which a thing can both change and remain the same, can undergo the most astonishing mutations and expansions and still constitute the operation of some basic and persistent structure. Indeed, one can argue as some have that the contemporary period, which includes all these spatial and technological innovations, may approximate Marx's abstract model more satisfactorily than the still semi-industrial and semi-agricultural societies of Marx's own day.[10] More modestly, however, I simply want to suggest that whatever the historical truth of the hypothesis about the cybernetic revolution, it is enough to register a widespread belief in it and in its effects, not merely on the part of elites but also in the populations of the First World states, for such a belief to constitute a social fact of the greatest importance, which cannot be dismissed as sheer error. In that case, one must also see Fitch's work dialectically, as an effort to restore the other part of the famous sentence, to remind us that it is people who still make this history, even if they make it 'in circumstances not of their own choosing'.

We must therefore look a little more closely into this question of the people who have made the spatial history of New York, and this brings us to the inner or more concrete conspiracy which Fitch dramatically wishes to disclose to us, complete with the names of the perpetrators and an account of their activities. We have already noted one level of the operation – that of New York's planners, who are also part of the circle of New York's financial and business elite; and Fitch has certainly named names here and given brief accounts of some of the careers of the players; but at a still relatively collective level, in which these concrete biographical people still represent a general class dynamic. It does not seem unfair to invoke the dialectic one more time by observing that, in so far as Fitch wishes to appeal to the activism of individuals in his political programme for the regeneration of New York, he is also obliged to identify specific individuals on the other side and to validate his claim that individuals can still accomplish things in history with an equal demonstration that individuals have already done so, and have brought us to this sorry pass by way of their agency as private people (and not as disembodied classes).

Ironically, and it is an irony he himself points out, there is a precedent for such an account of a specifically individual conspiracy against the city; and this lies in the identification of Robert Moses as the fundamental agent and villain in its transformations, an account we owe to Robert Caro's extraordinary biography, *The Powerbroker*. We will see in a moment

172

why Fitch needs to resist this particular account, suggesting that its function is to make Moses into the scapegoat for these developments: 'in retrospect it will turn out that Moses' greatest civic accomplishment was not the Coliseum or Jones Beach but taking the rap for two generations of New York City planning failures'.[11] Fair enough: every causal level invites the deeper digging for another one and sends us back another step, to construct a more fundamental 'causal level' behind it: was Moses really a world-historical actor, was he really acting on his own, and so on? And it is true that behind the richness of Caro's variegated accounts, there eventually looms a purely psychological dimension: because Moses was like that, because he wanted power and activity, because he had the genius to foresee all the possibilities, and so forth. Fitch's implicit critique is, however, more telling (and it tells against his own ultimate version of the narrative as well): the private individual Moses is not representative enough to bear the whole weight of the story, which demands an agent who is both individual and represent-ative of collectivity all at once.

Enter Nelson Rockefeller: for it is he, or rather the Rockefeller family themselves as a group of individuals, who will now offer the key to the mystery story and serve as the centre of Fitch's new version of the tale. I will quickly summarize this interesting new story: it begins with a disastrous mistake on the part of the Rockefeller family (or, more particularly, John D. Rockefeller Jr), which was to take out a twenty-one-year lease from Columbia University on the midtown plot of land on which Rockefeller Center now stands: we are in 1928, and from that date, Fitch tells us, 'to 1988 when they flip Rockefeller Center to the Japanese, understanding what the Rockefellers want is prerequisite to grasping what the city becomes'.[12] We need to ground that understanding in two facts: first, Rockefeller Center is initially a failure, that is to say, occupancy rates in the 1930s range only from '30 percent to 60 percent'[13] owing to its eccentric positioning in the midtown; many of the tenants being peers whom the Rockefellers have made special arrangements to attract (or to coerce, as the case may be). 'It was Nelson who had digested the results of the transit study which the family had commissioned to find out why Rockefeller Center was empty. The principal reason, the consultants explained, was that Rockefeller Center lacked access to mass transit. It was too far from Times Square. Too far from Grand Central. Mass transit was the key to healthy office development, the automobile was killing it.'[14] As we have already indicated, the motivation behind a development of this kind lies in the fabulous appreciation in value of the developed property: but under the twin circumstances of massive vacancies and the rental obligations to Columbia, the Rockefellers are unable to make good on these future prospects.

The second crucial fact, according to Fitch, is to be documented in Richardson Dillworth's testimony at Nelson Rockefeller's vice-presidential confirmation hearing in 1974,[15] which not only revealed 'that by far the bulk of the family's $1.3 billion wealth came from midtown – the equity in Rockefeller Center', but also the degree to which the family fortune had at that point 'dwindled spectacularly', and indeed, by the mid 1970s, 'shrunk by two-thirds'. This particular real estate investment thus marks a desperate crisis in the fortunes of the Rockefellers, a crisis that can only be surmounted in four ways: either the lease with Columbia is modified in their favour (understandably enough, the University is unwilling to comply), or it is abandoned altogether, with disastrous losses. Or the area immediately surrounding the Center is favourably developed by the Rockefellers themselves: a solution that in effect means pouring more good money in after bad. Or else, since 'other obstacles seemed insuperable without changing the structure of the city, ... this is precisely what the family now proceeded to do. Ultimately, the city officials proved far easier to manipulate than the trustees of Columbia University or the thirties real estate market'.[16] It is a breathtaking and Promethean proposition: to change the whole world in order to accommodate the self: even Fitch is somewhat embarrassed at his own daring. 'How could such a family [their civic and cultural achievements having been enumerated] be totally obsessed with such mean endeavors as driving hot dog sellers away from 42nd Street?' 'An explanation relying on the behavior of one family, it must be conceded, seems less than robust. ... Doctrinaire historical determinists will naturally insist that

New York would be "just the same" without the Rockefellers'. 'A focus on the family may annoy academic Marxists for whom the capitalist is only the personification of abstract capital and who believe, austerely, that any discussion of individuals in economic analysis represents a fatal concession to populism and empiricism'. And so on.[17]

On the contrary, Fitch here gives us a textbook demonstration of the 'logic of capital', and in particular of that Hegelian 'ruse of Reason' or 'ruse of History' whereby a collective process uses individuals for its own ends. The idea comes from Hegel's early study of Adam Smith and is in fact a transposition of the latter's well-known identification of the 'invisible hand' of the market. Discussions of Hegel's version mostly assume that the crucial distinction here runs between conscious action and unconscious meaning; I think it is better to posit a radical disjunction between the individual (and the meanings and motives of individual action) and the logic of the collective, or of History, of the systemic. From their point of view – and on Fitch's own interpretation – the Rockefellers were very conscious of their project, which was a completely rational one. As for the systemic consequences, we are of course free to suppose that they could not foresee them, or even that they did not care. But on the dialectical reading, those consequences are part and parcel of a systemic logic which is radically different from the logic of individual action, with which it can only rarely, and with great effort, be held together within the problematic confines of a single thought.

I need to make a brief digression at this point on the philosophical positions at stake here. Hegel was very conscious of chance, or, as we would call it today, of contingency;[18] and a necessary contingency is always foreseen in his larger systemic narratives, which however do not always insist on it explicitly, so that the occasional reader may be forgiven for overlooking Hegel's own commitment to it. Yet at the level of chance and contingency systemic processes are very far from being inevitable; they can be interrupted, nipped in the bud, deflected, slowed down, and so forth. Remember that Hegel's perspective is a retrospection, which only seeks to rediscover the necessity and the meaning of what has already happened: the famous owl of Minerva that flies at dusk. Perhaps, since contemporary historians have rediscovered the constitutive role of warfare in history with such gusto, a military analogy may be appropriate: the 'conditions not of our own making' can then be identified as the military situation, the terrain, the disposition of forces, and the like; the individual then in the synthesis of perception organizes all that data into a unified field in which the options and the opportunities become visible. It is this last which is the realm of individual creativity with respect to history, and, as we shall see later on, it holds for artistic and cultural creation just as much as for the individual capitalists.[19] A collective movement of resistance is on a somewhat different level, even though famously there are moments in which individual leaders also have just such strategic as well as tactical perceptions of possibility. But the ruse of History runs both ways; and if individual capitalists can sometimes be instrumental in working towards their own undoing (the deterioration of New York City is not a bad example), so also left movements sometimes unwittingly promote the 'cause' of their adversaries (in impelling them to new technological innovations, for example). A satisfactory conception of politics is one in which both the systemic and the individual are somehow coordinated (or, if you prefer, to use a popular slogan Fitch often parodies here, in which the global and the local are somehow reconnected).

But now we need to move more rapidly in two directions at once (perhaps these are indeed some version of the systemic and the local): one road leads us towards the individual buildings themselves; the other towards a further interrogation of finance capital and land speculation which can be expected to bring us at length to that knotty theoretical problem which the Marxian tradition quaintly designates as 'ground rent'. The building looms up first, or rather the complex of buildings, and it is best to respect its unavoidability. It is of course Rockefeller Center: the stake in all these manoeuvres, and the object of a good deal of interesting architectural analysis. Fitch seems relatively bemused by such discussions: 'the modern architectural equivalent of a medieval cathedral', he quotes Carol Krinsky as saying, correcting this seemingly positive assessment with Douglas Heskell's perception of the Center as 'some giant burial place' before washing his own hands of the matter: 'there is no way to confirm or disconfirm perceived symbolic values'.[20] I think he is mistaken about this: there are certainly ways of analyzing such 'perceived symbolic values' as social and historical facts (I don't know what 'confirm' or 'disconfirm' might mean here). What is clearer is that Fitch is not interested in doing so, and that in terms of his own analysis the cultural icing has little enough to do with the ingredients out of which the cake has been baked (along with the availability of the ovens, and so on). Oddly, this disjunction of symbolic value and economic activity is also registered by the work of one of the subtlest and most complex contemporary architectural theorists, Manfredo Tafuri himself, who has devoted a whole monograph to the context in which the Center is to be evaluated.

Tafuri's interpretive method can be described as follows: the premise is that, at least in this society (under capitalism), an individual building will always stand in contradiction with its urban context and also with its social function. The interesting buildings are those which try to resolve those contradictions through more or less ingenious formal and stylistic innovations. The resolutions are necessarily failures, because they remain in an aesthetic realm that is disjoined from the social one from which such contradictions spring; and also because social or systemic change would have to be total rather than piecemeal. So Tafuri's analyses tend to be a litany of failures, and the 'imaginary resolutions' are often described at a high level of abstraction, giving the picture of an interplay of 'isms' or disembodied styles, which it is left to the reader to restore to concrete perception.

In the case of Rockefeller Center, however, we may well face a redoubling of this situation: for Tafuri and his colleagues, on whose collective volume *The American City* I draw here, also seem to think that the situation of the American city (and the buildings to be constructed in it) is somehow doubly contradictory. The absence of a past, waves of immigration, construction on a tabula rasa: these are certainly features one would expect the Italian observer to insist on. But the Americans are contradicted twice over, doubly doomed so to speak, because in addition their very formal raw materials are borrowed European styles, which they can only coordinate and amalgamate in various ways, without seemingly being able to invent any new ones. In other words, the invention of the New is already impossible and contradictory in the general context of capitalism; but the eclecticism of a play of those already impossible styles in the US then replays that impossibility and those contradictions at one remove.

Tafuri's discussion of Rockefeller Center is embedded in a larger discussion of the symbolic value of the American skyscraper itself, which at the outset constitutes 'an organism that, by its very nature, defies all rules of proportion' and thus wishes to soar out of the city and against it as a 'unique event'.[21] Yet as the industrial city and its corporate organization progresses, 'the skyscraper as an "event", as an "anarchic individual" that, by projecting its image into the commercial center of the city, creates an unstable equilibrium between the independence of a single corporation and the organization of collective capital, no longer appear[s] to be a completely suitable structure'.[22] As I follow the complex and detailed history that Tafuri then outlines (running from the Chicago Tribune competition in 1922 all the way to the construction of Rockefeller Center itself in the early 1930s), I seem to be reading a dialectical narrative in which the skyscraper evolves away from its status as 'unique event', and towards a new conception of the enclave, within the city but apart from it, now reproducing something of the complexity of the city on a smaller scale: the 'enchanted mountain', in its failure to engage the city fabric in some new and innovative way, is thus doomed to make itself over into a miniature city within the city, and thus to abandon the fundamental contradiction it was called upon to resolve. Rockefeller Center will now serve as the climax of this development.

In Rockefeller Center (1931–1940), the anticipatory ideas of Saarinen, the programs of the Regional Plan of New York, Ferriss's images, and Hood's various pursuits were finally brought into synthesis. This statement is true in spite of the fact that Rockefeller Center was completely divorced from any regionalist conception and that it thoroughly ignored any urban considerations beyond the three midtown lots on which the complex was to rise. It was, in fact, a selective synthesis, the significance of which lies precisely in its choices and rejections. From Saarinen's Chicago lakefront, Rockefeller Center drew only its amplified scale and the coordinated unity of a skyscraper complex related to an open space provided with services for the public. From the recently developed taste for the International style, it accepted volumetric purity, without, however, renouncing the enrichments of Art Deco. From Adam's images of the new Manhattan, it extracted the concept of a contained and rational concentration, an oasis of order. Moreover, all the concepts accepted were stripped of any utopian character; Rockefeller Center in no way contested the established institutions or the current dynamics of the city. Indeed, it took its place in Manhattan as an island of 'equilibrated speculation' and emphasized in every way its character as a closed and circumscribed intervention, which nevertheless purported to serve as a model.[23]

And now the allegorical interpretation becomes clearer: the Center was 'an attempt to celebrate the reconciliation of the trusts and the collectivity on an urban scale'.[24] This, and not cultural window-dressing, is the symbolic significance of the building; and its eclectic play of styles – for Tafuri as superficial a decoration as for Fitch – has the function of signifying 'collective culture' to its general public and of documenting the claim of the Center to address public concerns, as much as to secure business and financial objectives.

Before turning to another related and even more contemporary analysis of Rockefeller Center, however, it may be worth recalling the emblematic value of the Center for the modernist tradition itself. Indeed, it figures prominently in what was surely for many years the fundamental text and ideological statement of architectural modernism, namely Siegfried Giedion's *Space, Time and Architecture*, which, promoting a new time–space aesthetic in the wake of Le Corbusier, in order to invent a viable contemporary alternative for the Baroque tradition of city planning, saw the fourteen associated buildings of the Center as a unique attempt to implant a new conception of urban design within the (to him intolerable) constriction of Manhattan's grid. The original fourteen buildings occupied 'an area of almost three city blocks (around twelve acres) ... cut out from New York's checkerboard grid'. These buildings, of variable height, and at least one of them, the RCA building, a skyscraper slab some seventy stories tall, 'are freely disposed in space and enclose an open area, the Rockefeller Plaza, which is used as an ice-skating rink throughout the winter'.[25]

In the light of what has been said, it will not be inappropriate to characterize Giedion's space–time concept, at least in the US context, as a Robert Moses aesthetic, in so far as his principal examples are the first great parkways (brand-new in this period), about which he celebrates the kinetic experience: 'Riding up and down the long sweeping grades produced an exhilarating dual feeling, one of being connected with the soil and yet of hovering just above it, a feeling like nothing else so much as sliding swiftly on skis through untouched snow down the sides of high mountains'.[26]

The bleakness of Tafuri's readings always stemmed from the principled absence in his work of any possible future aesthetic, any fantasized solution to the dilemmas of the capitalist city, any avant-garde path by which art might hope to make a contribution to a world-transformation which could for him only be economic and political. Obviously the modern movement itself meant precisely all these things, and Giedion's space–time concept, now so distant from us and so redolent of a bygone age, was an influential attempt to synthesize its various tendencies.

It implied a transcendence of individual experience that presumably also promised an expansion of it, in the world of the automobile and the airplane. Thus, of Rockefeller Center, Giedion asserts:

> nothing new or significant can be observed in looking over a map of the site. The ground plan reveals nothing. . . . The actual arrangement and disposition of the buildings can be seen and grasped only from the air. An air-view picture reveals that the various high buildings are spread out in an open arrangement . . . like the vanes of a windmill, the different volumes so placed that their shadows fall as little as possible upon one another. . . . Moving in the midst of the buildings through Rockefeller Plaza . . . one becomes conscious of new and unaccustomed interrelations between them. They cannot be grasped from any single position or embraced in any single view. . . . [This produces] an extraordinary new effect, some-

what like that of a rotating sphere of mirrored facets in a ballroom when the facets reflect whirling spots of light in all directions and in every dimension.[27]

This is not the place to evaluate the modernist aesthetic more comprehensively, but rather the moment to observe that – whatever the value of Giedion's aesthetic enthusiasm – it seems to have been wiped out by the proliferation of such buildings and spaces across Manhattan altogether: or perhaps one should say this negatively and suggest that the modernist euphoria was dependent on the relative scarcity of such new projects, spaces and constructions: Rockefeller Center is for the 1930s, and thereby for Giedion at that moment, a *novum*, something it no longer is for us.

When this space is utterly overbuilt, then, as it is today, the need arises for a rather different kind of aesthetic, which, as we have seen, Tafuri refuses to provide. But what Tafuri deplores and Giedion does not yet anticipate – a chaos of overbuilding and congestion – it is the originality of Rem Koolhaas to celebrate and to embrace. *Delirious New York* thus enthusiastically welcomes the contradictions Tafuri denounces, and makes of this resolute embrace of the irresolvable a new aesthetic of a very different kind from Giedion's: an aesthetic for which, however, Rockefeller Center again stands as a peculiarly central lesson.

Koolhaas's reading of the Center is of course embedded in his more general proposition about the enabling structure of the Manhattan grid; but what I want to underscore here is the specificity with which he is able to endow Tafuri's still very abstract formulation of the fundamental contradiction (the two discussions, as far as I can see, taking place completely independently of each other and without cross-reference). For now it becomes Raymond Hood's inner 'schizophrenia' as expressed, for example, in his impertinent combination of an immense parking garage with the solemnity of an enormous house of prayer in Columbus, Ohio, which makes him over into the fittest Hegelian instrument for Manhattan's 'ruse of Reason', allowing him 'simultaneously to derive energy and inspiration from Manhattan as irrational fantasy *and* to establish its unprecedented theorems in a series of strictly rational steps';[28] or, to take a slightly different formulation, to achieve an artefact (in this case, the McGraw-Hill Building) which 'looks like a fire raging inside an iceberg: the fire of Manhattanism inside the iceberg of Modernism'.[29]

But the more definitive account of the opposition will posit the term *congestion*, along with its novel solution in Hood's 'city within a city', namely to 'solve congestion by creating more congestion' and to interiorize it within the building complex itself.[30] The concept of congestion now condenses several different meanings: use and consumption, the urban, but also the business exploitation of the parcels, traffic along with ground rent, but also the foregrounding of the collective or popular, populist appeal. It can be seen that it is itself the mediation between all these hitherto distinct features of the phenomenon and the problem; just as Koolhaas's more general specification serves as the mediation between Tafuri's abstractions and a consideration of the concrete building complex in either architectural or commercial terms. The other term of the antithesis is less definitively formulated, probably because it runs the danger of endorsing the Center's taste or aesthetic: sometimes in Koolhaas's account it is simply 'beauty' ('the paradox of maximum congestion combined with maximum beauty'),[31] just as in Tafuri it is often simply 'spirituality'. But clearly enough this gesture towards the cultural realm and its function as a Barthesian 'sign' or connotation can itself be prolonged and incrementally specified. The crucial operation is the establishment of a mediation capable of translation in either direction: able to function as a characterization of the economic determinants of this construction within the city fully as much as it can offer directions for aesthetic analysis and cultural interpretation.

Put another way, these analyses seem both to demand and to evade the traditional academic question about the aesthetic, namely that of value. As a work of art, how is Rockefeller Center to be judged; indeed, does this question have any relevance at all in the present context? Both Tafuri and Koolhaas centre their discussions on the act of the architect himself: on what he confronts in the situation, let alone the raw materials and forms; on the deeper contradictions he must somehow resolve in order to build anything – and in particular on the tension between the urban fabric or totality and the individual building or monument (in this case the peculiar role and structure of the skyscraper). It is an analysis that can cut either way, as in the now time-honoured formula of imaginary toads in real gardens; or, as Kenneth Burke liked to put it, the interesting peculiarity of the slogan 'symbolic act' is that you can and must choose your emphasis in a necessarily binary way. The work may thus turn out to be a symbolic *act*, a real form of praxis in the symbolic realm; but it might also prove to be a merely *symbolic* act, an attempt to act in a realm in which action is impossible and does not exist as such. I thus have the feeling that for Tafuri, Rockefeller Center is this last – a merely symbolic act, which necessarily fails to resolve its contradictions; whereas for Koolhaas, it is the fact of creative and productive action within the symbolic that is the source of aesthetic excitement. But perhaps, on both accounts, the problem is simply that we have to do with a bad, or at best a mediocre, set of buildings: so that the question of value is then out of place and excluded from the outset. Yet in this context, in which the individual building seeks somehow to secure its place within the urban, and within a real city that already exists, is it possible that all buildings are bad, or at least failures in this sense? Or is the aesthetic of the individual building radically to be disjoined from the problem of the urban in such a way that the problems raised by each belong and remain in separate compartments (or dare I say in separate departments)?

But now I want to turn briefly to the other basic issue, the matter of 'ground rent', before making some hypotheses about the relationship between architecture and finance capital today. The problem of the value of land at best posed well-nigh insuperable difficulties for classical political economy, not least because in that period (the eighteenth and early nineteenth centuries) the process whereby traditional and often collective holdings were being commodified and privatized as Western capitalism developed was substantially incomplete: and this included the basic historical and structural tendency towards the commodification of farm labour, or in other words the transformation of peasants into agricultural workers, a process far more complete today than it was even at the time of Marx, let alone that of Ricardo. But the elimination of the peasantry as a feudal class or caste is not the same as the elimination of the problem of land values and ground rent. I must pay tribute here to David Harvey's *The Limits to Capital*, which is not only one of the most lucid and satisfying recent attempts to outline Marx's economic thought, but also perhaps the only one to tackle the thorny problem of ground rent in Marx, whose own analysis was cut short by his death, its published, posthumous version cobbled together by Engels. I don't want to get into the theory, but only to report that, according to Harvey's magisterial review and re-theorization (he offers us a plausible account of the more complicated scheme Marx might have elaborated had he lived), ground rent and value in land are both essential to the dynamic of capitalism and also a source of contradiction for it: if too much investment is immobilized in land, there are problems; if investment in land could be imagined as being out of the picture, there are equally grave problems in another direction. So the moment of ground rent, and that moment of finance capital which is organized around it, are permanent structural elements of the system, sometimes taking a secondary role and sinking into insignificance, sometimes, as in our own period, coming to the fore as though they were the principal locus of capitalist accumulation.

But what I mainly want to appeal to Harvey for is his account of the nature of value in land; you will remember, or can easily deduce, that if land has a value, this last cannot be explained by any labour theory of value. Labour can add value in the form of improvements; but labour cannot possibly be imagined to be the source of land value as it is for the value of industrial production. But land has value nonetheless: how to explain this paradox? Harvey suggests that for Marx the value of land is something like a structurally necessary fiction. And indeed he calls it precisely that, in the key expression 'fictitious capital' – 'a flow of money capital not backed by any commodity transaction'.[32] This is possible only because fictitious capital is oriented towards the expectation of future value: and thus with one stroke the value of land is revealed to be intimately related to the credit system, the stock market and finance capital generally: 'Under such conditions the land is treated as a pure financial asset which is bought and sold according to the rent it yields. Like all such forms of fictitious capital, what is traded is a claim upon future revenues, which means a claim upon future profits from the use of the land or, more directly, a claim upon future labor'.[33]

Now our series of mediations is complete, or at least more complete than it was: time and a new relationship to the future as a space of necessary expectation of revenue and capital accumulation – or, if you prefer, the structural reorganization of time itself into a kind of futures market – this is now the final link in the chain which leads from finance capital through land speculation to aesthetics and cultural production itself, or in other words, in our context, to architecture. All the historians of ideas tell us tirelessly about the way in which, in modernity, the emergence of the modality of various future tenses not only displaces the older sense of the past and of tradition, but also structures that new form of historicity which is ours. The effects are palpable in the history of ideas, and also, one would think, more immediately in the structure of narrative itself. Can all this be theorized in its effects on the architectural and spatial field? As far as I know, only Manfredo Tafuri and his philosophical collaborator Massimo Cacciari have evoked a 'planification of the future', which their discussion, however, limits to Keynesianism or, in other words, to liberal capital and social democracy. We have, however, posited this new colonization of the future as a fundamental tendency in capitalism itself, and the perpetual source of the perpetual recrudescence of finance capital and land speculation.

One can certainly begin a properly aesthetic exploration of these issues with a question about the way in which specific 'futures' – now in the financial as well as the temporal sense – come to be structural features of the newer architecture: something like planned obsolescence, if you like, in the certainty that the building will no longer ever have any aura of permanence, but will bear in its very raw materials the impending certainty of its own future demolition.

But I need to make at least a gesture towards fulfilling my initial programme – setting in place the chain of mediations that might lead from infrastructure (land speculation, finance capital) to superstructure (aesthetic form); I will take the short cut of cannibalizing the wonderful descriptions of Charles Jencks in his semiotics of what he calls 'late modernity' (a distinction that will not particularly concern us in the present context). Jencks first allows us to see the way not to do this: that of thematic self-reference, as when Anthony Lumsden's Branch Bank project in Bumi Daya 'alludes to the silver standard and an area of investment where the bank's money is possibly headed'.[34]

But then he also identifies at least two features (and very fundamental ones at that) which might well be appealed to to illustrate something of the formal overtones proper to a late finance capitalism. That these are, as he argues, extreme developments of the features of the modern, energetic distortions which end up turning this work against the very spirit of the modern, only reinforces the general argument: modernism to the second power no longer looks like modernism at all, but some other space altogether.

The two features I have in mind are 'extreme isometric space'[35] and, no doubt even more predictably, not just the glass skin but its 'enclosed skin volumes'.[36] Isometric space, however much it derived from the modernist 'free plan', becomes the very element of delirious equivalence itself, in which not even the monetary medium remains, and not only the contents but also the frames are now freed to endless metamorphosis: 'Mies' endless, universal space was becoming a reality, where ephemeral functions could come and go without messing up the absolute architecture above and below'.[37] The 'enclosed skin volumes' then illustrate another aspect of late capitalist abstraction, the way in which it dematerializes without signifying in any traditional way spirituality: 'breaking down the apparent mass, density, weight of a fifty storey building', as Jencks puts it.[38] The evolution of the curtain wall 'decreases the mass and weight while enhancing the volume and the contour – the difference between a brick and a balloon'.[39] What it would be important to develop is that both of these principles – features of the modern which are then projected into whole new and original spatial worlds in their own right – no longer operate according to the older modern binary oppositions. Weight or embodiment along with its progressive attenuation no longer posits the non-body or the spirit as an opposite; in the same way, where the free plan posited an older bourgeois space to be cancelled, the infinite new isometric kind cancels nothing, but simply develops under its own momentum like a new dimension. Without wishing to belabour the point, it strikes me that the abstract dimension or materialist sublimation of finance capital enjoys something of the same semi-autonomy as cyberspace.

'To the second power': this is more or less the formula in terms of which we have been imagining some new cultural logic beyond the modern one; and the formula can certainly be specified in any number of different ways: Barthesian connotation, for example, or reflection about reflection – provided only that it is not construed as increasing the magnitude of the 'first power' as in mathematical progressions. Probably Simmel's comparison with voyeurism does not quite do the trick,[40] particularly since he has to do with some 'first' or 'normal' finance capitalism only, and not the heightened forms of abstraction produced by our current variety, from which even those objects susceptible of voyeuristic pleasure seem to have disappeared. Whence, no doubt, the resurgence of ancient theories of the simulacrum, as some abstraction from beyond the already abstracted image. Jean Baudrillard's work is surely the most inventive exploration of the paradoxes and after-images of this new dimension of things, which he does not yet, I think, identify with finance capital; and I have already mentioned cyberspace, a rather different representational version of what cannot be represented and yet is more concrete – at least in cyberpunk SF like that of William Gibson – than the old modernist abstractions of cubism or classical SF itself.

Yet as we are certainly haunted by this particular spectre, perhaps it is in the ghost story itself – and particularly its postmodern varieties – that some very provisional analogy can be sought in conclusion. The ghost story is indeed virtually the architectural genre par excellence, wedded as it is to rooms and buildings ineradicably stained with the memory of gruesome events, material structures in which the past literally 'weighs like a nightmare on the brain of the living'. Yet just as the sense of the past and of history followed the extended family into oblivion, lacking the elders whose storytelling alone could inscribe it as sheer event into the listening minds of later generations, so also urban renewal seems everywhere in the process of sanitizing the ancient corridors and bedrooms to which alone a ghost might cling. (The haunting of open air sites, such as a gallows hill or a sacred burial ground, would seem to present a still earlier, pre-modern situation.)

Yet the time is still 'out of joint': and Derrida has restored to the ghost story and the matter of haunting a new and actual philosophical dignity it perhaps never had before, proposing to substitute, for the ontology of Heidegger (who cites these same words of Hamlet for his own purposes), a new kind of 'hauntology', the barely perceptible agitations in the air of a past abolished socially and collectively, yet still attempting to be reborn. (Significantly, Derrida includes the future among spectralities.)[41]

How is it to be imagined? One scarcely associates ghosts with high-rise buildings, even though I have heard of multi-storey apartment structures in Hong Kong which were said to be haunted;[42] yet perhaps the more fundamental narrative of a ghost story 'to the second power', of a properly postmodern ghost story, ordered by finance-capital spectralities rather than the old and more tangible kind, demands a narrative of the very search for a building to haunt in the first place. *Rouge* certainly preserves the classical ghost story's historical content:[43] the confrontation of the present with the past, in this instance the confrontation of the contemporary mode of production – the offices and the businesses of Hong Kong today (or rather yesterday, before 1997) – with what is still an *ancien régime* (if not a downright feudalism) of wealthy slackers and sophisticated establishments of hetairai, replete with gaming and sumptuary feasts, as well as erotic connoisseurship. In this pointed juxtaposition the moderns – bureaucrats and secretaries – are well aware of their bourgeois inferiority; nor does the suicide for love stand in any fundamental narrative tension with the decadence of the romantic 1930s. Save, perhaps, by accident, for the playboy fails to die and is finally unwilling to follow his glamorous partner into an eternal afterlife. He does not wish, so to speak, to be haunted; indeed, as a derelict old man in the present, he can scarcely be located in the first place. The traditional ghost story did not, surely, require mutual consent for a visitation – here it seems to; and the success or failure of the haunting never depended quite so much, as in this Hong Kong present-day, on the mediation of the present-day observers. To wish to be haunted; to long for the great passions that now exist only in the past; indeed, to survive in a bourgeois present as exotic cosmetics and costumes alone, as sheer postmodern 'nostalgia' trappings, as optional content within a stereotypical yet empty form: some first, 'classical' nostalgia as abstraction from the concrete object, alongside a second or more 'postmodern' one as nostalgia for nostalgia itself, a longing for the situation in which the process of abstraction might itself once again be possible; this is the source of our feeling that the newer moment is a return to realism – plots, agreeable buildings, decoration, melodies, and so on – when in fact it is only a replay of the empty stereotypes of all those things, and a vague memory of their fullness on the tip of the tongue.

Notes

Postmodernism and Consumer Society

1 Wayne C. Booth, *The Rhetoric of Irony* (Chicago, 1975).

2 Michael Herr, *Dispatches* (New York, 1977), pp. 8–9.

Theories of the Postmodern

1 The following analysis does not seem to me applicable to the work of the *boundary 2* group, who early on appropriated the term postmodernism in the rather different sense of a critique of establishment 'modernist' thought.

2 Written in spring 1982.

3 See his 'Modernity – An Incomplete Project', in *The Anti-Aesthetic*, Hal Foster, ed. (Port Townsend, 1983), pp. 3–15.

4 The specific politics associated with the Greens would seem to constitute a reaction to this situation rather than an exception from it.

5 See J.F. Lyotard, 'Answering the Question, What Is Postmodernism?', in *The Post Modern Condition* (Minneapolis, 1984), pp. 71–82; the book itself focuses primarily on science and epistemology rather than on culture.

6 See, in particular, Manfredo Tafuri, *Architecture and Utopia* (Cambridge, Mass., 1976) and, with Francesco Dal Co, *Modern Architecture* (New York, 1979) as well as my 'Architecture and the Critique of Ideology', in *The Ideologies of Theory*, vol. II (Minneapolis, 1988).

7 See my *Postmodernism, or, The Cultural Logic of Late Capitalism* (London, 1991).

8 See, for example, Charles Jencks, *Late-Modern Architecture* (New York, 1980); Jencks here, however, shifts his usage of the term from the designations for a cultural dominant or period style to the name for one aesthetic movement among others.

Marxism and Postmodernism

1 This essay, reprinted from *Postmodernism/Jameson/Critique*, ed. Douglas Kellner (Washington DC, 1989), concludes and responds to a collection of fourteen other essays commissioned to assess the relations of Marxism, poststructuralism and postmodernism.

2 Ernest Mandel, *Late Capitalism* (London, 1975).

3 Haynes Horne, 'Jameson's Strategies of Containment', in *Postmodernism/Jameson/Critique*, pp. 268–300.

4 Arno J. Mayer, *Why Did the Heavens Not Darken? The 'Final Solution' in History* (New York, 1988).

5 Gayatri Chakravorty Spivak, *In Other Worlds: Essays in Cultural Politics* (New York, 1987), p. 198.

6 Ronald L. Meek, *Social Science and the Ignoble Savage* (Cambridge, 1976).

7 Ibid., pp. 219–21.

8 Ibid., pp. 127–8.

9 Georg Lukács, *The Historical Novel* (Lincoln, Nebraska, 1983).

10 Tom Nairn, *The Break-up of Britain* (London, 1977).

11 Mike Featherstone, 'Postmodernism, Cultural Change and Social Practice', in *Postmodernism/Jameson/Critique*, pp. 117–38.

12 See also Fred Pfeil, 'Makin' Flippy-Floppy: Postmodernism and the Baby-Boom PMC', in *The Year Left I* (London, 1985).

13 David Gross, 'Marxism and Resistance: Fredric Jameson and the Moment of Postmodernism', in *Postmodernism/Jameson/Critique*, pp. 96–116.

14 'Periodizing the Sixties', in *The Ideologies of Theory*, vol. 2, pp. 178–208; and 'Postmodernism, or, The Cultural Logic of Late Capitalism', *New Left Review* 146 (July–August 1984).

15 Edward Soja, *Postmodern Geographies* (London, 1989).

The Antinomies of Postmodernity

1 Paul Virilio, *War and Cinema* (London, 1989), pp. 59–60.

2 Marcel Proust, *A la recherche du temps perdu*, vol. I (Paris, 1987), p. 36.

3 Tafuri, *Architecture and Utopia*, p. 70.

4 Ibid.

5 Ibid., p. 62.

6 Henri Lefebvre, *The Production of Space* (Oxford, 1991).

7 Claude Lévi-Strauss, translated as *The Savage Mind* (Chicago, 1966).

8 See Jacques Derrida, *Writing and Difference* (London, 1990).

9 See Ranajit Guha, *A Rule of Property for Bengal* (Paris and The Hague, 1963).

10 See Pierre-Philippe Rey, *Les Alliances de classes* (Paris, 1978).

11 Ursula Le Guin, *Always Coming Home* (London, 1985).

12 Samuel R. Delany, *Trouble on Triton: An Ambiguous Heterotopia* (Middleton, 1996).

13 For the identification of aesthetic modernism with Stalinism, see, in particular, Boris Groys, *Gesamtkunstwerk Stalin* (Munich, 1988); translated as *The Total Art of Stalinism: Avant-Garde, Aesthetic Dictatorship and Beyond* (Princeton, 1992).

'End of Art' or 'End of History'?

1 G.W.F. Hegel, *Aesthetik* (East Berlin, 1953).

2 Christ's body as transition: this is the point at which Hegel tries to think modernity. It is thus imagined – the modern – as the moment in which the individual body is somehow no longer fully meaningful in its own terms. If you think modernity scientifically, then, it is the moment of Copernicus: we (the human body) are no longer the measure, the centre of things. If you think it technologically, it is the moment when the tool, the graceful prosthesis and adjunct to the handicrafter's body, is transcended towards the machine, of which the individual body is itself the adjunct. If you think, finally, in economic terms, it is the moment in which commerce, grasped as a quintessential and profoundly human activity, is transcended towards a system – capitalism – in which money has a logic of its own and the cycles of the economic largely outstrip in their incomprehensibility the simple meaningfulness of good or bad luck, good or bad fortune, fulfilling a characteristic human destiny for good or ill, as opposed to suffering the seismographic shocks of systemic processes that can no longer be grasped or even represented in human categories.

3 Hegel, *Aesthetik*, pp. 102–3.

4 Perry Anderson, *A Zone of Engagement* (London, 1992).

5 Ibid., p. 327.

6 See Frederick Jackson Turner, *The Frontier in American History* (Mineola, 1996).

Transformations of the Image in Postmodernity

1 See chapter 8, 'Postmodernism and the Market', in *Postmodernism, or, The Cultural Logic of Late Capitalism*.

2 Richard Rorty, *Philosophy and the Mirror of Nature* (Princeton, 1981).

3 See my '"End of Art" or "End of History"?' in this volume, pp. 73–92.

4 Martin Jay, *Downcast Eyes: The Denigration of Vision in Twentieth-Century French Thought* (Berkeley, 1993).

5 Jonathan Crary, *Techniques of the Observer: On Vision and Modernity in the Nineteenth Century* (Cambridge, Mass., 1991).

6 But see my *Marxism and Form* (Princeton, 1981), chapter 4.

7 See 'Preface', Alejo Carpentier, *The Kingdom of this World* (London, 1990).

8 Michel Foucault, *Surveiller et punir* (Paris, 1975), p. 189; translated as *Discipline and Punish: The Birth of the Prison* (New York, 1995).

9 Aimé Césaire, *Aimé Césaire: Collected Poetry*, trans. Clayton Eshleman and Annette Smith (California, 1983), p. 35.

10 Alain Robbe-Grillet, *La Jalousie* (Paris, 1957), p. 80; translated as *Two Novels by Robbe-Grillet* (New York, 1989).

11 See my 'Postmodernism, or, The Cultural Logic of Late Capitalism'.

12 Karl-Heinz Bohrer, *Plötzlichkeit* (Frankfurt am Main, 1981); translated as *Suddenness: On the Moment of Aesthetic Appearance* (New York, 1994).

13 Antoine Compagnon, *Les Cinq paradoxes de la modernité* (Paris, 1990); translated by Franklin Philip as *The Five Paradoxes of Modernity* (New York, 1994). Translations are mine; but the second number given refers to the appropriate page of the English edition. Compagnon has added a new preface to the (somewhat modified) American version, in which he allows that, in the American context, his position might be considered a suitably qualified 'postmodern' one.

14 Ibid., p. 11/xvii.

15 Ibid., p. 75/39.

16 See Serge Guilbaut, *How New York Stole the Idea of Modern Art* (Chicago, 1983).

17 Compagnon, *Les Cinq paradoxes de la modernité*, p. 57/39.

18 Ibid., p. 79/57.

19 Ibid., p. 116/89.

20 Ibid., p. 115/89.

21 Ibid., p. 141/110–11.

22 Ibid., p. 178/144.

23 Ibid., p. 175/141.

24 André Malraux, *The Voices of Silence: Man and His Art* (Princeton, 1978), p. 98.

25 Theodor W. Adorno, *Aesthetische Theorie. Gesammelte Schriften*, vol. 7 (Frankfurt am Main, 1970), p. 17; translated as *Aesthetic Theory* (Minneapolis, 1997).

26 See chapter 7 of this volume for further discussion of Jarman.

27 Fredric Jameson *The Geopolitical Aesthetic* (London, 1992), pp. 97–101.

28 *Nouvel observateur*, 30 December 1993, pp. 8–9.

Culture and Finance Capital

1 Giovanni Arrighi, *The Long Twentieth Century* (London, 1994).

2 Rudolf Hilferding, *Finance Capital* (trans. London, 1985).

3 The signal exception is David Harvey's superb *Limits to Capital* (Chicago, 1982), a luminous presentation of Marxian economics, within which is embedded, where it may not have received the attention it merits, a whole new theory of finance capital (or, if you prefer, a reconstruction of some implicit Marxian theory of finance capital which Marx himself did not have time to complete), as well as of ground rent. The tension between Arrighi's diachronic account and Harvey's synchronic one is, to be sure, very important indeed, and undeveloped in the present essay, although I mean to deal with it elsewhere.

4 Arrighi, *The Long Twentieth Century*, p. 94.

5 Ibid., p. 6.

6 Fredric Jameson, *The Political Unconscious* (Ithaca, 1982).

7 C.B. MacPherson, *The Political Theory of Possessive Individualism* (Oxford, 1962).

8 Stéphane Mallarmé, 'Le livre, instrument spirituel', in *Oeuvres complètes* (Paris, 1945), p. 385.

9 Harry Braverman, *Labour and Monopoly Capital* (New York, 1976).

10 Wilhelm Worringer, *Abstraction and Empathy* (New York, 1963).

11 See, for a preliminary attempt, my 'Dualism and Marxism in Deleuze', *South Atlantic Quarterly*, Summer 1997, vol. 96, no. 3.

12 See, for more on land speculation, my 'One, two, three ... many mediations' in *ANYHOW*, edited by Cynthia Davidson (Cambridge, Mass., forthcoming).

13 Gilles Deleuze, *Cinema 1: The Movement Image* (Minneapolis, 1986, p. 175).

14 My rather opportunistic use of Jarman as an example in these two final chapters is not meant to offer any definitive assessment of mine on this serious and ambitious work, to which Jarman's tragically premature death, among so many, cannot but add a heightened significance. The distinction which interests me here is that between a painterly impulse and the mass-cultural visual developments outlined in this chapter. My impression has been that in Jarman the former has been deflected into the latter, so that, if one wants to say that these films are too visual (in the postmodern sense), one must add that they are not painterly enough. I would here wish to contrast the remarkable work of two great contemporary Indian filmmakers, Mani Kaul and Kumar Shahani, whose films address and satisfy the eye in a very different way; yet they are, on my view, essentially modernist filmmakers, and I hope it has become clear that it is also very far from my approach to postmodernity to wish that its artists simply 'return' to the 'modern' as such.

The Brick and the Balloon: Architecture, Idealism and Land Speculation

1 See, for a more comprehensive discussion, my forthcoming essay, 'The Theoretical Hesitation: Benjamin's Sociological Predecessor'. I also want to signal the related projects of Richard Dienst on debt as a postmodern phenomenon (see, for example, 'The Futures Market', in *Reading the Shape of the World*, ed. H. Schwarz and R. Dienst (Boulder, CO, 1996)); and also that of Christopher Newfield on corporate culture today (see, for example, his essays in *Social Text* 44 and 51, Fall 1995 and Summer 1997).

2 Translated in Georg Simmel, *On Individuality and Social Forms*, ed. D. N. Levine (Chicago, 1971), pp. 324–39.

3 See my essay 'Culture and Finance Capital', in this volume, pp. 136–61.

4 Simmel, *On Individuality and Social Forms*, p. 334. To which I would like to append the following:

The flexibility of money, as with so many of its qualities, is most clearly and emphatically expressed in the stock exchange, in which the money economy is crystallized as an independent structure just as political organization is crystallized in the state. The fluctuations in exchange prices frequently indicate subjective-psychological motivations, which, in their crudeness and independent movements, are totally out of proportion in relation to objective factors. It would certainly be superficial, however, to explain this by pointing out that price fluctuations correspond only rarely to real changes in the quality that the stock represents. For the significance of this quality for the market lies not only in the inner qualities of the State or the brewery, the mine or the bank, but in the relationship of these to all other stocks on the market and their conditions. Therefore, it does not affect their actual basis if, for instance, large insolvencies in Argentina depress the price of Chinese bonds, although the security of such bonds is no more affected by that event than by something that happens on the moon. For the value of these stocks, for all their external stability, none the less depends on the overall situation of the market, the fluctuations of which, at any one point, may for example make the further utilization of those returns less profitable. Over and above these stock market fluctuations, which even though they presuppose the synthesis of the single object with others are still objectively produced, there exists one factor that originates in speculation itself. These wagers on the future quoted price of one stock *themselves have the most considerable influence on such a price*. For instance, as soon as a powerful financial group, for reasons that have nothing to do with the quality of the stock, becomes interested in it, its quoted price will increase; conversely, a bearish group is able to bring about a fall in the quoted price by mere manipulation. Here the real value of the object appears to be the irrelevant substratus above which the movement of market values rises only because it has to be attached to some substance, or rather to some name. The relation between the real and final value of the object and its representation by a bond has lost all stability. This clearly shows the absolute flexibility of this form of value, a form that the objects have gained through money and which has completely detached them from their real basis. Now value follows, almost without resistance, the psychological impulses of the temper, of greed, of unfounded opinion, and it does this in such a striking manner since objective circumstances exist that could provide exact standards of valuation. But value in terms of the money form has made itself independent of its own roots and foundation in order to surrender itself completely to subjective energies. Here, where speculation itself may determine the fate of the object of speculation, the permeability and flexibility of the money form of values has found its most triumphant expression through subjectivity in its strictest sense.

Simmel, *Philosophy of Money*, trans. D. Frisby and T. Bottomore (London, 1978), pp. 325–6.

5 Robert Fitch, *The Assassination of New York* (London, 1996), p. 40.

6 Ibid., p. 60.

7 Ibid., p. xii.

8 In his book *The Long Twentieth Century* (London, 1994); for more on this work see my 'Culture and Finance Capital'.

9 Both descriptions specify the causal relationship between the informational developments they analyse and the increasing structural unemployment and ghettoization of the contemporary city. See Manuel Castells, *The Informational City* (Oxford, 1989), p. 228; or Saskia Sassen, *The Global City* (Princeton, 1991), p. 186.

10 Most notably Ernest Mandel, in *Late Capitalism* (London, 1975).

11 Fitch, *The Assassination of New York*, p. 149.

12 Ibid., pp. xvi–xvii.

13 Ibid., p. 86.

14 Ibid., p. 94.

15 Ibid., p. 189.

16 Ibid., p. 191.

17 Ibid., pp. 189, 226, xvii.

18 See Dieter Henrich, 'Hegels Theorie über den Zufall', in *Hegel im Kontext* (Frankfurt am Main, 1971).

19 Proust's interest in military strategy is in this connection most revealing indeed: see for example the discussions on the visit to Saint-Loup, during the latter's military service at Doncières, in *Le Côté de Guermantes*, from *A la recherche du temps perdu* (Paris, 1954).

20 Fitch, *The Assassination of New York*, pp. 186–7.

21 In Francesco Dal Co et al., *The American City* (Cambridge, Mass., 1979), p. 389.

22 Ibid., p. 390.

23 Ibid., p. 461.

24 Ibid., p. 483.

25 Siegfried Giedion, *Space, Time and Architecture* (1941; reprint, Cambridge, Mass., 1982), p. 845. I am grateful to Charles Jencks for reminding me of this basic text.

26 Ibid., p. 825.

27 Ibid., pp. 849–51.

28 Rem Koolhaas, *Delirious New York* (Oxford, 1978), p. 144.

29 Ibid., p. 142.

30 Ibid., p. 149.

31 Ibid., p. 153.

32 David Harvey, *The Limits to Capital* (Chicago, 1982), p. 265.

33 Ibid., p. 347.

34 Charles Jencks, *The New Moderns* (New York, 1990), p. 85.

35 Ibid., p. 81.

36 Ibid., p. 86.

37 Ibid., p. 81.

38 Ibid., p. 86.

39 Ibid., p. 85.

40 See Simmel, *Philosophy of Money*, p. 327:

Money thus provides a unique extension of the personality which does not seek to adorn itself with the possession of goods. Such a personality is indifferent to control over objects; it is satisfied with that momentary power over them, and while it appears as if this avoidance of any qualitative relationship to objects would not offer any extension and satisfaction to the person, the very act of buying is experienced as such a satisfaction, because the objects are absolutely obedient to money. Because of the completeness with which money and objects as money-values follow the impulses of the person, he is satisfied by a symbol of his domination over them which is otherwise obtained only through actual ownership. The enjoyment of this mere symbol of enjoyment may come close to the pathological, as in the following case related by a French novelist. An Englishman was a member of a bohemian group whose enjoyment in life consisted of his sponsorship of the wildest orgies, though he himself never joined in but always only paid for everybody – he appeared, said nothing, did nothing, paid for everything and disappeared. The one side of these dubious events – paying for them – must, in this man's experience, have stood for everything. One may readily assume that here is a case of one of those perverse satisfactions that has recently become the subject of sexual pathology. In comparison with ordinary extravagance, which stops at the first stage of possession and enjoyment and the mere squandering of money, the behaviour of this man is particularly eccentric because the enjoyments, represented here by their money equivalent, are so close and directly tempting to him. The absence of a positive owning and using of things on the one hand, and the fact on the other that the mere act of buying is experienced as a relationship between the person and the objects and as a personal satisfaction, can be explained by the expansion that the mere act of spending money affords to the person. Money builds a bridge between such people and objects. In crossing this bridge, the mind experiences the attraction of their possession even if it does in fact not attain it.

41 See my discussion in 'Marx's Purloined Letter', *New Left Review*, vol. 209, no. 4, 1995, pp. 86–120.

42 An unpublished paper by Kevin Heller explores the even more complex analogies in *Gremlins 2* (Joe Dante, 1990), not coincidentally filmed in Donald Trump's Tower.

43 Hong Kong, Stanley Kwan, 1987. I am indebted to Rey Chow for suggesting this reference.

Index

Adorno, Theodor 113
  Aesthetic Theory 101–2
  commodity form of modern art
    118
  culture and industry 135
  Dialectic of Enlightenment (with
    Horkheimer) 25
  Negative Dialectic 40
  on philosophy 81, 82
Aesthetic Theory (Adorno) 101–2
Aesthetics (Hegel) 80
Always Coming Home (Le Guin)
  69
American Graffiti (film) 7–8
Amin, Samir 91
An Andalusian Dog (film) 157
Anderson, Perry
  A Zone of Engagement 88
Arrighi, Giovanni
  The Long Twentieth Century
    136, 139–42, 144, 149, 151–4
  stages of capital development
    170
Ashbery, John 1
The Assassination of New York
  (Fitch) 166–77
Auerbach, Erich
  Mimesis 147

Baran and Sweezy
  Monopoly Capital 142

Barthes, Roland
  Mythologies 159–60
Bataille, Georges 65
Baudelaire, Charles 54–5, 113–17
Baudrillard, Jean 187
de Beauvoir, Simone 105
Being and Nothingness (Sartre)
  103–4
Bell, Daniel 170, 171
Benjamin, Walter 16, 47, 166
Bertolucci, Bernardo
  The Conformist 8
Body Heat (film) 9
Bohrer, Karl-Heinz
  Plötzlichkeit 113, 116, 117
Booth, Wayne 5
Brakhage, Stan 149, 160
  Dog Star Man 157–8
Braudel, Fernand 141, 170
Braverman, Harry
  Labor and Monopoly Capital
    149, 171
The Break-up of Britain (Nairn)
  42–3
Brecht, Berthold
  good old things 94
Buñuel, Luis 159–60
  An Andalusian Dog 157–8
  The Golden Age 157–8
Bürger, Peter 82, 84, 114–15, 118
Burke, Edmund 71

201

Burke, Kenneth 183
Burroughs, William 1

Cacciari, Massimo 185
Campagnon, Antoine
    The Five Paradoxes of
        Modernity 113–21
Capital (Marx)
    M-C-M' formula 141, 151–2
Capitalism and Schizophrenia
    (Deleuze and Guattari) 152
Caravaggio (film) 124–5
Caro, Robert
    The Powerbroker 172–3
Carpentier, Alejo 105
Castells, Manuel 171
Césaire, Aimé 107–8
Chinatown (film) 8, 9
Cissé, Souleymane
    Yeelen/The Light 126–7
Clash 1
La Condition humaine (Malraux)
    122
The Conformist (film) 8
Corneau, Alain
    Tous les matins du monde
        132–3
Crary, Jonathan
    Techniques of the Observer 103

Dash, Julie 128
Daughters of the Dust (film) 128
Debord, Guy
    The Society of the Spectacle 110
Delany, Samuel
    Trouble on Triton 69
Deleuze, Gilles 64, 140, 150
    Capitalism and Schizophrenia
        (with Guattari) 152
    naturalist image 158
Derrida, Jacques 64–5, 188
Descartes, René 155
    Discourse on Method 104
Dialectic of Enlightenment
    (Adorno and Horkheimer) 25
Dillworth, Richardson 174

Discourse on Method (Descartes)
    104
Dispatches (Herr) 16
Doctorow, E.L. 10
Dog Star Man (film) 157–8
The Double Life of Véronique
    (film) 133
Downcast Eyes (Jay) 103

Eliot, T.S. 2, 7
Engels, Friedrich 184

Fanon, Frantz 104–5
Featherstone, Mike 44–5
Finance Capital (Hilferding) 138
Fitch, Robert
    The Assassination of New York
        166–77
The Five Paradoxes of Modernity
    (Campagnon) 113–21
Fleischer, Richard
    Soylent Green 126
Foucault, Michel
    categorizing work 3
    History of Sexuality 106–7
    Otherness and reification
        105–10
Frankfurt School 56
Freud, Sigmund
    tribal dream analysis 32
Frida (film) 128
From Bauhaus to Our House
    (Wolfe) 22
'The Frontier in American History'
    (Turner) 90, 92
Fukuyama, Francis 73
    The End of History 89–91
    and Kojève 87, 89

Gandhi, Mohandas (Mahatma) 97
Gang of Four 1
Gehry, Frank 10
Giddens, Anthony 165
Giedion, Siegfried
    Space, Time and Architecture
        179–83

Glass, Philip 1
Godard, Jean-Luc 1, 133
The Godfather (film) 129
The Golden Age (film) 157
Graves, Michael 10
Gravity's Rainbow (Pynchon) 158
Greenberg, Clement 116
Gross, David 47
Grundrisse (Marx) 68, 139
Guattari, Felix 150
  Capitalism and Schizophrenia
    (with Deleuze) 152

Haacke, Hans 75
Habermas, Jürgen 25–6
Harvey, David
  The Limits to Capital 184–5
Hassan, Ihab 22
Hauser, Arnold
  Social History of Art 145–6
Hayek, Friedrich A. 137
Hegel, Georg W.F. 133
  end of art 73, 76–92
  history 29
  use of individual in collective
    process 175
Heidegger, Martin 113, 131, 188
  and Sartre's Look 103–4
Herr, Michael
  Dispatches 16
Heskell, Douglas 176–7
Hilferding, Rudolf 143
  Finance Capital 138
  *Imperialism: the Highest Stage
    of Capitalism* 138
History of Sexuality (Foucault)
  106–7
Hood, Raymond 178, 181–2
Horkheimer, Max
  culture and industry 135
  Dialectic of Enlightenment (with
    Adorno) 25
Horne, Haynes 38

Ikhnaton 146
*Imperialism: the Highest Stage of
  Capitalism* (Hilferding) 138

Jacob, Jane 70, 167
La Jalousie (Robbe-Grillet) 108–9
Jameson, Fredric
  The Political Unconscious 44,
    144
Jarman, Derek
  Caravaggio 124–5
  Last of England 157–8, 159
Jay, Martin
  Downcast Eyes 103
Je vous salue Marie (film) 133
Jencks, Charles 29, 30
  features of late modernity 186–7
Joyce, James
  'High Oxen of the Sun' chapter
    17–18
  now classic 18–19
  Ulysses 149
Julian, Isaac 128
Jünger, Ernst 113

Kahlo, Frida 128
Kant, Immanuel
  Beauty 83–4, 86
  space and time 58
  Third Critique 101–2
  time and space 51
Kasdan, Lawrence
  Body Heat 9
Kellner, Doug 34
Kieslówski, Krzysztof
  The Double Life of Véronique
    133
  Three Colours Blue 133
Kojève, Alexandre 60
  end of history debate 73
  and Fukuyama 87, 89
  master-slave struggle 103
Koolhaas, Rem 181–3
Kramer, Hilton 29, 119
  The New Criterion 23–4, 113
Krinsky, Carol 176–7

Labor and Monopoly Capital
  (Braverman) 149, 171
Lacoue-Labarthe, Philippe 83

Landau, Sol 48
Last of England (film) 157–8, 159
Late Capitalism (Mandel) 35, 139
Latino Bar (film) 127–8
Lawrence, D.H. 4
Le Guin, Ursula
 Always Coming Home 69
Learning from Las Vegas (Venturi)
 1
Leduc, Paul
 Frida 128
 Latino Bar 127–8
Lefebvre, Henri
 The Production of Space 63–4
Lenin, V. I. 139
 imperialism 34, 143
Lévi-Strauss, Claude
 La Pensée sauvage 64–5
The Limits to Capital (Harvey)
 184–5
Locke, John 145
The Long Twentieth Century
 (Arrighi) 136, 139–42, 144,
 149, 151–4
Loos, Adolf 71
Lucas, George
 American Graffiti 7–8
 Star Wars 8
Lucia (film) 130–31
Luhmann, Niklas 164
Lukács, Georg 27, 42, 133, 145
 modernist reification 148
Lumsden, Anthony 186
Lyotard, Jean-François 26–9
 post-modern before modern 113

Machiavelli, Niccolo 164
MacPherson, C.B. 144
Madness and Civilization
 (Foucault) 105
Mallarmé, Stéphane 147
Malraux, André
 La Condition humaine 122
 Voices of Silence 120–23
Mandel, Ernest
 Late Capitalism 35, 139

Mann, Thomas 17
Marx, Karl and Marxism 7, 79
 aesthetics 112
 class 48
 end of history 89–91
 Grundrisse 139
 Harvey's outline 184–5
 human relationships and trade
 146
 ideals 30
 literary critics and money
 145
 logic of capital 169
 M-C-M′ formula from *Capital*
 141, 151–2
 model of capital development
 41, 171–2
 modernism 148
 outer limits of a global market
 68
 in postmodern context 33–4,
 94–6
 rural idiocy 70
 Tafuri and Lyotard's political
 ambivalence 27–8
 third stage of capitalism 34–7
Mayer, Arno 55–6
 *Why Did the Heavens Not
 Darken?* 38
Meek, Ronald L. 41
Merleau-Ponty, Maurice 104
'Metropolis and Mental Life'
 (Simmel) 143, 151, 165–6
Mimesis (Auerbach) 147
Monopoly Capital (Sweezy and
 Baran) 142
Moore, Charles 10
Moses, Robert 172–3, 180
Mythologies (Barthes) 159–60

Nairn, Tom
 The Break-up of Britain 42–3
Negative Dialectic (Adorno) 40
The New Criterion (journal) 23–4,
 113

Nietzsche, Friedrich
   in postmodern context 94–5,
   95–6

The Opportunist (film) 130–31
Orwell, George
   'Politics and the English
      Language' 4–5

Parmenides 58–9, 60
La Pensée sauvage (Lévi-Strauss)
   64–5
Philosophy of Money (Simmel) 165
Picasso, Pablo 7
   now classic 18–19
Plato 82
Plötzlichkeit (Bohrer) 113, 116,
   117
Polanski, Roman
   Chinatown 8, 9
The Political Unconscious
   (Jameson) 44, 144
'Politics and the English Language'
   (Orwell) 4–5
Portman, John
   The Bonaventure Hotel 11–16
Postmodern Geographies (Soja) 49
The Powerbroker (Caro) 172–3
The Production of Space (Lefebvre)
   63–4
Proust, Marcel 7, 52, 54–5, 149
Pynchon, Thomas 1
   Gravity's Rainbow 158

Ragtime (film) 10
Raiders of the Lost Ark (film) 8
Reagan, Ronald 137
Reed, Ishmael 1
Rey, Pierre-Philippe 67
Richelieu, Cardinal Armand Jean
   du Plessis 164
Ricoeur, Paul 55
Riley, Terry 1
Robbe-Grillet, Alain
   La Jalousie 108–9
Rockefeller, Nelson 173–4

Rockefeller family 173–5
Rorty, Richard 94
Russell, Ken 155, 157–8

Sartre, Jean-Paul 55
   the Look in *Being and
      Nothingness* 103–4
Sassen, Saskia 171
Scott, Sir Walter 42–3
Simmel, Georg 187
   'Metropolis and Mental Life'
      143, 151, 165–6
   Philosophy of Money 165
Smith, Adam 41, 149, 175
Social History of Art (Hauser)
   145–6
The Society of the Spectacle
   (Debord) 110
Soja, Edward
   Postmodern Geographies 49
Solas, Humberto
   Lucia 130–31
   The Opportunist 130–31
Soylent Green (film) 126
Space, Time and Architecture
   (Giedion) 179–83
Spivak, Gayatri 40
Star Wars (film) 8
Stevens, Wallace 2, 4
Sweezy and Baran
   Monopoly Capital 142

Tafuri, Manfredo 27–9, 177–83
   intellectual work 56, 57
Talking Heads 1
Techniques of the Observer
   (Crary) 103
Thatcher, Margaret 137
Third Critique (Kant) 101–2
Three Colours Blue (film) 133
Tous les matins du monde (film)
   132–3
Trouble on Triton (Delany) 69
Turner, Frederick Jackson
   'The Frontier in American
      History' 90, 92

INDEX

Ulysses (Joyce) 149
  'High Oxen of the Sun' chapter
  17–18

Valéry, Paul 51–2
Venturi, Robert 10
  Learning from Las Vegas 1
Villiers de L'Isle, Adam 52
Virilio, Paul
  War and Cinema 52–3
Voices of Silence (Malraux)
  120–23

Wallerstein, Immanuel 93
War and Cinema (Virilio)
  52–3
Warhol, Andy 1

*Why Did the Heavens Not
  Darken?* (Mayer) 38
Wilde, Oscar 145
Williams, Raymond 69
Willis, Paul 110
Wittfogel, Karl
  Oriental Despotism 96
Wolfe, Tom 29
  From Bauhaus to Our House 22
Worringer, Wilhelm 151

Yeelen/The Light (film) 126–7

Zeno of Elea 58
Zola, Emile 31
A Zone of Engagement (Anderson)
  88